.Lydgate's Reson and Sensuallyte: Vol. I

EARLY ENGLISH TEXT SOCIETY

Extra Series, No. 84

Lydgate's
Reson and Sensuallyte

EDITED FROM

BODLEIAN MS. FAIRFAX 16

AND

BRITISH MUSEUM
ADDITIONAL MS. 29729

BY

ERNST SIEPER

VOLUME I
THE MANUSCRIPTS, TEXT
GLOSSARY

Published for
THE EARLY ENGLISH TEXT SOCIETY
by the
OXFORD UNIVERSITY PRESS
LONDON   NEW YORK   TORONTO

OXFORD
UNIVERSITY PRESS

Great Clarendon Street, Oxford OX2 6DP
United Kingdom

Oxford University Press is a department of the University of Oxford.
It furthers the University's objective of excellence in research, scholarship,
and education by publishing worldwide. Oxford is a registered trade mark of
Oxford University Press in the UK and in certain other countries

First Edition published in 1901
Reprinted 1965

Published in the United States of America by Oxford University Press
198 Madison Avenue, New York, NY 10016, United States of America

British Library Cataloguing in Publication Data
Data available

Library of Congress Cataloging in Publication Data
Data available

Extra Series, 84

ISBN 978-0-19-722567-7

PREFACE.

THE task of preparing an edition of the present work of Lydgate was committed to me in the beginning of the year 1896. It had originally been undertaken by Professor Schick, who came to an understanding with the Director of the Early English Text Society, the result of which was that the task was handed over to me. Shortly afterwards I went to England, and there I spent almost two years busying myself in the preparation of this edition and in the study of other works of the school of Chaucer. On my return to Germany I published first that part of my researches which concerned the original of Lydgate's poem, namely, *Les Échecs Amoureux.*[1] I had hoped that the text of the English poem, and the studies connected with it, would have followed closely afterwards. But the fulfilment of this purpose was unexpectedly delayed by other tasks, and by the pressure of university lectures until last summer, when, by the permission of the authorities of the University of Munich, I was granted time and opportunity to return to England and bring my work to a close.

With the consent of Dr. Furnivall, the materials of this work have been divided into two volumes. The present is the first volume, containing the text and, what naturally belongs to it, an account of the MSS. and a glossary. The second volume will contain chapters on the metre, grammar, authorship and date of the poem, Lydgate's style, the French original, and notes. In the last chapter but one I hope to supplement to some extent what I have already said in my book on *Les Échecs Amoureux*, especially as regards the second half of the Old French poem, and the Paris commentaries of the same. I had proposed to myself an enquiry

---

[1] *Les Échecs Amoureux*, eine altfranzösische Nachahmung des Rosenromans und ihre englische Übertragung : Litterarhistorische Forschungen, herausgegeben von Joseph Schick und M. Frh. v. Waldberg. IX. Heft. Weimar, 1898.

into the relation of *Les Échecs Amoureux* to the encyclopædic works of the Middle Ages, but I have handed it on to my pupil, Mr. E. Höefler. The result will appear shortly, and will, I hope, be found to give a worthy treatment of the subject.

It is hoped that the principles here followed in the presentation of the text will not need explanation. I trust the reader will agree with me in having decided to discuss the variations of spelling in Stowe all together in a separate paragraph of the introduction rather than to note each variant in the text. One word may be added on the punctuation of the poem. It is quite impossible to apply any principle of punctuation to Lydgate's text with rigorous consistency. For instance, such expressions as "of entente," "in especial," "withoute strif," are often thrown in as mere stopgaps, without any particular meaning. In such cases they are, as a rule, placed between commas. But in other places they are so closely connected with preceding or following words that they cannot be separated from them by a comma. As a general rule, I have preferred to err on the side of over- rather than of under-punctuation. This should ensure, at any rate, that the meaning is made clear.

The English side-notes are Dr. Furnivall's work : but as I was authorized to alter them if I pleased, and have ventured to make use of that permission in one or two instances, I must be held responsible to some extent for them also. The Glossary is designed, in the first instance, for practical purposes. Cross-references from one word to another are as far as possible avoided. Rare word-forms and difficulties in the text are sufficiently treated in the Notes.

There remains for me the duty of expressing my thanks to many helpers and friends. In the first place, to the Early English Text Society and its Director, Dr. Furnivall. The E. E. T. S. had a copy of the Fairfax MS. of *Reason and Sensuality* taken, which made it possible for me to begin work on the book before I started for England. Further, the Society was good enough to undertake the cost of copying several other MSS. in English libraries, at Paris and at Dresden, which seemed.to me necessary for this edition. To Dr. Furnivall personally also I am indebted for the constant encouragement and kindness which he shewed me during my visits to England. My friend, the Rev. S. C. Gayford, has given me, throughout the whole course of my work, advice and help of all kinds, and I owe to him my sincere thanks. I must thankfully acknowledge also the help of other English friends, Mr. C. Brough,

Mr. Arthur Thomas and Miss N. Lacy. To the officials of the British Museum, of the Bodleian Library, and of the National Library in Paris, I am much obliged for their unfailing assistance. To Professor K. Weyman of Munich I owe several excellent suggestions for the correct reading of the Latin marginal notes. And, above all, it is a deep pleasure for me to express my heartfelt gratitude to my honoured master, Professor Schick, to whom this work is dedicated.

E. SIEPER.

Oxford, August 1901.

*

ERRATA.

l. 2197 : put the comma after *fairest*.

p. 96, marginal note : read *tibia* for the *tubea* of the MSS.

l. 3686 : no comma after *pereles*.

p. 145, ll. 5546 f., not 5545 f., are added in the margin.

INTRODUCTION.

THE MANUSCRIPTS.

OUR poem has come down to us in two MS.-copies: Fairfax 16 and Additional 29,729.

1. FAIRFAX 16. F.

Bodleiana, Oxford. A vellum MS. of about the middle of the fifteenth century,[1] containing a number of poems by Chaucer and other poets. Skeat, in the introduction to his edition of Chaucer's *Minor Poems* (p. xl), points out the orthographical peculiarities of this valuable MS. See also Warton-Hazlitt, iii, 61 Note; Schick, *Temple of Glas*, p. xviii f.; Krausser, *Complaint of the 'Black Knight*, Heidelberger Dissertation, 1896, p. 1 f. Our poem extends from fol. 202–300 *a*. From fol. 300 *b* to 305 *a* are blank pages, probably for the remainder of this unfinished work.

It is written in single columns, thirty-eight lines to a full column. The text is not illuminated, but the first letter of each line is ornamented with a flourish or two in red. Frequently the initials of proper names as well as the letter I are coloured in the same manner: proper names are also underlined in red. The lines begin with capital letters. There is only one initial which is elaborately decorated, and that is the **T** on the first page: the letter itself is blue, and the ornamentation is red. The heading of the several chapters and paragraphs are also in red; so are the explanatory notes, which are written in Latin on the margin: in fact, all the writing except the text itself is in red.

One line (1180) is wanting. Other missing lines have been added in the margin: 88, 334, 420, 574, 613, 954, 2504, 3254, 3470, 3664, 4450, 4749, 5546–47, 5912, 6457. From whom do these lines originate? Stowe, who has supplied corrections in other places[2] of this MS., has nothing to do with them; for firstly, the

---

[1] At the beginning of the MS. we find the date 1450.
[2] Cp. Schick, *Temple of Glas*, p. xix.

handwriting differs entirely from that of Stowe, and secondly,
the orthography of these additional lines does· not have all the
characteristics of his <u>MSS</u>. To judge from the handwriting, I
am inclined to believe that they are written by Shirley himself. It
is true there are slight variations in the handwriting, but these are
easily explained by the altered position of the hand when writing on
the margin. It is more difficult to make the orthography of these
additional lines agree with that of the proper text.

However it be, it is certain that the marginal additions are
not mere commentaries, but taken from a complete manuscript.
The subjoined list will serve to illustrate this : The lines on the
margin—all printed in italics—contain each a certain word (sometimes at the beginning of the verse, sometimes in the first half of ·it),
which appears also in the preceding or following line.

1. 1. 88.	*In a morwe so as I lay*
	In my bed within a cloos
2. 1. 334.	*Though she sempt flouryng in youthe*
	Th[r]ogh freshnesse of hir visage
3. ·1. 420.	*Cloystred rounde with bright[e] sterres*
	Hir hed was cercled environ)
4. 1. 574.	*Wheche god a-bove hayth yove to the*
	Which thou shuldest neuer cesse
5. 1. 2503.	For elles thou ne mayst nat chese
	But thow shalt thy tyme lese
6. 1. 4749.	*[As hor]ryble and foule also*
	As ys the paleys of Pluto
7. 1. 5546.	*Ten without[e] dowse regarde*
	Yonge fresh and lusty of visag[es]
	As with-out wer ten ymages
8. 1. 5912.	*And for hit was gretly to drede*
	Lyst for disuse throgh ydelnesse
9. 1. 6456.	As the vertu most Royal
	And this vertu specialy

We see here at once, how it is that the verses have dropped out
of the text : the scribe has been led astray by the presence of the
same, or a similar word in the corresponding part of the preceding
or following line, and so one verse has been left out, an error which
is not infrequent in manuscripts. In some cases the copyist, after
having begun a line, carelessly allowed his eyes to wander into the
next one, the latter part of which thus completed the verse.

This accounts for the erroneous "Thogh" in l. 335, which is, in
fact, the "Thogh" of the foregoing line.

l. 2503 originally ran "For elles thou shalt thy tyme ·lese."

Here the latter half of l. 2504 had been added to the first part of
l. 2503; but later on "shalt thy tyme lese" has been crossed out
and the correct words substituted.

In brief, there is no doubt that the writer of F was sometimes
led by the delusive likeness of two words from one line into the
following one; and as almost all the marginal lines strengthen, if
they do not prove, this hypothesis, I think we are not wrong in
holding that they are original.

Concerning the title, we find it given in the table of fol. 2*b* as:
" The booke of⁴ þe Autoure how he plaid at þe Chesse and was mated
of⁴ a Feerse." But the poem itself bears the heading " Resoṇ and
sensuallyte compylid by Iohn Lydgat."

These words appear in a later hand, which is undoubtedly that
of Stowe, the writer of the Additional MS. Whether the latter
title is original, and therefore supplied from another MS., or an
invention of Stowe, will be discussed later on.

2. ADDITIONAL 297,29. A.

Purchased by the British Museum at Messrs. Puttick's, July 15,
1874.

The original owner was John Stowe, who wrote it in 1558, as is
distinctly stated in the following entry on the last page: "This
boke perteynythe to John stowe, and was by hym wryten in þᵉ yere
of owr Lord 1558." In another entry, written upside down at the
foot of this page, Stowe tells us, when he commenced writing: "This
20ᵉᵗʰ day of Jun wasse thys bowcke begonne."

The MS. consists of poems which are either by Lydgate, or have
some relation to him. Therefore Stowe gave his book the following
title (fol. 2): " Danne Lidigate monke of Burye his Woorke."

Alongside of this appear the words " written by Stowe." The
handwriting is small, neat, and of a more recent date. A little
further down follows the additional note: " And A translation of
Virgils Aneyd / dedicated to prince Arthur sonne to kinge Henrye
the seventh."

Another note on this page refers to Lydgate's life. It was
evidently penned by the same hand. We shall consider it in a later
chapter.

This MS. is of the highest importance for the study of Lydgate.
Bale probably gained much of his knowledge from it. Especially

are some of the minor occasional poems of great interest. It offers a field as yet unexplored for the student of Lydgate. A synopsis of its contents would therefore seem to be acceptable.

Fol. 2 *a*: short poem, " out of Master blomfelds boke a pece of þe battayll of þe psalms."

Fol. 3 *a–*4 *b*: poem in seventeen stanzas. Title and the refrain of every stanza: "Quid eligam ignoro."

Fol. 4 *b*–5 *a*: " how the plage was sesyd in rome." The name of John Lydgate is added to this title and the " Explicit."

Fol. 6 *a* and *b*: poem dedicated to Lydgate. The first line of the title has been partly cut off, so that it is unreadable; the second shows the words: " booke dwelyng at wyndsor." Colophon: " explicit per Magistrum bwrgh ad Joannem) lidgate." [1]

Fol. 6 *b* and 7 *a*: " A leson to kepe well þe tonge out of Magister Hanlay's booke." The author, as it is apparent by the colophon, is again Magister Benedictus Burgh.

Fol. 7 *a*–8 *a*: poem on the seven deadly sins. The title: "Remembar man thow art but wormes mette " recurs as the refrain of every stanza.

Fol. 8 *a*–9 *a*: "Epitaphy of kynge Edward þe fowrthe." The name of John Lydgate, in title and colophon originally given as the name of the author, has been corrected to that of Skelton. The poem shows some more rather careless corrections, which are partly cancelled.

Fol. 9 *b* and 10 *a*: " A balad made by John lydgat of þe ymage of owr lady."

Fol. 10 *a* and *b*: satirical poem with the refrain: " conveyede by lyne ryght as a rammes horne." Colophon: " quod John ludgate / writen out of Magister philyppes boke."

Fol. 11 *a*–16 *b*: "The 15 oes." Colophon: " Explicit / the xv. Oes compilid by John lydgat monke of bury / and were here wryten out of mastar stantons boke / by John stowe."

The rest of the page is filled out with a small poem of Lydgate on "the 9 properties of wyne."

Fol. 16 *b*: blank.

Fol. 17–83 *a*: "the sege of worthy thebes." The first part of the title is cut off, only the words " Monke of bwrye " are readable,

---

[1] " Magister bowrgh " as well as "John Lidgate " were, there is no doubt, also contained in the first line. Perhaps this line began as follows: "Magister bowrgh his poemys of John Lidgate." It is impossible to make out what the rest was.

but both title as given above and name of author (John lydgatt) appear in the colophon. With many marginal notes in red and black ink.

Fol. 84 *a*–86 *a*: "a tretis of the kynges coronacion Henry the VI. made by the monke of bury John lidgatt anno 1430 þᵉ 6. of november.[1]

Fol. 87–121 *b*: "The court of sapyence compylyd by John lydgate."

Fol. 122 *a*–123 *a*: thanksgiving song of Mary. Each stanza is preceded by a sentence of the Magnificat. After the "Amen" at the end follows the name of Lydgate.

Fol. 123 *a*–124 *a*: "the songe of Just mesure." This title only in the colophon. At the beginning and end Lydgate's name.

Fol. 124 *b*–126 *a*: "Amor vincit omnia mentiris quoþ pecunia." Below the title and in the colophon appears the name of Lydgate.

Fol. 126 *a* and 126 *b*: a poetical paraphrase of the following sentences: "terram terra tegat; demon peccata resumat; Mundus res habeat; spiritus alta petat." At the end: "Amen / quod Robartus peet" (!).

Fol. 126 *b*–127 *b*: "verses of þᵉ sawter, whiche þat kynge herry the v. whom god assoyle by gret devocion vsyd in his chapell etc., translatid by þᵉ Monke Lydegat dan John."

Fol. 127 *b*–129 *b*: "a balade whych John Lydgate the monke of bery wrott & made at þᵉ commaundement of þᵉ quene Kateryn,[2] as in here sportes she wallkyd by the medowes that were late mowen in the monthe of July." The colophon is followed by an envoy.

Fol. 129 *b*–130 *a*: song of repentance. Without title. Colophon: "finis / lidgat."

Fol. 130 *a* and *b*: "see myche say lytell & lerne to soffar in tyme." The poem begins and concludes with these maxims, of which it is a paraphrase. No title. After the "Explicit" Lydgate's name.

Fol. 130 *b* and 131 *a*: song of praise to Mary. Each stanza commencing with "Heyl."

Fol. 131 *a* and *b*: exhortation of the crucified Saviour, which, in the last stanza, is followed by a prayer.

Fol. 131 *b* and 132 *a*: poem of three stanzas, with the refrain: "Is this fortune: not I or infortune / thowgh I go lowse I tyed am

---

[1] This ceremony was performed at Paris, December 17, 1430.
[2] Married 1420, and two years afterwards became a widow.

wit*h* a leyne." Between stanza one and two we read : " Le dis de lidgate."

Fol. 132 *a* commences a collection of poems introduced by the following entry : "Here be-ginneth serteu thing*es* of John lydgat / copied out of þᵉ boke of John Sherley." This series is continued as far as fol. 179, where we read in a colophon : " Here endeth þᵉ workes of John lidgate w*hich* John Stow hath caused to be coppyed out of an owld booke sometyme wrytten by John sherleye as is aboue made mencyvn / John sherley wrat in þᵉ tyme of John lydgate in his lyffe / tyme." On the first pages the handwriting is that of Stowe, but from fol. 134 his work has been carried on by some one else, who also wrote the above-mentioned note of introduction, which, it is clear, was put in afterwards. The words " caused to be copied " in the final note also seem to indicate that Stowe was not the only writer of these poems out of Sherley's book.

There are three more small entries on fol. 132 *a* :

1. "a seyng of da*ñ* John Lydgat." Two stanzas. The first speaks of "fowr thyngs that makyth ma*ñ* A fooll," and the second of "fowr thyngs cawsyng gret folye."

2. proverbe.

3. dictum de senioribus.

Fol. 132 *b* : "balade de bone counseyle," only one stanza.

Fol. 132 *b*–134 *a* : ".A letar made in wyse of balad by daun John Lydgat / brought by A pursyvaunt in wyse of momers dys- guysyd to fore þᵉ mayre of london estfeld vpon the twelffthe nyght of cristmasse,"[1] etc. The poem contains numerous historical and geographical names as well as classical references which are partly explained in marginal notes.

Fol. 1̣34 *a*–135 *b* : " A lettar made by John lidgat for a mom-*m*ynge whiche þᵉ gold smythes of london shewyd before Eestfyld þᵉ mayr on candylmas day at nyght this letar was presentyd by an Harold callyd fortune."

Fol. 135 *b*–136 *b* : " a balade made by daun John Lidgate at elltham in cristmasse ffor amomyng to fore the kynge and the Quene."

Fol. 136 *b*–140 *a* : poem in five-beat iambics with the following heading : " Nowe foloweth here the maner of a bille by weye of supplycation put to the kynge holdinge his noble fest of crystmasse

---

[1] By the side of this heading the following note : "william estfeld meresar mayre anno domini 1430, also þᵉ second tyme mayre anno 1438."

in the castell of hartford as in dysguysinge of þe rude vpplandishe
people complayninge on ther wyues *with* the boystrus answere of ther
wyues / deuysed by lidgate / at þᵉ requeste of the countrowlore /
Brys slayn at louiers."[1]

Fol. 140 *a*–144 *a*: "... the deuyse of a desguysinge to fore the
grete estates of this land than beinge at london made by lidgate daun
John the munke of bury" etc. A poem of the same metre as *Reason
and Sensuality,* and also in other respects very much resembling it.

Fol. 144 *a*–145 *b*: "the deuyse of amomynge to for the kynge
Henry the sixte beinge in his castell of wyndsore the fest of hys
crismasse holdinge ther made by lidgate dame John the munke of
bury how pampull[2] (!) and the floure delys came first to the kynges
of fraunce by myracles at reynes."

Fol. 145 *b*–161 *a*: a series of ballads by Lydgate :—

1. A ballad "gyuen vnto þᵉ kyng Henry and to his moder the
quene Kateryne sittyng at þᵉ mete vpon the yeares day in the castell
of Hertford."

2. A translation of "gloriosa dicta sunt de te," etc.

As we read in the heading, the author made this poem at "thyn-
staunce of the bushope of excestre."

3. Two ballads entitled "of good counsayle;" the first is char-
acterized by its heading as a translation out of the latin.

4. A ballad "translated out of frenche."

5. "a balade made at the reuerence of our lady."

6. "a balade w*hich* lydegate wrote at þᵉ request of a squyer þat
serued in loues courte."

7. A ballad "at þᵉ reuerence of my lady of Holand, and of my
lord of glouscester to fore þᵉ daye of there maryage in þᵉ desyrous
tyme of ther true louynge."

8. "a balade sayde by agentillwoman which loued aman of gret
estate."

Fol. 161 *a*–166 *a*: "a sayenge of þᵉ nightingalle" by Lydgate.

Fol. 166 *a*–168 *b*: "an ordonaunce of a presesyon of þᵉ feste of
corpus cristie made in london by dame John lydegate."

Fol. 169 *a* and *b*: "seuen balades mad by dame John lydgate
of þᵉ sodeine fall of certayne princes of ffraunce and engelond, now
late in our dayes."

---

[1] Louviers, town of France, dep. Eure, near Rouen. It was taken and
sacked by Edward III. and again by Henry V.

[2] Stands for þ ampull (ampulla).

Fol. 169 *b*–170 *b* : "a balade ryall now late made by dame John lydgate þᵉ munke of bury ymagyned by him *within* þe tyme of his translation of bocas by þᵉ commaundement of my lord of glocester."

Fol. 170 *b*–177 *b* : "þe lyffe of saynt margret." Lydgate translated the poem, as the heading shows : "at þᵉ request of my lady of Huntingeton some tyme þᵉ countes of þᵉ marche."

Fol. 177 *b*–179 *a* : "kalundare of John shirley, w*hi*ch," as is added in the heading, "he sett in þᵉ beginninge of his booke."

Fol. 179 *b*–183 *a* : "þᵉ prologe of John lydgattes testament whiche I fownd in M*agister* stantons boke." This poem appears again in the handwriting of Stowe.

Fol. 183 *b* : blank.

Fol. 184 *a*–286 *b* : our poem.

Fol. 287 *a*–288 *a* : "þᵉ fyfteɳ ooes drawen," as we learn from the colophon, "oute of latyn vnto engelishe by lidgate."

On the last page we find, beside the statements above mentioned, two small poetical entries : the first with the heading "boccius de *con*solatio (!) philosophie ; " the second, warning the false pity of ever-weeping women.

Now coming to our own poem it extends as already mentioned from fol. 184 *a*–236 *b*. Like F it is written in single columns. Only one line (88) is in the margin. There is no attempt at illumination or other ornament. The Latin comments on the margin are also written in black ink. On the last pages some of these marginal lines are cut off at the end. The handwriting shows that Stowe and his assistants in the preceding pages took turns in the work of copying.

3. RELATION OF THE TWO MSS.

There is no doubt that our poem found its way into the Addit. MS. from F. Some of the corrections supplied in various places of F, as has already been hinted, by Stowe, show conclusively that he used this MS., but even in our poem there are traces of Stowe's pen. The title has been filled in by him, and further below we find the two nouns of this title, where they occur in the body of the text, added in the margin also in his handwriting. But the texts themselves prove, when compared, that A is a mere copy from F. In all essentials they agree perfectly. Only where F contains manifest errors, Stowe has substituted conjectures which we have partly adopted. Occasionally also, obsolete forms which the copyist did not understand, were replaced by more current expressions. Thus "the same" is sometimes found instead of "thilke." Six verses are left out: 1930, 4409, 4450, 4715, 6440–41. In the last two of these omitted verses, we find a fresh proof that A was copied from F. These lines (6440 and 6441) happen to be at the end of fol. 291 *b* of F. Stowe having written up to this point had just completed a page. So turning over and beginning a fresh column, he could easily fall into the mistake of forgetting the few verses left and beginning a fresh page of F.

Thus, though Stowe's copy, on the whole, proves fairly exact, as far as the text itself is concerned, his orthography is far from being what we might call conservative.

We need hardly mention the fact that he often wrongly adds or omits an "e" at the end of a word. This misuse of the final "e" is not astonishing in a MS. written at a time when the true use of it had been lost for about two centuries. Neither should we be surprised by the confusion of "s" and "c" in words of Romance origin, which is, of course, due to the fact that there was no phonetic difference between these letters. But a most remarkable characteristic is the scribe's excessive fondness for the letter "y" instead of "i." In this respect he goes much farther than the writer of F; an "i" of the letter is usually replaced by "y." Examples: him—hym, his—hyr, scripture—scrypture, Appetite—Appetyt, wille—wyll, fille —fyll, etc. Frequently we find "y" also in verbal inflexions substituted for "e": disposen—disposyn, feleth—felyth, serveth— servyth, couched—couchyd. These alterations seem to be more or less arbitrary. A similar arbitrary method is employed with regard to the joining or separating of words. Thus the indefinite article often appears connected with its noun, while, on the other hand, compound verbs are resolved into their constituent parts: a wounde —awounde, a cedre—aseder; be kam—bekam, overtake—over take, perserved—per served.

All other differences are in the direction of the modern system of spelling.

1. Obsolete forms of prepositions, conjunctions, pronouns disappear: ageyn[e]s—ageynst, swich—such, yif—if, hit—it.

2. With a few exceptions the "ea" of modern orthography has taken the place of the "e" in F: seson—season, bemes—beames, mene—meane, appered—appeared, reherse—rehearse, hed—head.

3. "u" has been altered either into "w" or "v": ansuere—

answer, thou—thow, duellen—dwellen ; dyuerse—dyvers, gouerne—
governe, euery—every, haue—have.

4. "er" has been replaced by "ar," even where this alteration
does not agree with the present pronunciation. This is the case both
in unaccented and accented syllables : after—aftar, tother—tothar,
water—watar, serve—sarve, hert—hart, mervelous—marveylous,
sterres—starres.

5. The consonant following a short vowel is mostly doubled : al
—all, shal—shall, wil—will, ful—full, wel—well, hil—hyll, bakward—backward, egal—egall. The practice is by no means confined
to final consonants : shalt—shallt.

6. The expedient of doubling a letter to express the long vowel
sound is not adopted : thus Stowe writes " non " where in F we find
"noon." Other instances : alsoo—also, treen—tren, oonly—only,
stoon—ston, shoon—shon, seeth—seth.

7. Endings in Romance words like " dre," " tre," " ble," " bre "
appear in Stowe's MS. generally as " der," " ter " (" tar "), " bell,"
" ber." Instances : metre—mytar, considre—consider, remembre—
remember, agreable—agreabell, perdurable—perdurabell.

8. The " r " in such words as " thrust," " briddes " is shifted :
thurst, byrdes.

If we add, in conclusion, that the O.E. forms of the possessive
pronouns are supplanted by those of O.N. origin, I think we have
touched on the salient points of Stowe's alterations.

Reason and Sensuality.

[*MS. Fairfax* 16 (*Bodleian Library*), *leaf* 202.]

Reson) and sensuallyte compylid by John Lydgat.

To alle folkys vertuouse,
   That gentil ben) and amerouse,
Which love the faire pley notable
Of the chesse, most delytable,   4
Whith alle her hoole ful entente :
To hem thys boke y wil presente ;
Where they shal fynde and sen Anoon),
How that I, nat yore agoon),   8
Was of a Fers so Fortunat
In-to a corner dryve and maat,
Of hir[e[that, withoute lye,
Koude ful many iupartye,   12
And hir draughtes in swich wise
So disposen and devise
That vlixes, to reknen alle,
To hir ne was nat peregalle.   16
   But first or I do specifye
Myn) entent, for to vnwrie,
Or ferther in this boke procede,
I prey hem all that shal hyt rede,   20
Wherso hyt plese hem outher greve,
Nat be to hasty to repreve
Thys werke, in hyndring¹ of my name,
Ther-vpon) to sette a blame.   24
For many oon), in metre and prose,
That nouther kan) the text nor glose,

I present this book to all lovers of Chess.

It tells how

I was mated by a Queen,

who was cleverer than Ulysses.

I ask my readers not to be hasty in blaming me.

The Author.	Wil ful[1] ofte at prime face [1] ful] om. A.

Som̃ thing⸳ hindren̄ and difface,   28
Or they can̄ any lake espye,
Oonly of malyce and envye
Or collateral necligence ;

But if my work offends any careful reader,

But who that of good dilligence   32
Lyst bysye him to don̄ his cure
To sen and rede thys scripture,
And feleth̄ fully the sentence,
Yif hee therin kan fynde offence,   36
My wille is this, that he observe
Me to repreve, as y desserve,

[leaf 202, bk.]
I hope he'll scold me, and correct what is wrong.

Besechinge him for to directe
Al that ys mys, and to correcte :   40
This pray I him of hert entere.
Now wille ye than this matere
Considre wel, and han a sight⸳,
And ye shal fynde anoone ryght⸳   44
By and by in this scripture
Of my matynge the Aventure.

¶ Cy comence Lauctour soñ trayte.

Fortune has

After this Fortune sone,
Which̄ ofter changeth̄ as the mone,   48
Had throgh̄ hir subtil gyn be-gon̄ne
To yive me drynke of her ton̄ne,
Of which she hath̄, with̄-oute wer⸳,[2]   [2] wer] wher F. A.

2 tuns in her cellar ;

Couched tweyn̄ in hir celler :   52
That oon̄ ful of prosperite,
The tother of aduersyte,
Myd hir wonderful taverne,
Wyth̄ the which she dooth̄ gouerne   56
Euery maner creature,
With-oute[n] ordre or mesure,
By a maner ful dyuerse.

one full of delicious drink,

The ton̄ of hem she kan̄ reverse   60
With̄ a drynke ful preciouse,
Ryght⸳ sote and ryght⸳ delyciouse,
Of which̄ no man̄ kan̄ drynk hys fille,
Thogh̄ he haue plente at his wille,   64

So ful hyt is of fals delyte,
Throgħ his gredy Appetite,
So ydropyke is hys lust
That plenty non may stavnche his thrust. 68

    The tother drynke, in sothfastnesse, the other full
of bitterness.
Ys so ful of bitternesse
To hem that taste it, this no fable,
Lothsome and alle habomynable. 72

And of this ilke drynkes tweyne These she
serves to folk,
Serveth fortune, in certeyne, with joy or
sorrow.
To alle foolkys eve and morowe, [leaf 203]
Some witħ Joye and some witħ sorowe, 76
After fortune lyst ordeyne.

And thus, wheɲ I had do my peyne When I had
tasted both,
To knowe sothely, in sentence,
The verray trewe difference 80
Of this drynkys ful notable :
First of the swetnesse delytable
And of the tothris bitternesse,
Whicħ broghte meɲ in gret distresse, 84
Causynge hem her lyve to lothe ;

And whaɲ y knyw the kynde of bothe :
The same tyme, this¹ no nay, ¹ this] this is F. A.
In a morowe so as I lay [This line is inserted in the margin; 88 I lay in bed
also in A.]
In my bed wytħiɲ a cloos,
Whaɲ the clere sonɲe Aroos one spring
morning.
In grene ver ful of delyt,
Whicħ prikketħ witħ his appetyt 92
This lusty hertys amerouse,
The sesoɲ is so graciouse,
For this sesoɲ, with-outeɲ fayle, Spring
clothes the
Clotheħ witħ newe apparayle 96 earth anew.
Alle the erthe, this verray trewe,
Witħ many sondry dyuers hewe ;
The same tyme, in special,
The day and nyghť be lycħ egal. 100

¶ Cy parle Lauctour de prime temps.

This is the lusty sesoɲ newe
Which euery thing causetħ renewe

The Author.
And reioyssheth in his kynde,
Commonly as men) may fynde   104

Spring's white and red flowers
In these herbes white and rede,
Which spryngen in the grene mede,
Norysshed wyth the sonne shene,
So that alle the soyl ys grene,   108

[leaf 203, bk.]
Al ouersprad with sondry floures,
With bavme dewed and soote shoures,
Both hil and wale on) euery syde,

make the earth look like the starrd Heaven.
So that the erthe, of verrey pride,   112
Semeth of beaute to be evene
Vnto the bryghte sterred hevene.
Hys mantel ys so lusty hewed,
Wyth sondry floures al renewed   116
And wyth mottes fressh and fyne,
Which as any sterres shyne ;

Trees are new clad in green,
And euery bough, braunch, and tre,
Clad newe in grene, men) may se,   120
By kyndely disposicion)
Ech to bere fryut in ther seson).

springs are crystal-clear ;
And the wellys thanne appere
As cristal or quyk syluer clere,   124
Out of her veynes as they sprynge,
And in ther lusty stremes bringe :
Al plente and habondaunce
And fulsomnesse of al plesaunce,   128
Makyng the soyl so fressh and fair ;

the air is mild,
And so attempre was the air
That ther' ne was, in sothfastnesse,
Of colde nor hoot[e] no duresse ;   132
The bryghte sonne, y yow ensure,
Hys bemes sprad by swhich mesure.

the wind most sweet ;
And Zepherus, the wynde moost soote,
Enspired bothe croope and roote   136
Of herbes and of floures newe,
That they wern) alway fressh of hewe
And with her blosmes ful habounde,

the silver dew is like pearls on the grass.
And the siluer dropes rounde   140
Lych perles fret vpon) the grene ;
And euery greyn), with-oute wene,

Out of the erthe gan tappere,

Eue*r*ech be kynde in ther manere.

And thus the erthe, sooth to seyne,

Enforced him to gete ageyne

Hys beaute olde and his fairenesse,

That wynter slough with his duresse ;

And with his ornementz newe

He made him faire and fresh of hewe,

As a mayde in hir beaute

That shal of newe wedded be,

To seme pleynly to hir spouse

More agreable and graciouse,

For which she taketh, with-oute fayle,

Hyr beest and rychest apparayle.

   And thus in semblable[1] wise

The erthe.did him self disgise,

To shew him fair, lusty, and clere,

After the seso*n* of the yere ;

Wha*n* briddes in ther Armonye

Synge and make*n* melodye

In the seso*n* most benygne,

As nature lyst assigne ;

Wha*n* eche be kynde cheseth his make

And besy ben her nest to make,

Lych as techeth hem nature

To make, longe for tendure,

And her lignes to sustene,

And to Recure, thus I mene,

Ageyn the harmys and gret[2] damage,

That wynter wroughte with his rage,

And eue*r*y maner creature,

Of verray kynde, did his cure

To be glad and eke joyouse

For the seso*n* graciouse ;

And dyd also her besy peyne,

With hool herte and nat f[e]yne,

To serve love and to be trewe

In that lusty seso*n* newe.

144

In Spring

[leaf 204]

the earth regains its old beauty which Winter kild,

148

and is like a newly-wedded bride.

152

156

[1] semblable] semblalle F. semblabell A.

160

Birds make melody,

164

mate, and build their nests.

168

[2] and gret] and the gret F. A.

172

All creatures rejoice,

176

and serve Love.

180

The Author.

[leaf 204, bk.]

¶ **Here sheweth thauctour how natu[r]e appered vn-to hym.**

In the glad
spring-time,

The same tyme, in sothfastenesse,
   For verray ioye and gladnesse,
Yt fil in-to my remembraunce
To thynke vpoɲ the atemp*er*aunce   184
Of the noble, fresh*e* tyme,

n April,

In Apprile, whaɲ the firthe p*r*ime
Hath broghtᵗ in ver ful fair of syghtᵗ,
Whaɲ eu*er*y hert ys glad and lyghtᵗ   188
And him reioysseth with plesaunce,
For the grete suffysaunce
That they ha fou*n*de by disport :
The same tyme y toke comfort   192
Myn obs*er*vances for to kepe,

I lay half
awake,

Nouther in slombre nor a-slepe,
But for Ioye al wakynge,
To here the briddes chau*n*te and synge   196
Oɲ fressh*e* brau*n*ches in certeyɲ,
That to slepe me thoughtᵗ veyɲ.

to hear the
warbling
birds.

I was so ententyf for to here
Her wherbles and her notys clere   200
That myɲ ymagynacioɲ
So strong was in conclusyoɲ,
I was ravysshed, as thought*e* me,
Bothe to here hem and to se :   204

Suddenly a
lovely lady
appeard to
me,

That sodenly, in myɲ avys,
I saugh a lady of gret prys,
Most excellent of beaute,
Appere sodeynly to me :   208
Whos fairenesse whaɲ I gaɲ be-holde,
For fere myɲ hert[e] gan to colde
And drough bakward of sodeyɲ drede,
Whaɲ I behelde hir woman-hede   212

whos beauty
shed light on
all the place.

And the beaute of hir face,
The whiche aboute*n* al the place

[leaf 205]

Caste so mervelous a lyghtᵗ,
So clere, so p*er*cynge and so bryghtᵗ,   216
That the goddesse Proserpyne

With al hir bryghte stonys fyne
And hir ryche perles clere
To hir beaute ne myght¹ appere.   220
They were so percyng and so chene,
That I ne myghte nat sustene
In hir presence to abyde,
But went bak and stood asyde,   224
Til at the last[e], in certeyn,
I Forced me [onward] ageyn),
Hert and body, in sothnesse.
   And tho y felt so gret swetnesse   228
Through my chambre, out of Doute,
Both withinne and with-oute,
Lych as hyt had[de] ben) at al
Ful of avmber oriental,   232
Of Aloe, and of muske newe,
And ful of Rosis fresh of hewe ;
And of al[le] thinges soote,
Of herbe, greyn), or any roote,   236
That man) kan) wisshen) or devise,
Vern there in her best[e] wise,
To shewen) and exemplyfye,
And also for to magnifye   240
The presence and the noblesse
Of thys hevenly emperesse,
Most digne, in sothe, to vere corovne,
Whos worthinesse y wil expovne   244
And descryve hir excellence,
Yif ȝe wil yive me audience.

¶ How the Lady nature gouerneth the Worlde.

This emperesse, y yow ensure,
I-called was Dame Nature,   248
The whiche in euery Region)
Is most worthy of Renoun,
Nat oonly touchinge hir beaute,
But moost eke of Auctorite ;   252
For this is she that is stallyd
And the quene of kynde called,
For she ys lady and maistresse

The Author.
At first, the Lady's beauty

made me draw back.

Then I came forward.

Her scent was

like amber,

musk and roses.

This Heavenly Empress

was Lady Nature,
[leaf 205, bk.]

Queen of all Creation.

The Author.	And vnder god the chefe goddesse,	256
Nature rules the earth,	The whiche of erthe, this no dout,	
	Hath gouernaunce rounde about,	
	To whom al thing must enclyne.	
	For, through purveance dyvyne,	260
	No man) may contrarie nor with-seye	
	Nor hir lawes disobeye,	
	Which ben so just and agreable,	
	And passyngly so resonable,	264
	And therwith al so ynly faire,	
	That this lady debonayre	
	Hath sothly syttynge in hir stalle	
the planets and stars,	Power of planetes alle	268
	And of the brighte sterrys clere,	
	Euerych mevyng in his spere,	
the revolving of the firmament,	And tournyng of the firmament	
	From) Est in-to the Occydent,	272
	Gouernance eke of the hevene,	
	Of Plyades and sterres sevene,	
	That so lustely do[1] shyne,	[1] do] F. A.
and of the 9 spheres which make Heavenly harmony.	And mevyng of the speres[2] nyne,	[2] speres] steres F. A.
	Which in ther heuenly armonye	277
	Make so soote a melodye,	
	By acorde celestiall,	
	In ther concourse eternall,	280
	That they be both[e] crop and roote	
	Of musyk and of songis soote.	
	And she, throgh her excellence,	
	Be the heuenly influence,	284
	And hir pover which ys eterne,	
[leaf 206]	The elementez dothe gouerne	
She governs the elements,	In ther werkyng ful contrayre.	
	And this lady debonayre	288
unites and severs them.	Doth hem somwhile a-corde in oon),	
	And after severeth hem anoon),	
	And devydeth hem a-sonder:	
	The ton here and the tother yonder,	292
	In ther naturel mouciouns	
	Thorogh dyuers transmutaciouns,	
	As men may see, y yow ensure.	

And this lady, Dame nature,   296   *The Author.*
Throgh hir myght', this verray trewe,   Nature
Alle erthely thing repaireth newe   repairs all
                                                              earthly
By naturel reuolucioñ   things,
And new[e] generacioñ,   300
To contynywe and hañ in mynde
Eche thinge in his ovne kynde,
Which she seth faylle and transmywe,
As yt is of kynde dywe,   304
By naturel disposicioñ,
To tourne to corrupcioñ.
For which this lady in hir forge   and in her
                                                              Forge even
Newe and newe ay doth forge   308   makes new
Thyngys so mervelous and queynte,   quaint
                                                              things.
And in her labour kañ not feynte,
But bysy ys euer in oõñ,
That to discrive hem euerychoñ   312
No mañ alyve hath wytte therto :
Aristotiles nor Plato.

¶ Here speketh thauctour of the beaute of Nature.

Touching' the beaute and fayrenesse   Her beauty
Of [t]his honourabill goddesse,   316
Ther was no mañ her alyve   no man can
                                                              describe or
That konnyng hadde to discryve
The excellence of hir beaute,
Nor comprehende in no degre   320   understand.
Hyr semelynesse, hyr womanhede,
For al beaute hyt dyd excede.   [leaf 206, bk.]
For she was, shortly for to telle,
Verray exaumple and eke the welle   324
Of al beaute in this worlde here,
For douteles, withoute were,
Yf she shal shortly be commended,   *Nota*
There was no thing to be amended.   328
For she sempte, by hir vysage   She lookt
                                                              young.
To be but yonge and tendir of age.
For iñ the face of this quene   In her face
                                                              no spot was
Ther was no spoote nor frovnce sene.   332   seen.

The Author.
For this no nay, as yt is kouthe,

Yet, young
as Nature
lookt,
Though she sempt flouryng in youthe [This line added in the margin.]
Th[r]ogh[1] fresħnesse of hir visage, [1] Th[r]ogh] thorow A.

she was so
old that no
man could
number her
days.
She was ful fer y-ronne in age, 336
That no man koude nor myght anon
Noumbre hir yeres euerychon,
Nor covnte hem alle in hys devys,
Nat Aristotle that was so wys. 340
And hyt sat wel, as by reson,
Vn-to her condicion
For to be fal[le] fer in age.
She was so prudent and so sage, 344

She never
changed.
In al hir werkys ferme and stable, *nota*
And neuer founde variable.

. ¶ **Now, after descripcioun of hir beaute, I shall
declare the maner of hir clothyng.**

She wore a
Touchyng the clothyng and vesture
    Of this lady, Dame Nature, 348
First in hir noble apparaylle
She had vpon of ryche entaylle,
Above[n] alle hir garnementys, 351

Mantle of
the Four
Elements,
Wrought of foure elementys,[2] [2] elementys] elemenentys F.
A mantel large hir self to shroude,
Which y ne comprehende koude,
Nor discrive in my konnynge.
The nature of euery thinge 356

which
pictured all
Creation,
For ther was wrogħt in portreyture,
The resemblaunce and the fygure

[leaf 207]
Of alle that vnto god obeyes,

and the Ideas
of it in God's
mind.
And exemplarie of ydeyes, 360
Ful longe aforn or they weren wrought,
Compassed in dyvyne thougħ[t].
For this lady, fressħest of hewe,

She works
day and
night,
Werketħ euer and forgeth newe, 364
Day and nyght, in her entent,

weaving her
garment.
Wevyng in hir garnement
Thynges dyuers ful habounde,
That she be nat naked founde. 368
For Antropos, hir self to wreke,

Doth ful many thredes breke,

The whiche of malyce kan) manace

The portreytures to difface

And the wonderful figures

Of the ymages and peyntures,

Maugre lachesys and cloto,

Whereof grete ioy[e] hath Pluto,

Cerberus, which devoureth al,

Y mene the porter infernal,

That al consumeth in her rage.

But to recuren hir Damage

She wirketh ay, and cesseth noght',

On) thinges in hir mantel wrought';

For ther was no thyng vnder hevene

That man) kan) thynke outher nevene,[1]

Wher yt of foule, wher yt of fayr,

Or briddes fleyng in the ayr,

Nor fysshes noone, out of drede,

With siluer skales whyte and rede,

That men) ther myghte sen) and fynde,

And portrey[e]de in her kynde

With colour[e]s to hem lyche,

And prest in her mantel ryche.

Man) was set in the hyest place

Towarde heven) erecte hys face,

Cleymyng hys diwe herytage

Be the syght of his visage,

To make a demonstracion) :

He passeth bestys of reson),

Hys eye vp-cast ryght' as lyne,

Where as bestes don) enclyne

Her hedes to the erthe lowe,

To shewe shortely and to knowe

By these signes, in sentence,

The grete, myghty difference

Of man), whos soule ys immortaH,

And other thinges bestiaH.

Side notes:

372

376

380

383

388

392

400

404

The Author.

Tho' Fate and Hell are ever destroy- ing her work,

Nature never stops repairing it.

[1] nevene] mevene F. A.

¶ Vnde *Ouidius* de *transformatis* : prona q[ue] *cum* spectent *etc.*

¶ Os hom*ini* sublime dedit, celum*que* vi- dere // Iussit et erectos ad celum tendere vultus.

Man was set faceward to heaven,

[leaf 207, bk.]

with eyes upcast, while beasts look down.

¶ **Of tharray of natures hede.**

Nature's

    Touching thatire and the Rychesse
      That this wonderful goddesse   408
Had oꝛ her hede, to tel[le] blyve,
I ha no konnyng to discrive ;

hair shone like the sun. Whos here shooꝛ as the sonne bryght,
That cast about[e] swych a lyght,   412
So persyng pleynly and so shene,
That I myghte nat sustene
To beholde the bryghtnesse
Nor the excellent fairnesse.   416

Her head reacht the Stars, For vp to the sterres rede
This lady raughte with hir hede,
And as I koude loke aferris,   419
Cloystred rounde with bryght[e] sterres,   [This line added in the margin.]
which circled it. Hir hed was cercled environ,
That Argus, in conclusioꝛ,
With hys hundred eyen bryght
The noumbre of hem nat tel[le][1] myght.   424

In her Crown were the 7 Planets.   And iu hir corovne, high as hevene,   [1] tel[le]] tell A.
Were[2] set the planetis sevene.   [2] were] where F.
And as me thought, I saugh my selve
In hir cercle sygnes twelve,   428
In ther course, out of Doute,
Froꝛ Est to West goynge aboute,
That the ryche corovne shene
Of Adriane, the fresshe quene,   432
[leaf 208] Was nat so lusty to be-holde.
And thus thys lady, as y tolde,
Vpoꝛ hir hede arrayed was,
Bryghter thaꝛ stoꝛ, cristal, or[3] glas   [3] or] or or F. 436

¶ **How the goddesse nature spake vnto**
the Auctour.

This Goddess Nature

    This noble goddesse honurable,
      Debonayre, and amyable,
Fressh of hewe as eny Rose,
spoke to me. Gaꝛ to me for to vnclose   440
And to discure hir talent
And the sonime of hir entent.

And tho, as I reherse kan),   *Nature*
Her tale anoon) thus she began) :   444
" My childe," quod she, " thou art to blame,   blamed me
And vn-to the yt is gret shame,
Thy self so longe to encombre,
Thus to slepe and to slombre   448   for sleeping
                                                               in the glad
This glade morwe fresĥ and lygĥt',   morning,
Whan) Phebus with his bemys bryght'
Ys reysed vp so hygĥ alofte,
And on) the herbes tendre and softe   452
The bawmy dropes siluer fair
Vapoured hatĥ vp in the ayr ;
And ther leves white and rede
Dotĥ vpon) her stalke to sprede,   456
And herest, how the briddes synge   when the
                                                          birds were
For gladnesse of the morwenynge,   singing.
Preysing god, as they best may,
Syngyng ther hourys of the day ;   460
And thou, of slouthe and necligence,
Dost vnto kynde grete offence,
Of verray wilful ydelnesse,
The whicĥ ys lady and maistresse   464
Of vicys al[le], this no drede.
Wherfore arys and take good hede,   She bade me
                                                          rise and do
Of wyt and of discrecion),   some work.
To do somme occupacion),   468   [leaf 208, bk.]
And draw the first to somme place,
For thyn) encrese, oonly of grace,
Wher as vertu dotĥ habounde,
Slouthe and vices to confounde."   472

¶ How the Auctour ansuerde to Nature.   *The Author.*

Whan she had shewyd hir sentence,
This lady most of excellence,
As she that was bothe fair and good,
Astonyed first ful still y stoode,   476   I was too
                                                               amazed to
And longe a-bood, in certeyn),   speak.
Or y durst ansuere ageyn),
What for drede, what for shame,
Desirous to knowe her name.   480

C

But tho in hast[e] this goddesse,
But Nature Oonly of her gentilesse,
To put me out of drede and fere,
Of al that me lyst enquire,   484
Or what so that me lyst devyse
cheerd me up, Yaf me answere in goodly wyse,
Benyg[n]e of chere and eke of face.
    And tho supprised with hir grace,   488
Out of my drede y gan abrayde,
And vnto hir[e] thus I seyde:
and so I "Ha ye, that be chefe goddesse,
Callyd quene and eke maistresse   492
Of euery thyng in this worlde here,
Which so goodly lyst appere
And shewe yow to my symplesse,
thankt her I thanke vn-to your high nóblesse   496
And eke to yóur magnificence,
Felynge wel by your presence
That your comyng douteles
Ys for my good and grete encres,   500
for her visit, Me so goodely to vysite,
Of entent, me to excite
Alle vertues for to sywe,
And vices pleynly to eschiwe,   504
[leaf 209] That wel y ought[e], of resoŋ,
To yive to yow a grete guerdoŋ.
and promist
to obey her For whiche, in sothe, til that y deye,
with all my
heart. I wil in euery thyng obeye,   508
With al my hert and al [my] myght,
To your plesaunce, as hyt ys ryght,
And ther-to do my bysy peyne,
Lych as your self list ordeyne."   512

¶ How nature Declareth to the Auctour
hir entent.

Nature then **T**his lady tho, ful wel apayed,
    Quod she to me: "thow hast wel sayed,
For which I wil, in sentence,
That thow yive me Audience;   516
bade me For more y wil the nat[1] respite   [1] the nat] not the A.

" But that thou goo for to visyte

Rounde thys worlde in lengthe and brede,

And considre, and take good hede,   520

Yf ther fayle in my wirkynge

Of fairenesse any thynge,

Or of beaute ther wanteth ought'   523

And of wyssdome that may be sought ;

To fyn, that thou maist comprehende

The mater, and thy self amende,

To preyse the lorde eternal,

The whiche made and caused[1] al,   [1] caused] causeth A.   528

And is him silf so iuste and stable

And of pover pardurable ;

The which for man), in hys werkynge,

Made and wroughte euery thing :   532

Beste and foule, as thou maist see,

And sondry fysshes in the see,

And trees with her blosmys newe,

Herbes and floures fressh of hewe :   536

To fyn), he shulde him not excuse,

Duely hem for to vse,

And nat distroyen) hem in veyn).

" For al this worlde, in certeyn),   540

Was maad, as I reherse kan),

For profyt oonly of A man),

That he sholde han the souereynte

Of al thys noblesse and bewte,   544

Havynge in verray existence

The lordshippe and the excellence

And the chefe prerogatyfe,

As he that ys superlatyfe   548

Of thing commytted to his cure,

As most souereyn) creature.

For whiche these olde clerkes all

The lesse worlde lyst to call,   ¶ Mundus homo minor est.   552

For hys noblesse and reson)

And also for hys high renoun.

For, by recorde of olde scripture,

Hyt founden ys in hys nature,   556

So many propurte notable,

Marginal notes:

Nature.

go round the World, and see if anywhere her work fails in beauty,

[This line added in the margin.]

so that I may praise God

who made everything for Man,—

beast,

fish,

tree,

flower,—

[leaf 209, bk.]

that he should be lord of all.

This is why Man was cald the 'less World.'

Man is like God, as well as like the World.

" That man ys sothely resemblable

Man is like
the World,
Vn-to the worlde, this no doute,

Whiche ys so grete and rounde aboute.　　　560

for all it holds
is seen in him.
For what this worlde dothe contene,

Parcel therof men may sene

Within a man ful clerly shyne,　　　¶ relucet in homine.

As nature doth him enclyne　　　564

He is like God
too.
Lych to the goddys immortall

That be a-bove celestiall,

To whom a man, for hys noblesse,

Ys[1] half lyke throgh hys worthynesse.　　¹ Ys] Ye F.A. 568

And since he
is so,
" Now man, sithe thou art semblable

To goddys that ben pardurable,

he ought to
keep from
vice,
Thow owest wel to do thy peyne

Thy self fro vices to restreyne,　　　572

Knowyng the grete dignyte

Wheche god a-bove hayth yove to[2] the,　　[This line added in the margin.]

Which thou shuldest neuer cesse　　² to] om. A.

and grow in
virtue.
In vertu al wey to encresse.　　　576

And euer in oon be ententive

To be perfyte of thy lyve,

And certes elles to thy name

Hyt is rebukyng and gret shame."　　　580

¶ How the Auctour answerde to nature.

[leaf 210]
I say it is a
" Lady," quod I, " and maistresse

And vnder god cheffe goddesse

Of al this worlde, as semeth me,

great dignity
for man to
be like God;
Hyt is a ful grete dignite　　　584

The whiche is yoven vn-to man,

Yf he by vertu siwe kan

To be lyke in condicion,

As god hath yove to him reson.　　　588

And yf he haue therin delyte,

He shal deserve ful gret merite,

Thorgh the werkes honourable,

To his noblesse covenable,　　　592

And gret guerdon, whan he hath do,

And I acorde wel therto.　　　Auctor.

but it is hard
But hyt is harde, who kan discerne,

" A man) him self so to governe,   596
And for to do hys bysy peyne   for man to
For to acheve and atteyne   attain per-
                                                                                     fection,
Vnto so higħ perfeccion),
And yit haue y affeccion)   600   tho' I want
Wyth al my hool[e] wyt and mynde   to reach it.
Therto a way[e] for to fynde."

¶ Nature.   *Nature.*

"Certys and thou wilt nat feyne,   Nature tells
                                                                                     me I can do
Thow shalt mowe wel the wey atteyne,   604   so,
And fynally the pathe acheve,
Of whiche no man) the shal repreve ;
Yf thou lyst wyrken) as the sage,
Begynne anoone thy viage,   608
As I ha seyde the ther to forne,
Lyst thy travayle be nat lorne.
For in thy bed thus to soiourne   if I'll not
                                                                                     lie in bed,
To gret harme hyt wil the tourne.   612
And fyrst considre weħ in thy syght   [This line added in
                                                                               the margin.]
Too goo the wey[e] that is ryght,   but go the
                                                                                     right way,
And haue in mynde euer amonge   or road,
In thy passage thou goo nat wronge,   616
Nor erre nat in thin entent.   [leaf 210, bk.]
For in thys worlde here present
Be so many dyuers thynges,
Wonderful in ther werkynges,   620
And weyes, somme freysħ and feyre,
And somme also that be contreyre,
The whiche, in sotħ, who taketħ hede,
Ful dyuersely a man) kan) lede ;   624
For which I wil that thou be wyse,   and take
                                                                                     care not to
And that thow) goo be good avyse,   wander from
                                                                                     it.
That in the fyn) thou erre nought.
But cast profoundly in thy thought,   628
As thou gost in thys worlde here,
To erre nat in no manere."

¶ The Auctour ansuerde vn-to nature.

" Ha, lady myn)," tho quod I,

The Author.
I ask Nature
to teach me
the right way.

" For goddys sake hath mercy   632
To teche me, and sey nat nay,
Whicħ ys the verray ryghte way,
Vnto me most profitable !
This prey y yow, of hert[e] stable. "   636

Nature

¶ **Nature.**

And she ne lyst no lenger duelle,
But in al hast[e] gan me telle
And seyde : " thou shalt fynde trewe,
Ther be ful many weyes newe,   640
Wonderful and ryghť dyuers,
Bothe good and eke pervers,
Of whicħ, yif I shal nat feyne,

says there
are two ways,

In especial[1] ther be tweyne,   [1] especial] special A.   644
And thou mayst chese[n], in substaunce,
Whiche ys most to thy plesaunce :

one to the
East,

The toon gyneth in thorient
And gooth towarde thoccident,
And lenger' ther lyst nat soiourne
But ageynwarde doth retourne,
Takyng hys gynnyng of entent
By exaumple of the firmament.   651

¶ Oriens signiﬁcat celestia et diuina / et occidens temporalia et terrena / et ideo prima via que incipit ab oriente et tandem reuertitur ibidem est via racionis que incipit

[leaf 211]
the other to
the West.

The tother from' the west certeyn)
Towarde the est tourneth ageyn),
The ryghte wey, but then) anoon),
Whan) that he hath hys cours [y]-goon),
By a maner ful contraire
Ageyn) westwarde he doth repaire.
But vnderstond and take good hede,
Whicħ thou shalt sywe[n] in dede   660
And mayntene witħ al thy myghť,
As the way that ys most ryghť.
For fynally, in sentence,
Of hem thys ys the difference :   664

¶ a consideracione celestium et eternorum et leuiter transeundo per ista terrena semper redit et finaliter se conuertit ad eterna / Alia vero via que incipit ab occidente signiﬁcat viam sensus qui adheret communiter magis temporalibus et terrenis.

The East

Thorient, whicħ ys so bryghť
And casteth forth so clere a lyghť,

betokens
Heavenly
things.

Betokeneth in especiall
Thinges that be celestiall   *¶ Verba expositoris in latino et translatoris in anglico.*   668
And thinges, as I kan) diffyne,

" That be [1] verrely dyvyne.

For whicħ, in conclusyon),

This is the wey[e] of Reson) 672 The Eastern way is the way of Reason ;

Which causeth man), thys no nay,

For to goo the ryghte way

Which hath his gynnyng in the Est.

But the tother of the west 676 the Western, of Sensuality.

Ys, who that kan) beholde and se,

The wey of sensualyte,

Which set his entente in al

To thinges that be temporal, 680

Passynge and transytorie,

And fulfylled of veyn) glorie.

¶ **Now speketh the auctour of the two vertues
that nature hath yive to mañ.**

" G od the which of hys goodnesse, · God has

As to forne y dyd expresse, 684

As he that bothe may and kan),

Hath yove and graunted vnto man) given man

Many vertu in substaunce, [leaf 211, bk.]

Throgħ hys myghty purveyaunce, 688

Twoo maners of knowlychynge,

As he that is most souereyn) kynge,

And thys myghty lorde also

Hath graunted hym vertues two, 692 two Virtues,

That ben) in pris of gret noblesse,

Which conveye him and eke dresse

And conduyte him, out of drede,

In euery thing, whan) he hath nede. 696

The first, withbout[e] werre or stryf, ¶ Virtus sensitiua per quam homo grosso modo cognoscit et sentit.

Called the vertu sensytif, 1. sensitive, by which he perceives things,

By which he feleth and doth knowe

Thinges, bothen) high and lowe, 700

Which to forn) him be present,

Conceyvynge in hys entent

Foreyn thinges accidental :

I mene thus, in special, 704

As is recorded in scriptures,

As ben) colours and figures

Nature.
" And many sondry eke sauours,

feels heat
and cold,
Hoot and colde in storm) and shours, 708

And, shortly also to compyle,

Other formes that be sotyle,

Naturely, as hyt ys dywe,

Of hys kynde to pursywe 712

and what
pleases or
offends him;
Thinges that be to his plesaunce,

And eschewe hem that do greuaunce,

And flen) fro hem that ben) odible;

Whiche[1] vertu namyd ys sensible, [1] Whiche] With F.

And is, as y reherse kan), 717

Yove to beste and eke to man),

But vn-to man) him to governe

More perfytly, who kan) discerne. 720

2. Under-
standing
The[2] tother vertu, out of drede, [2] The] To F. A.

Myn) ovne frende, who taketh hede,

Ys called, in conclusion),

and Reason,
Vnderstondyng and reson), ¶ Intellectus *et* racio. 724

By whiche of ryght', with-out[e] shame,

Of a man) he bereth the name,

[leaf 212]
And throgh clere[3] intelligence [3] clere] clene A.

by which he
differs from
beasts,
Fro bestes bereth the difference, 728

And of nature ys resemblable

and is like
Gods,
To goddys that be pardurable;

Knowynge throgh hys dignite

Many thinges that be secre; 732

Wher sensityf, this is certeyn),

Is in knowynge but foreyn),

As of the barke which is withoute

For-derked with a maner doute, 736

Of thing*es* which by accident

Ne ben) but out-warde (but) apparent,

And ne kan no ferther wy*n*ne

To know the prevy pithe withynne; 740

Wher as man), in sentence,

By reson) hath intelligence

seeking to
know divine
and spiritual
things.
To make hys wytt to enclyne,

To knowe thinges that be dyvyne, 744

Lastyng and perpetuel,

Hevenly and espirituel,

" Of heven) and of the firmament,   *Nature.*

And of euery element,   748

Whos wyt ys so clere y-founde,   Man's under-
                                                   standing
So p*er*fyt pleynly and profounde,   pierces earth
                                                   and heaven.
That he p*er*ceth erthe and hevene

And fer above the sterris sevene,   752

So that he hath of eu*er*y thing

Verray p*er*fyt knowlechyng

In his secret ynwarde syght',

So that this vertu to no wyght',   756

Of reson) and entendement,

I mene as in this lyve p*re*sent,

Is yiven) oonly but to man).

And as me semeth trewly than),   760

He sholde, who so kan) discerne,   He should
                                                   rule himself
Oonly by reson) him governe,   .by Reason
                                                   alone.
Lyst that he, whiche wer grete shame,   ¶ Concludendo qu*od*
                                        no*n* sit dign*us* ha-
Be depryved of hys name.   bere nomen hominis.

¶ How nature procedeth ferther to speke   [leaf 212, bk.]
of these twoo vertues.

"Yet ferthermore, as hyt is skylle,

To tel[le] the y haue grete wille,

How this vertu sensityf   Man's feel-
                                                   ings often
Hath oft[e] sythe ful gret stryf   768   strive with
                                                   Reason,
With reson), the myghty quene,

And hir quarel doth sustene

Ageyns hir ful Rigorously,

And many sythe ful folyly   772

Ys to that lady debonaire

In her werkyng ful contraire,   and thwart
                                                   her work.
No thing of hir opinion) ;

For, fynaly, lyche as reson)   776

Vnto vertu ay accordeth,

So sensualyte discordeth,   Sensuality
                                                   desires only
And hath noon) other appetit   bodily de-
                                                   light.
But in bodely delyt,   780

Al set to worldly vanyte.

And this a gret dyuersyte

Atwene her condicion) ;

Nature.
" For euer at contradiccioṇ   784
Beṇ thise tweyne douteles,
Ay at discorde, and selde in pes,
To our purpos in special.

Reason
But Reysoṇ, that goueṛneth al,   788
I dar afferme hyt nat in veyṇ,
Holdeth the wey[e], most certeyṇ,

guides men
to the whole-
som East,
Tournyng towarde thorient̛,
Most holsoṃ and convenient   792
To oṇ entent who haveth grace
Therin[1] to walkyṇ and to trace.   [1] Therin] Wherin F. A.

while Sensu-
ality
Al be that sensualyte
Causeth meṇ, who that kaṇ se,   796
Of wilfulnes euer amonge,

sends them
to the wrong
West
To go the wey[e] that is wronge,
Which westward euer doth enclyne,

[leaf 213]
Fer̛[2] out of the ryght[e] lyne ;   [2] Fer] for A.   800

of false plea-
sure.
Ful of plesaunce and fals delyte,
And of flesshly appetyte.
But my counsayl and myṇ avys
Ys : that thou be war and wys   804

This, men
should leave,
To leve[3] the wey, this holde I best,   [3] leve] love A.
Which that ledeth in-to West,

and go East-
ward,
And go alway, lyst thou be shent,
The wey toward the orient,   808
Which is a wey most covenable
And to manne resonable.

as the West
road
Al be the tother wey[e] seme   ¶ *i. e.* via sensualitatis.
Fair and fressh, as folkes deme,   812
And wonder sote in special

pleases only
bestial folk.
To swich as be but bestial,
The which I rede the teschiwe,
Of honeste, as hyt is diwe.   816

¶ How nature charged him to goo the wey of vertu and of Resoṇ).

Start then
with Virtue
and Reason.
" Begynne the wey[e], ech sesoṇ,
First at vertu and resoṇ,
And fle ech thing that they dispreyse,
And vp to god thy hert[e] reyse,   820

" And love him ouer al[le] thinge,

Nat declynyng fro hys biddyng !

And her with al take good hede

Both to love him and to drede

As thy lorde most souereyne ;   825

And to forn) thyn) eyen) tweyne

Most enterly lat him be set !

For thou, in soth, mayst' do no bet,

And, lych to hys *commaundement*,

Set thy desire and thyn) entent

To thinges that be celestiaH,

And dispise ther with aH   832

Erthely thinges transitorye,

And remembre in thy memorye[1]

Al swich worldly vanyte !

Love ryghtwisnesse and pite,   836

And as ferforth as thou kan),

Do to eny maner man),

Bothe of high and lowh degre,

As thou woldest he did to the !   840

And do no man no maner wronge,

But make thy self myghty and stronge

With al thyn) hool entencion)

To holde the wey[e] of reson),   844

The which, in soth, yif thou take hede,

Doth a man) to heven) lede,

The verray trewe, ryghte way,

Fro when) thou came, this is no nay,   848

And fynaly, yif thou take hede,

Thider ageyn) thou must *procede*.

Be ryghtful eke at al[le] dawes

Especial vnto my lawes,   852

As reson) wil of verray ryght',

And kepe the wel with al thy myght'

Fro thilke wey that ledeth wrong !

And eke eschiwe and make the strong   856

Pleynly ageyn[e]s alle tho

That the wronge wey[e] go !

I mene swich, as thou shalt fynde,

That falsly wirke ageyn[e]s kynde ;   860

Nature.

Love God ;

¶ Ita exhortabat*ur* Cipio a *patre* suo et ab avo suo vt sibi in somno videbatur.

fear Him as a Sovereign.

¶ Celestia spectato / semp*er* humana *contemn*ito It*em* pat*er* Iustitia*m* cole et pie-tate*m* / Ea eni*m* est via in cel*um*.

Set your mind on Heavenly things ; despise earthly.

[1] memorye] memoire F.   [leaf 213, bk.]

Do to every man as you would he should do to you.

¶ Viam racio*n*is tene.   Hold to Rea-son's road, which leads to Heaven.

Keep from the wrong road,

and oppose all who go it.

Nature. " The whiche for her gret offence
                   Oft[e] falle in the sentence

Genius is
the priest of
Nature,
                   Of my prest called Genivs.   ¶ Genivs sacerdos nature.
                   For, truly, thou shalt fynde hyt thus :   864
                   That his power is Auctorised
                   And throgħ the world eke solemnysed,

and curses
all who act
against her
laws.
                   To a-coursen alle tho
                   That ageyn) my lawes do.   868
                   For whiche, by the rede of me,

So, do as
Reason,
[leaf 214]
                   Do, as reson) techetħ the,
                   And thy wittis hool enclyne
                   To rewle the by hir doctrine,   872
                   Whom) that y love of hert entere

Nature's sis-
ter, bids,
                   As myn) ovne suster dere !
                   And she, in sootħ, lyst nat discorde
                   For nought' to whicħ I me accorde.   876
                   We be so ful of oon) acorde

for she and
Nature ever
agree.
                   That atwene vs ys no discorde,
                   And fully eke of oon) assent,
                   As he that hath entendement   880
                   May vnderstonde of newe and olde.
                   And shortly thus I haue the tolde
                   The wey[e] whicħ thou shalt eschewe,
                   And whiche of ryght' thou shalt pursewe,   884
                   Lycħ as to forn) I haue discryved,
                   Til tyme that thou be arived
                   Vp at the port of al solace.

And may
God send you
grace not to
fail !
                   And god the sende mygħt' and grace,   888
                   That thou erre nat nor faylle,
                   But that my wordes may avaylle
                   To al that may profyte the !
                   In sotħ, thou gest no more of me,   892
                   The surplus haue in remembraunce,
                   And fynaly, as in substaunce,
                   Do as the lyst, lo, this the ende !
                   For now fro the y must wende."   896

          ¶ How nature departed away, and how the auctour
             began his passage to visite the Worlde, As
             nature yaf him counsaylle.

And sodenly, y yow ensure, *The Author.*
Whan͛ this lady, dame Nature, Nature leaves me.
Departed was, y lefte allone
Solytary in gret mone, 900
Ful angwysshous in wo and peyne,
And hir absence gan compleyne.
And in al hast, whan͛ne she was goon͛,
Out of my bed I roose anoon͛, 904 [leaf 214, bk.] I get up,
And myd of my dool and sorwe
I clad[de] me that glade morwe, dress,
Which͛, in soth͛, gaf me corage
For to gynne my passage. 908
And sothly, lych͛ as she me bad,
In al hast whan͛ I was clad
And redy eke in myn͛ array,
I went[e] forth the same day, 912 and go into a big field
Vpon͛ my wey[e], in certeyn͛,
In-to a felde ful large and pleyn͛
To sen the seson͛ delytable,
Which͛ was to me ful profitable 916
And ryght͛ holsom͛ douteles ;
The whiche wey, in soth͛, y ches,
Couered with͛ flour[e]s fressh͛ and grene full of flowers,
By vertu of the lusty quene, 920
Callyd Flora, the goddesse,
That myn͛ hert[e] for gladnesse
Supprised was oonly to se
Of thilke[1] place the beaute, [1] thilke] the same A. 924
To my plesaunce most covenable
And of syght͛ most delytable. fair to see.
But in a while, this no nay,
I was disloggyd of my way, 928 But I wander from my path :
That I left anoone ryght͛
Therof bothe mynde and syght͛.
For thylke[2] seson͛ of the yere [2] thylke] the same A.
The ayre so atempere was and clere, 932 the air is so mild,
And also, as myn͛ Auctour tellys,
The freshnes of the clere wellys, the springs so fresh.
That fro the movntes were descended,
Which͛ ne myghte be amended, 936

The Author.

Made the cold[e] siluer stremes

Sunshine is on the streams.

To shyne ageyɲ the sonɲe bemes.
The Ryvers with a soot[e] sovne
That be the wallys ronne dovne . . .   940

[leaf 215]

And some also meɲ myghte see
Flowyng fro the salt[e] see,

Rivers bear large ships.

Somme so myghty and so large
To bere a gret shiþ or a barge,   944
The which, in many sondry wyse,
Serveden for marchandyse,
And wern also ful profitable
And vn-to manɲe ryght' vayllable.   948

Mountains are high.

I saugh also ful high mouɲtaynes,
The holtis hore and large playnes,
The medwes that wer inly fair,
And also eke in my repair   952

Wild beasts range forests.

The wodes grene and the forestis,
Rennyng full oft[1] wylde bestis,[2]
The whiche dide her besy cure
For to gete ther pasture,   956

[1] oft] of A.
[[2] This line is added in the margin.]

The sea is tempestuous;

The see sommwhile ful hidouse
Of wawes eke tempest[u]ouse,
Ful of fisshes·gret and smale,
And also eke, this is no tale,   960

the sky full of stars.

The hevene, who so taketh hede,
Ful of bryghte sterris rede.
And in my walke I saugh also
Many other merveyles mo   964
That truely, as thoughte me,
For the grete dyuersyte,
And for the thinges so vnkouthe,
Est and West, north and southe,   968
Which I behelde in many caas,

I forget all past events,

That al my lyf which passed was
Was clene out of my remembraunce,

so delightful are these worldly sights.

For the fals[e], veyɲ plesaunce   972
Of thys worldly vanyte,
Whiche sempte pleynly vn-to me
Of his facoɲ so graciouse,
So lusty and delyciouse,   976

That I was feble in my devis
Of wysdaṁ for to yive a pris
To eue*r*y thing, and dul of mynde, [leaf 215, bk.]
To preyse hit lyke his ovne kynde : 980 I am too
dull to praise
Earth's beau-
My ku*n*nynge was to feble and feynt, ties as they
deserve;
And so witḣ ignoraunce y-meynt.[1]   [1] y-meynt] I-mixitt A.
And yet felt y, in sothfastnesse,
Lyche a maner of suetnesse 984
Entre*n* in-to my corage,
Ay as y went in my passage,
Whycḣ was to me, y yow ensure,
Ryghṫ p*r*ofytable to my Norture ; 988 but they pro-
fit me.
And of the surplus of my thoughṫ,
Of thinges that I knyw ryghṫ noughṫ
I abood no lenger space,
But wonder lyghtly let hem pace. 992

¶ How the auctour mette sodeynly iij goddesse[s] and I. god whicḣ conveyde hem.

And, shortly, ferther to p*r*ocede
In my way, or I toke hede,
Al allone with-oute guyde,
My*n* eye so as I caste a-syde, 996
Ther was a pathe, with-out[e] lye,
In whiche I saugḣ a companye, I see four
Ful excellent of ther beaute,
And foure ther wern, as thoghte me, 1000
That ther ne was no ma*n* a-lyve
The whiche koude in sotḣ discryve
Her gret[e] fairenesse half a ryghṫ. fairest folk,
who ray forth
For they yaf as gret a lyghṫ 1004 light like the
stars in a
As sterris in the frosty nyghṫ, frosty night.
Whan*n*e walkne is most bryghṫ,
Witḣ-oute cloude or any skye,
That who that sey hem witḣ his eye, 1008
He myghṫ afferme*n* in certey*n*,
And recorde hyt wel, and sey*n*,
By apparence of her figures,
They wern noo*n* erthely creatures, 1012
But rather, who considered al,

Dyvine and eke celestial,

Who that wer wys and tooke good hede.

Of these
four folk,   And or that I ferther procede,   1016

Thys ys myn) entencion)

To make a[1] bref descripcion   [1] make a] make of a F. A.

Of hem, sothly, as ye shal se.

three are
Ladies,   And in novmbre ther wer thre,   1020

Ladyes of gret apparaille,

Among[e] whiche, this no faylle,

Ther was oon) hem to conveye,

Vnto whom they did obeye.   1024

And al[le] iij, thys no fable,

famous God-
desses.   Wer goddesses honourable

Of al this worlde, most famous ;

Myn) Auctour truly telleth thus.   1028

¶ Her the auctour maketh a descripcioun of Pallas.

The first is
Lady Pallas,   The first of hem y-named was,

As seyth my boke, Dame Pallas,

A goddes of ful gret renoun,

And by lyne descended doun

Fro the goddys high kynrede,

daughter of
Jupiter,   Doughter, pleynly, as I rede,

Of[1] Iubiter, the booke seyth thus,

sister of
Apollo,   And Suster also to Phebus.

And Iubiter, as clerkes write   1037

And in her bookes lyst endyte,

Is taken), so as they discerneth,

For the lord that al governeth,   1040

To whom) Pallas, lyk as they lere,

Ys his ovne doghtre dere,

Called so for hyr[2] prudence,

chief Goddess
of Wisdom.   As chef goddesse of sapience,   1044

In tokne, trewly, as yt is,

That alle wisdam descended is

Fro[3] god a-bove and al prudence,

And therfore, for hir excellence,

She called is, and that of olde,

Doughter to god, as I haue tolde,

¶ Iubiter apud poetas accipitur *multis* modis : al*iquando* pro deo vero *et* summo, sicut hic, cum dic*itur* q*uod* Pallas est filia Iouis *et* hoc est iuxta illud / *Omnis* sap*i*encia A domino deo est / al*iquando* capi*tur* pro planeta, al*iquando* pro celo al*iquando* pro igne vel aere super[i]ori al*iquando* eciam historialiter accipitur *pro* rege Crete.

nota
[2] hyr] hys F.   his A.

[3] Fro] for F. A.

¶ Pallas dom*ina* dea belli q*ue* interpretatur Idem q*uod* sap*i*encia v[e]l prudencia que in bello est m*ultum* necessaria.

Rede poetis, and ye shal se, [leaf 216, bk.]
And for hir gret[e][1] dignite,   [1] gret[e]] gretar A.   1052   *The Author.*
As she that may most availe,
Named the goddese of bataile,   Pallas is the
Of Armes, and of chyvalrye.   Goddess of
Battle.
In tokne, who that kaŋ espye,   1056
Wysdam, yif I shal nat tarye,
In werre[2] ys ful necessarye.   [2] werre] warrous A.
And she yiveth honour and glorie,
And vnto knyghtes eke victorye,   1060   She gives
Wher as she is fauourable ;   Victory to
whom she
And this lady honourable,   favours,
Who that euer be leve or lothe,
Thilke tyme, whaŋ she ys wrothe,   1064
Frowardly of hir nature,
Ys cause of discomfyture
To many ooŋ that may not chese,
And causeth hem her lyf to lese.   1068   and Death
and Shame
And somme she puteth in gret shame   to others.
To lese her honour and her name,
And many a noble Regioŋ
She hath brought' to confusioŋ,   1072
As grounde of' meschef and of sorwe.
And she also, both eve and morwe,   She takes
Idleness from
Thys myght'y lady and goddesse,   men,
Fro meŋ[3] avoydeth ydelnesse,   [3] men] man A.   1076
And maketh hem ful prudently
For to lyve vertuously,   and makes
them virtu-
Her lyfe by wisdaŋ to amende,   ous, wise,
And in her wyt to comprehende   1080
Secretys which that be dyvyne.
And she kaŋ folkes eke enclyne,
Both in werre and eke debat,
To beŋ ewrous and fortunat ;   1084   fortunate,
And maŋ, be kynde corumpable,
She kaŋ make pardurable,
Yf she be vertu him gouerne,   [leaf 217]
Lyk goddys for to be eterne,   1088   and heirs of
eternal life.
To lyveŋ in that perfyt lyfe
Wher[4] Ioye ys ay with-out[e] stryfe,   [4] Wher] whos A.

D

The Author. The whyche shal haue ende neuer,

But ay contwne and p*er*seuer   1092

In blysse, the whicħ, as I kan) telle,

Al worldly Ioy[e] dotħ excelle.

¶ Here descryuetħ the auctour the beaute and the maner of Pallas.

Lady Pallas

This lady, vn-to my devys,

    That was most excellent and wys,   1096

is passing
fair; and
Passyng fair for to beholde,

Lyche[1] to forn) as I yow tolde.   [1] Lyche] lyth F.

For, fynaly, in hir figure

Reserved was al mesure   1100

That, yif she shal be comp*r*ehended,   *nota.*

Ther was no thyng to be amended.

her hue fresh,
And hir colour and hir hiwe

Was eu*ere* y-lychc fresħ and nywe,   1104

And yet this lady, wys and sage,

tho she is old.
Was ryght' olde and of gret age,

No thing stondynge out of Ioynt

But ay abydynge in oo poynt,   1108

Her beauty
and wisdom
do not fade:
Whos beaute fade may nor falle,

For wisdam neuer may apalle,

Nor of Nature neuer sterve,   ¶ Sapiencia no*n* mar-
    cescit vn*de* appellat*ur*

she is cald
Minerva,
For whicħ she called ys Mynerve,   Minerva *id est* [im-]
    mortalis.

That ys to seyne in special   1113

or immortal.
A thing that ys ay inmortal.

Her eyes are
like torches.
And hir ey[e]n), in certeyn)

Resemblede vnto torchys tweyn),   1116

Whicħ brenten ay y-lyche bryght'   ¶ Hoc dicit*ur* quia sa-
    piens clare et p*er*fecte

Witħ-out eclypsyng of her lyght'.   videt et sapiencia illu-
    mi*n*at intellectum.

And fortħ I passe in sothnesse

Al hir beaute to expresse,   1120

[leaf 217, bk.]
For wel wote y, I sholde faylle,

Having of oo thing gret mervaille :

Her height
varies:
That hir gretnesse was vnstable,

And founden) ofte ryght' chaungeable :   1124

Somwhile amonge, I dar ensure,   ¶ Hoc dicit*ur* p*r*opter
    considerac*i*onem *ter-*

now ordi-
nary,
Comon)[2] she was of hir stature,   *renorum.*
    [2] Comon] cemon F. A.

And so*m*mwhile she wex so long   1127

That to the hevene she raught' amonge ;
And as myn) Auctour seyth certeyn),
The which ne writ no thing in veyn),
Sommwhile she persed of entent
Fer a-bove the firmament
And the sterris clere and bright',
That men) loste of hir the syght',
Tyl that hir lyst ageyn) retourne
Lowe in erthe to soiourne,
And openly, as hyt was seyn),
Took hir gretnesse new ageyn),
Whos mevyng[e] to devyse
I-shewed was in treble wyse,
As ye han herd aforn) declare.
And, certys, now I wil not spare
For to don) my besy cure
To discriven hir vesture,
With-outen) any more delay,
And the maner of hir array.

Margin notes:
¶ Propter consideracionem celestium. — *The Author.*
1131 — then rising above the stars
¶ Propter consideracionem diuinorum.
1136 — till she pleases to shrink to earth.
1140
1144 — I'll now describe her clothing.

¶ Of the vesture of Pallas the goddesse.

Hir clothing was, this no fable,
Ryght' worthy and ryght' honourable
Wroght and wove, this noo tale,
With sotil thredes softe and smale,
Of mater nat corompable,
The werk of which, in comparable,
Was also, who took good hede,
That, also god me save, and spede,
And me defende from al damage,
I kan) nat tel in no langage
What thing hyt was to my knowyng'.
For hyt was no erthly thing',
Nor wroght' be crafte of mannes hande,
Who that kan) wel vnderstande ;
For Pallas, which that ys goddesse,
And of wevyng chef maistresse,
Wroght' hyt, yif I shal nat feyn),
With hir ovne handis tweyn).
I knew yt wel, me lyst nat lye,

Margin notes:
1148
It is wrought of unrotting threads,
1152
1156
[leaf 218]
not woven by hand of man,
1160
nota
but by her own Goddess-hands.
1164

First whan͛ the werke y dide espye,

More fresh of hewe than͛ may flours,   1167

And wroght yt was of .iij. colours,   ¶ Hoc *dicitur* propter tres
                                                       partes ph*ilosoph*ie.

The whiche thre do signifye

The *partyes* of Philosophie,

Of which, by ryght͛ and nat of wrong,   1171

Pallas medleth euer among,   ¶ Pallas dea sap*iencie* in-
                                                       tromittit se ex m*atre*
Whos mantel, who that vnderstood,   de tribus partib*us* phi-
                                                       losophie.
Was long and wyde, large and brood,

As yt sat wel, of honeste,

To a lady of high degre   1176

To be arayed in this cas.

Swich was the mantel of Pallas,

And lyke myn͛ auctour in scripture

[1]Makythe mensyon of her armoure.[1]   [1—1] *om.* F. 1180

¶ Here descryveth the Auctour the armys of Pallas.

O f verray ryght͛, both hygh and lowe,
       Yt longeth to yow for to knowe,

And to emprynte in your memorye,   ¶ Pallas d*icitur* armata
                                                       quia sapiens *debet*
That Pallas, for to han victorye,   ha*b*ere m*u*ltiplic*em*
                                                       armaturam duar*um*
Shal eve and morwe armed be   virtutum.

In novmbre͛ with armvres thre :

First on͛ hir hede, be gouernaunce,

A bryght͛ helme of a-temperaunce,   1188

Harder than Iren͛ outher stel,

For to endure and last[e] wel,

Which maked was of swych temprure,   ¶ Deb*et* enim sapiens
                                                       ha*b*ere galeam tem-
That pollex swerde ne noon͛ armure   perancie,

May do therto no violence.   1193

And eke also, in hir diffence,

From al hir fon͛ hir self to were,

In her ryght͛ honde she had a spere,   1196

Which named was, in sothfastnesse,

The egal launce of ryght͛wysnesse,   ¶ Lanceam iusticie, et
                                                       scutum paciencie.
To loke that no wrong be do.

In hir lyfte hande she had also   1200

A myghty shelde of pacience

Ther-with to make resistence

AgeyꝚ al vices, out of drede ;

In whiche shelde, lyke as I rede, 1204

An hed was wroght¹ ful mervelous

Of a best[e] monstruous.

But thilke tyme, as I took hede,

Her helme was voyded from hir hede, 1208

Castyng in myꝚ oppiniouꝚ,

She did hyt of EntenciouꝚ,

That I myght¹ in the self[e] place

Sen the beaute of hir face, 1212

And ther-vpouꝚ be Iuge and deme.

And, truly, as me dide seme,

About hir hede environe

I saugh a passyng ryche corovne, 1216

Excellyng alle, I yow ensure,

The corovne except of Dame Nature.

But of ResouꝚ I dar wel seyꝚ,

And afferme hyt in certeyꝚ : 1220

The corovne of Pallas, the goddesse,

Surmountede al[le] of rychesse,

To which was nouꝚ egal nor Evene,

For of the highe god of hevene 1224

Hyt forged was, ful yore agouꝚ,

With many a noble ryche stouꝚ,

By a maner espicial.

And with this corovne most royal 1228

This ilke lorde, which ys most wys,

Corowned hir in paradys,

For hir beaute and high prudence, *nota*

Pallas, goddesse of sapience, 1232

Ther-by for to signifye,

Who that truly kaꝚ espye,

That verray wysdam hath no delyt,

Ne² no maner of appetyt 1236

In worldly thing most transitorie.

    And as hyt ys put in memorie,

The same **Pallas**, as I toke hede,

Fleyng had about her hede 1240

Of Cynetys ful grete novmbre,

Makyng in maner of an ovmbre,

The Author.

With her wynges ay flykeryng,　　　　　1243

To don̄ hir sport witħ her pleyng,[1]　　¹ pleyng] preyinge A.

¶ Ista sunt verba trans-atoris.
Whicħ thing to my fantasye

Of wisdam̄ may signyfye :　　　¶ Secundum q*uod* ipse op-pinat*ur* q*uod* q*ui*l*ibet* sapi*en*s deberet *habere* respectum *ad* finem *et* ex prudenci*a* diem mortis preuidere que cuil*ibet* hom*i*ni hic mortali est incerta.

And as the Swan sings before his death,
So as the **Swan**, this is no nay,

Syngetħ to forn̄ his fatal day,

With werbles ful of melodye,　　　　　1249

To shewen̄ in her armonye,

Of kynde as she is enclyned,

How the threde shal be vntwyned　　　1252

Of hir lyf, bookys seyn̄ so,

By antropos, and broke a-two :

so men (who are reason-able beasts)
So eue*r*y man̄, in caas semblable,

Whicħ is a best[e] resonable,　　　　　1256

Shulde aduerte, and han in mynde,

And vnclose his eyen̄ blynde,

should re-member that they must die,
To sen̄ aforn, it ys no Iape,

How he the dethe may nat eskape,　　　1260

Whan̄ Antropos the hour hath set,

And sen, sitħ it may be no bet,

That al our lyf, wyth-out[e] were,　　　1263

Ys but a maner exile here,　　　¶ Vn*de* sic*ut* olor sui funeris est preco / ita deberet q*ui*l*ibet* vir-tuosus gaudere de morte temporali q*ue* non

Of whicħ he ougħt[e] to be sad,

And ageynward lygħt⁺ and glad,　　　¶ est nisi transmutacio quedam ad vitam

[leaf 219, bk.]
And think[e], how he ys a man̄,　　　eternam vnde paul*us*

and should sing, before they quit this strifeful life,
Of vertu syng[e] witħ the swan̄,　　　de hoc mundo fessus

To forn̄ the tyme in special　　　cupiebat dissolui et esse cum chr*ist*o.

That called is his day fatal,

And sen, how this present lyf

Ys ful of werre and [of] strif,　　　　　1272

That to departe with al hys mygħt⁺

He sholde be botħ glad and lygħt⁺,

　　　¶ **Hoc est filius sap*ienc*ie.**

As Pallas childe, for to discerne,

to go to life eternal.
How he shal go to lyf eterne　　　　　1276

Fer a-bove the sterrys clere.

Now no more of thys matere,

But first, so as I vndertook,　　　¶ Huc vsque verba translatoris.

To the processe of my book　　　　　1280

I wil retourne, and that ful blywe,

The Author.

Tharray of Iuno to discryve.

¶ Here descryveth the auctour the maner and the array of the secounde goddesse Iuno.

Next Pallas, as hyt ys founde,

After Pallas came Juno,

Foloweth Iuno, the secounde,   **1284**

The myghty lady and maistresse,   nota

And chefe goddesse of rychesse,

And in poetys, as yt is ryff,

Called **Iubiteris** wyff.   **1288** wife of Jupiter,

The whiche, throgh his gret[e] myght,

Both ageyn reson and ryght,

Caste hys olde fader doun

who turnd his father

From hys myghty Region,   **1292** Saturn out of·Heaven

Robbyng him of his rychesse,

In-to myschefe and gret distresse,

I mene the grete god Satourne,

In pouerte for to soiourne,   **1296** into poverty,

Out of his myghty Royal Se ;

And eke also of cruelte

Made him lese, I yow ensure,

Hys membres of engendrure.   **1300** [leaf 220] and also castrated him.

The whiche was, so as I rede,

Passyngly a cruel dede,

With-out[e] merci outher grace

So hys fader to enchace   **1304**

Out of hys kyngdam forto duelle.

For this Satourne, as bookes telle,

This Saturn

With his lokkys hoore and gray,

Held his kyngdam many day,   **1308**

That ther was noon vn-to him lyche.

He was so myghty and so ryche,

was rich,

That throgh his noble high estate

The worlde was called aureate,   **1312** and cald 'aureate,' he had so much gold.

Ther was of golde so gret plente,

Devoyded al of skarsete,

Hyt was so haboundant at al,

But lich as I reherse shal,   **1316**

Iubiter hath hyt empeyred,

That we be now of gold dispeyred,

For hit ys now, with-out[e] wene,

Tourned in-to siluer shene,   1320

Wel wors then) hyt was founde aforn),

Fer exiled and y-lorne ;

For in the worlde that now is founde,

Ther be but fewe that habounde   1324

With gold, siluer, or swych metal ;

For now the world, in special,

Is vnnethe, who look wel,

Nouther of Coper, nor of stel,   1328

Nouther of led[e], Tyn), nor Bras.

For hyt is wel wors than) it was,

Damaged by ful fals allay.

Swich falsnesse regneth now this day, 1332

Thorgh coveytise, that feyth ys gon) ; *nota*

For now vnnethe ther ys noon)

That loueth but for lucre of gode,   *nota*

So vnkynde is blood to blode ;   1336

Who lyst assay[e], he shal fynde,

How the worlde ys wax vnkynde,

And in falshede doth him delyte.

Herof no·more I wil now[1] write,   1340

But to **Iuno** tourne ageyn), [1] I wil now] now wyll I A.

The whiche, lych as clerk*es* seyn),

Is of this world goddesse and quene,

Rede her bokes, and ye shal sene,   1344

Wife to Iubiter, the grete,

Next Satourne, kyng of Crete,

Corbed, croked, feble, and colde,

Lych to forn) as I ha tolde,   1348

Cibeles eke, his moder dere, ¶ Cibeles fuit mat*er* Iouis secun-
            d*um* opinionem poetar*um*.

So that **Iuno**, as ye may lere,

Descended ys, yif ye take hede,

Passyngly of high kynrede,   1352

Of noble generacion),

And of gret domynacion). [2] *nota* ¶ Iuno d*icitur* dea diui-
              ciar*um* eo q*uod* ille Aer
For she is quene and eke goddesse[2] inferior circumdat ter-
              ram in qua om*ne*s the-
Of worldly tresour and rychesse, sauri *et* om*ne*s diuicie
              continentur / vnde sig-
And hem gouerneth, sooth to sey, ni*fi*cat vitam actiuam
              que debet*ur* diuitib*us*.

For fortune doth hir lust obey, The Author.

The gerful lady with hir whel, Fortune obeys Juno,

That blynd is and seth[1] neuer a del ; [1] seth] seith A. 1360

For erthely tresour, in certeyn,

Is holy put in her demeyn ;

For **Iuno** is the tresourere, who is Treasurer ;

And fortune hir awmonere. 1364 Fortune is Almoner.

¶ Here discriveth the auctour hir beaute and hir array.

This goddesse of hir nature ¶ Quia diuicie alliciunt corda hominum et specialiter cupidorum. Juno was beautiful ;

    Was ryght' faire, y yow ensure ;

She stood so in ech mannys grace,

It neded noght' to papphe hir face, 1368 her face didn't need paint.

For she was, bothe fer' and nere,

Ryght' agreable of look and chere,

Whos beaute wolde neuer cesse . nota Folk lookt at her all day

To make folkys faste presse 1372 untired,,

Vpon) hir to stare and muse, [leaf 221]

And al the day her look to vse,

With-outen) eny werynesse,

For to beholden) hir fairenesse, 1376

Of which no man) wex feynt nor dul,

Nor therof was replet nor ful,

Nor myght' nor power had[de] noon) and couldn't leave her,

Out of the place for to goon), 1380

But euere ylyche desirous,

Al thogh that cruel Cerberus tho Cerberus tore them to bits.

Sholde haue rent hem and y-gnawe,

And her throte asonder drawe. 1384

For the nerer that they went,

Ay the more her hert[e] brent,

And the more gan) presse and siwe,

Without[e] power to remywe. 1388

¶ And with hir beaute moste notable

She had atyre ryght' honourable, She wore a

In myn) Auctour as hyt is tolde :

A sur-cote on) of clothe of golde, 1392 surcoat of cloth of gold.

Of sotil shap ryght' wonderful,

That my kunnyng ys to dul,

The Author. Thogĥ I studied al my lyve,

To declare hyt and descryve,   1396

Juno's sur-
coat Wrogħt' and wove witĥ sondry flours ;

And an hundred folde colours

Men) in her clothing myghte fynde,

was deckt
with jewels. Fret[1] ful of ryche stonys ynde,   [1] Fret] firt A.   1400

The whiche bekam) hir wonder wele ;

Wherby men) myghte know and fele,

By hir abyte large and longe,

That she of frendes was rygĥt stronge,   1404

And myghty[2] also of rychesse.   [2] myghty] myghte A.

For she of tresour was goddesse,

In al this worlde noon) to hir lyche,

And of gold and stonys ryche,   1408

White, blyw[e] grene, and rede,

[leaf 221, bk.]
She wore a
Crown She had a corowne vpon) hir hede,

Passyng ryche of apparaylle.

But of oo thing I gan) mervaylle :   1412

That she gan) ay hir hede to wrye,

As sempte me, vnder a skye,

And as I coude espye and knowe,

ringd by a
Rainbow. Me thought', I sawgĥ a Reyne-bowe   1416

Of blywe and rede and watiry grene,

The whicĥ environ) of this quene

Went, so as I kan) devise,

About hir hede in cercle wise.   1420

In her hand
was a Sceptre. And in hir hande, as I behelde,

A ful ryche sceptre she helde

To shewe, in euery mannys[3] syght',   [3] mannys] mans A.

That she was a quene of ryght'.   1424

Ther sawgĥ I also, out of doute,

Siwyng after a gret route

Peacocks
with angels'
feathers fol-
lowd her. Pokokes, that yaf a gret lyght'

Wytĥ her Aungelys fethers bryght',   1428

About hir fete, for plesaunce,

In maner of an obseruaunce,

Did her dever hir to serve,

The bet hir grace to disserve.   1432

¶ **Her descryveth the Auctour the maner**
and the array of Venus.

Myn̄ auctour pleynly telleth thus :
    The thridde[1] goddesse was Venus,   ¶ *Venus id est car-*   The 3rd
nalis concupiscen-   Goddess was
Which, with her excelent visage,   *cia vel planeta que*   Venus,
inclinat ad concu-
Descended was of gret lynage,   *pisceneciam et sig-*
nificat vitam vo-
Doughtre, lych as ye han̄ herd,   *luptuosam que de-*   daughter of
betur carnalibus.   Saturn,
To saturne with his frosty berd,   [1] thridde] thyrde A.
As ye shal here, ceriously,
Conceyved wonder straungely,   1440
In the silve same wyse
As ye aforn̄ han̄ herd deuyse,
And eke in bokes ys remembred :
How that Saturne was dismembred,   1444   [leaf 222]
whom his
I mene thus, by fatal ewre,   son Jupiter
gelded,
Lost hys membres of engendrure
By Iubyter, hys sone and ayre,   [2] nouther] neither A.
Which was nouther[2] good nor faire ;   1448
But throgh his myght' and high renoun,
He put him from his region̄,   dethroned,
And on̄ hys fader took gret wrake ;
For the membres that y of spake   1452
He cast hem in the salt[e] see,   and cast into
the sea,
Of which the natyvite
Gan̄ first, as bookes lyst expresse,   wherefrom
Venus
Of feyre venus, the goddesse.   1456   rose.
For writyng of poetis halt   ¶ *id est* tenet.
That she roos of the foom̄ most salt
Which ryseth in the wawes felle,
That fynaly, as clerkes telle,   1460
The See was moder to Venus,   *nota*   The Sea was
her mother,
And hir fader Saturnus,   Saturn her
father.
As clerkys make mencion̄
Touching hir generacion̄.   1464
She hath also, of kyndly ryght',
Gret lordshippe and ryght' gret myght',
By influence of hir werkynges,
In gouernaunce of worldly thinges ;   1468
For she doth leden and eke guye

The Author.
Venus rules
all who love.

The amerouse constablerye,
Enclynyng by fleshly appetyte
Folkys, for to haue delyte   1472
To serve love and to obeye,
Wherso she do hem lyve or deye.

¶ Her maketh thauctour a descripcion of hir myght.

Who lyst to know hir pover pleyn,
     He shal fynden, in certeyn,   1476
Hir lordshippe gret, in special,
For, sothely, she comaundeth al,

[leaf 222, bk.]

No one can
disobey her.

What so hir lyst, this no nay,
For ther is platly non that may   1480
Dysobey[e]n hir byddyng :
Nouther emperour nor kyng,
Duk nor other creature,
But mavgre hem they must endure   1484
Vnder hir myghty obeysaunce,
So disposyd[1] ys hir chaunce.   [1] disposyd] disposposyd F., disposposed A.

No Goddess

For other goddesse ys ther non,
For to rekene hem euerychon,   1488

does such
wonders as
she :

That so gret merveyles doth ;
For hyt ys she the whiche, in soth,

she turns
peace to war,
and strife
to unity.

Kan, whan hir lyst, both nyghe and ferre,
Pes I-tournen in-to werre,   1492
And she kan bringe ageyn taccord
Folke that stonden at discord.
And this lady, Dame Venus,

She makes
folk misers
and generous.

Kan make folkys covetous   1496
To spend her good and lytel charge,
And the Negarde to be large ;
And thorgh hir myght, which ys dyvyne,

She humbles
the proud,

She the proude kan enclyne   1500
To lownesse and humilyte,
And the deynouse meke to be,
The daungerouse eke debonaire,
And do the soleyn speke faire,   1504

and makes
the angry,
mild.

The envyous to be amyable,
And the angry to be tretable ;

And she kan also, in certeyn,
Hertys which that be vileyn
Disposen hem to gentilesse,
To honour, and to worthynesse,
Leve her port vnkouth and straunge,
And the cowarde she kan chaunge
To be manful, and gete a name,
And maken fer to springe his fame,
And atteyne to gret noblesse,
Oonly throgh his high prowesse.
And she kan maken ageynwarde
The hardy for to be cowarde,
Throgh hir gery influence,
And throgh hir proude violence;
Hygh and low she kan eke drawe
Obey the boundes of hir lawe.
Ageyn hir myght' ther is no went;
For in the highe firmament
The goddys alle, as hyt is skyl,
Must enclyne to hir wil:
Bothe **Iubiter**, and eke Phebus,
Mars, saturne, and mercurius,
They fynde kan non existence,
Ageyn hir power no diffence,
But wolde echon, as clerkes telle,
Ay with hir abyde and duelle.
So strongely she kan hem assaylle
That no diffence may hem avaylle.

The Author.	
1508	Venus makes
1512	cowards, manful;
1516	[leaf 223] and the brave, cowards.
1520	
1524	
	Gods obey her too.
1528	
	Against her is no defence.
1532	

¶ **Her maketh thauctour A descripcion of hir beaute and of hir array.**

Now wil I make a smale lesson
    Of hir array and hir fason:
Venus was fresh and yonge of age,
And passyng fair of hir visage,
That, touchyng sothly hir beaute,
Was noon so faire, in no contre,
Nor non that myghte countrevaylle
Of ryche atyre nor apparaylle
To hir, in soth, no maner wyse.

1536	
	She is fresh, young and fair.
1540	

The Author.	For, finaly,[1] to hir servise	[1] finaly] fynall A. 1544

For, finaly,[1] to hir servise   [1] finaly] fynall A.   1544
She drougħ al tho by violence
Swicħ as kam in hir presence,

Venus has glad, laugh-ing eyes.
[leaf 223, bk.]

Benigne of port, wyth chere smyling',
Hyr' eyen) glade ay laughyng',   1548
Lyght' of corage, of' wil chaungable,
Selde or neuer founde stable,
Variaunt of hir manere :

She changes every hour.

For an hour to-gedre y-fere[2]   [2] y-fere] y fre F. A. 1552
She na-bood in oo degre,
Throgħ hir mutabilite ;
Queynte of array, who lyst take hede,

Her coat is laced with red.

A cote y-lacyd al of Rede,   1556
Rycher than outher silke or golde,
But the mater is nat tolde
Wher-of yt was y-made or wrogħt',
Nor, pleynly, I ne coude noght'   1560
Deme, wherof yt sholde be.
But wel I wot, men) mygħte se

It fits her like a skin.

Hir shappe throgħ-out, so was hit maked,
Lycħ as she had in sotħ be naked ;   1564
A lace of golde, ful ryche at al,
Gyrt about hir medil smal,

She has rings on her fin-gers,

On) her fyngres eu*e*rychon)
Rynges with many ryche ston).   1568
And thogħ she were a quene certeyn),
Yet ther was no corovne seyn)
Of gold nor' stonys on) hir hede,

and roses round her head.

But she had of roses rede   1572
·In stede therof a chapelet
As compas rounde ful freshly set.
For kerchef pleynly had she non),

Her hair shines like gold wire. Her right hand holds a fiery brand.

Whos here as eny gold wyre shon),   1576
And hild also in hir ryght' honde,   [3] as a kole] as kole A.
Rede as a kole,[3] A firy bronde,   ¶ Hoc fingunt poete propter ardorem libidinis.
Castyng sparklys fer a-broode,
Rounde al the place wher she stood,   1580
Of whiche thing I took hede eke ;
That fire whicħ is y-callyd greke   ¶ Ignis grecus.
Ys nat so p*er*ilouse nor so rage,

Nor so dredful of damage ;　　　　　　　1584　*The Author.*

[leaf 224]

For fire ys noɴ, to rekne al,

That may of force be egal

Venus's fire is most piercing.

To venus fire in pᵉrsyngᵗ,

Nor of hete lyke in brennyngᵗ,　　　　　1588

Nor so dredful harme to do.

In hir lyft hond she held also

In her left hand she holds a Golden Apple.

An appul rounde of gold ful ryche,

That tresour noɴ ther-to was lyche,　　　1592

Who loke aryghtᵗ, I dar wel say.

Thus haue I tolde yow hir array,

Save as mynɴ Auctour lyst to write.

Ther was gret novmbre of dowes white,　1596

White doves fly round her head.

Rounde about hyr hede fleyng,

Of entent, to my semyng,

As hyt wer for attendaunce,

To Venus for to do plesaunce.　　　　　1600

¶ Her descriveth thauctour, how Mercure conveyde the thre goddesse[s].

Now haue I tolde in substaunce
　　　The maner and the gouernaunce

Of thre goddesses by and by,

As ye haue herde, ceriously,　　　　　1604

Of Pallas, Iuno, and Venus.

But now vnto Mercurius

Mercury was

I must in hast my stile dresse

To al the maner to expresse :　　　　　1608

First of his natiuite,

And eke also, how that he

begotten in adultery.

Was getynɴ in a¹-vowtrie,　　　　¹ a] *om.* A.

As poetys specefie,　　　　　　　　1612

And reherse eke in thys cas

That Iubiter his fader was ;

Jupiter was his father,

And also eke, lyɔ̄ as they feynɴ,

He be-gat him, in certeynɴ,　¶ Ista filia vocabatᵘʳ a poetis pleias vel Maya.　1616

Of a mayde ful entere,

Which was Atlas doghter dere,

Atlas's' daughter his mother.

The myghty geaunt strong and large,

[leaf 224, bk.]

Whiche vpoɴ him took the charge　　　1620

The Author. Vpon) his bak, of verray mygħt',

To bere the hevene, and stond vprygħt'.

And thogħ Mercure was thus borne,

Lycħ as I haue told to forn),[1]   [1] to forn] beforne A.   1624

Iuno, **Iubiter[e]s** Wyfe,

Made quarel non nor stryf,

Nor was wrothe for this offence,

But took hyt al in pacience ;   1628

But bisyly dide hir cure   ¶ Hoc signi/icat quod
diuicijs pascuntur
To yive him mylke to hys norture :   sapientes vel elo-
quentes vel merca-
The whiche thinges dotħ signifye   tores.

That wisdam and philosophie   1632

Yfostred ben) witħ rychesse,

And also eke I dar expresse,

Marchaundyse nor eloquence

Ne shold[e] ha noon) excellence,   1636

But **Iuno**, goddesse of rychesse,

Ne dyde her hool[e] besynesse

To yive hem mylke to her fosterynge,[2]   [2] fosterynge] for-
string F.
Ellis in veyn) wer her werkyng.   1640

And thogħ this **Iuno**, as I fynde,

Was stepmoder, as be kynde,

Of hir pappis softe as silke

She brougħ[te] fortħ and gaf eke mylke,   1644

Poetis pleynly write thus,

Vnto this[3] god Mercurius,   [3] this] his F. A.

Al thogħ ful selde, as men) may se,

That stepmodres kynde be   1648

To children) born) out of wed-lok,

Or geten) of a foreyn) stok ;

Stepmodres han hem in hatrede,

As hyt shewetħ ofte in dede,   1652

Thogħ Iuno of gentilesse

Shewed[e] gret kyndenesse,

To Mercure, as ye may se,

A god of gret Auctorite.   1656

For he is lorde most facounde,

The whiche sothly doth habounde

To be except in al langage,

And eke to haven) avauntage,   1660

Marginal notes (left):
Juno made no strife over Jupiter's adultery,
but nurst his bastard, Mercury,
making him wise and eloquent.
She fed him from her own breasts,
tho step-mothers generally hate their step-children.
[leaf 225]

Oonly by crafte, to do his cure,   *The Author.*

To set in ordre and mesure   Mercury
is the God

Euery worde, that no thing skape,   of words

Throgh negligence, for no rape,   1664

And, specialy, to be reserved[1]   ¹ reserved] reseyved F. A.

That peyse[2] and novmbre be obser*v*ed,   *id est* pondus.

Throgh rethoryke, as in sentence,   ² peyse] poyse A.

And, by craft of eloquence,   1668 and eloquence,

First to examyne in his thought',

And for noon) hast to sey ryght' nought'

Vnavised, fer nor nere.

This god is also messagere   1672 and Messenger of

Of the court celestial,   the celestial
court,

For to report in special   to report
the secrets

The secre thingis of the hevene,   1675 of Heaven.

Of sterris, and of planetis sevene.   ¶ Potest exponi per hoc
quod Phebus est deus

And eke this god Mercurius   sapiencie et³ Mercurius eloquencie *quia*

Is [y]called with Phebus,   semper eloquencia
bene convenit sapien-
tibus.

Be synguler aqueyntance,   ³ et] and A.

And for special alliaunce,   1680

He is to Phebus, in certeyn),

By office maked chau*m*berleyn), ¶ Quia *semper* est pro- He is Cham-
pinquus soli. berlain and

Called eke hys secretairye   Secretary to
Apollo.

And ther with al his chefe notairie. 1684

¶ Her reherseth thauctour of the power of Mercuri*us*.

This god hath also gret povste   Mercury

  In heuene, and ryght' gret dignite,

And passing Dominacion)

In al the heuenly region),   1688

In erthe also in many wise :

Specialy in marchandyse,   is the pro-
tector of

Prudent Marchaundes to diffende, Merchants,
[leaf 225, bk.]

And her estatis to amende,   1692

And in welthe to contune

Maugre assautys of fortune.

And this god of eloquence   and is skild
in calcula-

Hath also gret experience   1696 tion.

In crafte of calculacion)

E

The Author. And eke in computacioɴ.

And also eke he dotħ habounde

In sotyltes ful profounde,   1700

Mercury gives know-ledge to philosophers And yivetħ, by his influence,

Bothe wysdaɴ and science

To philosophres and prophetis

Of many merveyl*es* and secretis,   1704

Whicħ exceden in werching

Al[le] mannys knowleching,

and fore-knowledge to prophets. And futire thingis ooɴ and alle,   1707

To telle[1] aforne, how hyt shal falle.   [1] To telle] Til F., Tyl A.

¶ Her descriveth thauctour Alle hys shappe and his array.

He is very beautiful: This ilke god of whicħ I telle

    Of shap and beaute dyd excelle,

Of whom the face was yong and whyte,

To be-holde of gret delyte,   1712

And al his membres lower dou*n*

Of rygħt' good p*r*oporsioɴ,

his nose long, Hys eyeɴ gray, his nase longe,

Hys mouthe rygħt' smal, nat set a-wronge,   1716

his teeth white, Hys tetħe eke white as evory,

Wel set in ordre by and by,

Hys body smal, and avenant',

Quik, lusty, fresħ, and rygħt' plesant',   1720

his face glad. Glad of contynaunce and chere,

Lyke an heuenly messagere,

That ther was no maner lak.

His robe is A ryche robe vpoɴ his bak,   1724

Whos[2] colour, sothly, was nat stable,   [2] Whos] Was F. A.

But dyuers, and variable,

[leaf 226] And of mony sondry hewe :

ever chang-ing colour. Chaungyng alwey newe and newe,   1728

Now blak, now white, now Iawne and rede,   ¶ Hoc *potest* ex-poni *quod* cum bonis est bo-*nus* cum malis mal*us* vel eci-am de sermone convenienter.

Now grene and perse, who took hede ;

For neuer in o poynt he a-bood,

So wonderly witħ him yt stood,

Mervelous in his lyknesse.   1733

And as he lad[de] the goddesse,

He helde a yerde in his ryght honde,

That so mervelous a wonde ¶ *id est* virga. 1736

Was neuer sen, to rekne al,

Nor that myght be peregal

Vnto this yerde dout[e]les,

Nat the yerde of Moyses : 1740

For the wertu, who look a-ryght,

Was of so gret[e] force and myght

That afferme ful wel I dar,

How this god which that hit bar, 1744

I mene this god Mercurius,

Maugre the myght of Cerberus

And the princes eke of helle,

Maugre ther myght, I dar wel telle, 1748

By vertu oonly of this wonde,

Which that he holdeth in his honde,

Drough out the soules, oon by oon,

Maugre the princes euerychoon, 1752

And made hem quyte from her baundon,

Out of that derk[e] region :

Olde poetys writen so ;

And many another merveyl mo 1756

They endyte of his povere.

And as I gan neghe nere,

Avysely as I behelde,

In his lifte honde A flowte he helde, 1760

When so him list the longe day,

Ther with to pipe and make play,

Oonly him self for to disporte,

And his hert[e] to comforte 1764

Wyth the sugred armonye,

Which gaf so soote a melodye

That no man koude him selfe so kepe,

But hyt wolde make him slepe. 1768

Of so gret vertu was the sovne,

As yt ys made mensiovne,

That hit passed of force and myght

Sirenes song, who look a-ryght, 1772

Which ar meremaydenes of the se,

And vntweyne departed be,

The Author.	Half fysħ and women), bookes seyn),	
Mermaids' singing is not to be compared with Mercury's flute,	But al her syngyng was in weyn)	1776
	To be compared, in sothnesse,	
	Vnto the excellent swetnesse	
	Of this Floyte[1] melodious, [1] Floyte] flowte A.	
	By force of whicħ Mercurius	1780
which sent Argus to sleep,	Made Argus slepe, this no drede,	
	For al the eyen) in his hede,	
	That were an hundred as be novmbre,[2] [2] novmbre] nvmbred A.	
	But the songe gan) him encombre,	1784
	That diffence koude he noon),	
	But that he slept witħ euery-choon),	
and made him lose his head.	Lost his hede for his trespace ;	
	Ther was as tho noon) other grace.	1788
	For Iubiter hadde of entent	
	Yiven) him in comaundement	
	To Mercurie, to do so,	
	For the love of Dame Yo, ¶ Yo fuit filia ynachi.	1792
	That Doghtre was to ynachus,	
	Methamorphoseos telleth thus,	
	To make hir fre from) al servage,	
	Inly fair of hir visage. ¶ *scilicet* Mercurius.	1796
Mercury wears a curvd Sword,	And by his syde he had a swerde,	
	Sharpe to shaue a mannys berde,	
	Wonder kene the poynt to forn),	
	Cromped ageyn), as is an horn),	1800
	Of entayle and of fasson)	
	Lyche the blade of a fawchon),	
[leaf 227] better than that of Hector or Achilles :	That I suppose, hercules,	
	Hector of troy, nor achilles,	1804
	Whicħ were so noble in bataylle,	
	Had no swerd of swicħ entaylle,	
	Wherin) they myght' hem self assure,	
	Nor so tempred for to endure ;	1808
it slew Argus.	For witħ this swerde, most ful of drede,	
	Argus was slayn) and lost his hede.	
	And for to make men) afferde,	
	Of entent he bereth this suerde,	1812
	For vengeaunce and for diffence,	
	For al[le] tho that do offençe	

AgeyꝞ his myght' hem to constreyꝞ.

And he hath also wynges tweyꝞ,   1816   Mercury has
two wings,

Fressħ, and shene, and no thing pale,

To fleeꝞ botħ onꝞ hille and wale,   to fly o'er hill
and vale.

Lycħ hys desire on mont' and pleyꝞ;

Of whos abood ys no[n] certeyꝞ,   1820

So swift ys he in his passage.

And as I lyft vp my visage,

I ganꝞ beholde, in special,

Kome in a pathe that was but smal,   1824   I see him
guiding

Conveyed by Mercurius,   *nota*   Pallas, Juno
and Venus

Pallas, Iuno, and **Venus,**

Ech arrayed lycħ a quene,

As any Aungel bryght' and shene.   1828

I went ageyꝞ hem, as I koude,

Thought' I wolde me nat shroude;

For as hyt semed, al[le] thre

Took her way towardys me   1832   towards me,

Of onꝞ entent with chere and look;

And thogħ I slept, myn hert awook,

Thus thoght' I tho in my dremyng;   in my dream.

And at the poynt of her metyng,   1836

I, so as me sempte dewe,

Ful humblely ganꝞ hem salewe,   I salute the
Goddesses;

WhanꝞ I espyed by her chere

Tyme opportune and best leysere,   1840

With al mynꝞ hool[e] dilligence

To hem I did[e] reuerence.   [leaf 227, bk.]

And they goodly, as thoughte me,   and they re-
ceive me in

Acceptede al thing' at degre   1844   friendly wise.

In ryght' wonder frendly wyse,

As the processe shal devyse.

¶ **Here maketh thauctour mension, how Mercure
shewed and declared the cause why he broght
the thre goddesses wyth hym.**

Mercurie, in al the hast he kanꝞ,   *nota*   Mercury
speaks to me.

    Vn-to me his tale ganꝞ   1848

Prudently, and lyst nat spare,

And seyde: " frende, I shal declare

Mercury tells me the three Goddesses are sent to me by Jupiter, to get my opinion on the Judgment of Paris,

" To the the cause [of] our comyng,

From **Iubiter**, the hevenly kyng,   1852

To the of purpose pleynly sent

For to yive a Iugement,

And to shew vs thin advys

Vpon the doom of Dam **Paris**,   1856

Which ys wreten in bokes olde,

who gave Venus the Apple,

That yaf the Appul, rounde of golde,

To freshe Venus, the goddesse,

Specyaly for hir fairenesse,   1860

and left Pallas and Juno.

And left **Pallas** and **Iuno**,

The story platly telleth so,

As of clerkys ys devysed.

Wher-vpon be wel avysed   1864

Prudently theron to deme,

Iustly, as hyt doth the seme,

Wher thow felyst in thy thoght,

His Iugement was good or noght.   1868

But short[e]ly first, in sentence,

I shal yive the euydence,

Mercury states that before the Siege of Troy,

First expovne, as hyt is good,

Of alle the mater, how hit stood :   1872

Whylom to for the sege of troye,

Whan they flourede in her Ioye,

when Helen was ravisht,

And wyth stronge honde dyd her peyne

To ravyshe the quene heleyne,   1876

Pelleus held a feast at his wedding of Thetis, on

The same tyme, kyng **Pelleus**,

Ful ryche, and wys, and ryght famous,

Helde a feste, as hit is ryfe,

At the weddyng of his wyf,   1880

Which **Thetys** highte, this the fyne ;[1]   [1] fyne] syne F.

whom he begat Achilles.

Of whiche two, be ryghtful lyne,

Descended grete Achilles,

Ful renomed in werre and pes   1884

Amonges grekes, as of renoun.

And as hit ys made mensyon

That Pelleus, this noble kyng,

Vpon the day of his weddyng,   1888

Made a feste within his halle

Of the grete estatis alle

[leaf 228]

"Throgh out grece, that ther was now

Mercury.

But they wer present euerychon) ;   1892   At Pelleus's wedding-

And also eke, in special,   feast all the Gods and

Alle the goddys celestial,   Goddesses were present,

And goddesses, this no fayle,

In ther rychest apparayle,   1896

Al echon) ther wer present ;

For ther was noon) that was absent,

Syttyng at the kynges borde,

Except the goddesse of discorde,   ¶ Invidia.   1900   except the Goddess of Discord.

Lych as bookes specifye,

Which, of malis and envye,

Of rancour pale and appallyd,

Be-cause that she was nat callyd,   1904   She, because she wasn't invited,

Cast of malys at the lest

To distroube hem at her[1] fest,   [1] her] the A.

Both in high and lowe estate,

For to make hem at debate ;   1908

And gan) anoon) in cruel wise   [leaf 228, bk.] made a

A mortal Appul to devyse,   Golden Apple,

Rounde of golde, with lettres grave,

Which seyd[e] that she shold hyt have,   1912

Oonly by gifte and other noon),   to be given to the fairest

Which fairest was of euerychoon),   woman,

Of al that seten) at the borde.

And thus this goddesse of discorde   1916

With hir sleyght' and sotil gynne,

Sodeynly kam[2] fleyng in,   [2] kam] kan F.

Deynous of port and eke of syght',

Threwe the appul anon) ryght'   1920   and threw it on the feast-table.

Among hem at the table doun.

And whan) they hadde in-speccion)

Of the Appul and writyng',

And conceyvede the menyng' :   1924

Shortly, in conclusion),

Al was turned vpe so doun.

For al her ioy[e] and gladnesse   ¶ Invidia omnia subuertit.   Then all their joy was turnd

Was turned in-to hevynesse,   1928   into gloom.

And the plesaunce of eche estate

[3]Was platly tourned to debate,[3]   [3—3] om. A.

Mercury.
"Both of higĥ and eke of lowe,
By the fals[e] sede y-sowe   1932
Hatred made   Of this lady, Dame hatrede,   *nota*
To-rent and owgly in her wede,   ¶ *id est* Invidia uel discordia.
Whicĥ of entent kam) so ferre
them
. quarrel;   For to sette hem al at werre.   1936
for each
wanted the   For eue*r*ycĥ bysy was in dede
Apple;   The ryche appul to possede,
To reioysshe yt dide her myght',
And gan) pretende a tytle of ryght',   1940
By excellence of ther beaute.
specially   And specialy atwixen) thre
Pallas, Juno
and Venus.   Roos first thys stryfe contagious :
Pallas, Iuno, and Venus,   1944
Who fairest was, and did excelle
Of beaute for to bere the belle,
And of the Appul, by reson)
[leaf 229]   For to han possession).   1948
They wran-   And eche gan) other hyt denye,
gled
And gan to holde chaun*p*artye
To resiste and to[1] wythstonde,   [1] to] do F.A.
till Jupiter   Til Iubiter took al on) honde,   1952
And lyst nat to be rekkeles,
To stynte noyse, and make pes,
And al rancour for to fyne,
declared it   Fynally gan) determyne :   1956
That al of oon) opinion),
Witĥ-out[e] contradiccion),
should go by   Shold[e] stonden at devys
the Judg-
ment of   And Iugyment of [Dam] Paris,   1960
Paris.   Whicĥ sholde, by gret dilligence,
He should   By diffynityf sentence,
decide who
should have   Yive a doom among these thre,
the Apple.   Whicĥ that shal, for hir beaute,   1964
The Appul wyn*n*e of verray ryght'.
And I my self anoon*e* ryght',
As Iubiter com*m*anded me,
Ladde hem witĥ me al[le] thre,   1968
Whan) the son*n*e shoon) ful shene,
In-to a wood[e] fressĥ and grene

" Besyde Troy, whicħ **Ida** hight¹,

¶ Ida fuit nomen silue iux*ta* ciuitatem troianain.

Mercury.

Wonder delytable of syght¹;

1972

Wher as Paris, whoo took kepe,

Lay on the playn and kept[e] shepe;

Paris was a herd on Mount Ida,

For he an Erde was that tyde,

And **Oenonye** by hys syde,

¶ Oenonia fuit amasia paridis.

and Oenone was his

Hys *par*amour of tender age,

1977　paramour.

Inly fair of hir visage.

And whan I kam, wher as he lay,

I ne made noo delay,

1980

But tolde him by and by the cas

Of the goddesses, how it was,

Mercury told him he had to decide

As I ha put in remembrau*n*ce,

And Iubiteres ordynaunce,

1984

As I ha tolde her eu*er*y del,

[leaf 229, bk.]

And bad him for to avise him wel,

between the 3 Goddesses.

Vpon this nyw vnkouth*e* striff

To yive a doom dyffynityff.

1988

And al[le] thre, stondynge besyde,

¶ Quelib*et*¹ illar*um* pr*e*posuit pro p*ar*te sua.

Gan ful besyly prevyde,

¹ Quelib*et*] Quolib*et* F.

Eche for hyr part ful dilligent,

Witħ many myghty Argument,

1992

Tatteyne to ther entencio*n*,

By many strong suasio*n*.

And Iuno first, whicħ is goddesse

no*ta*

Juno promist Paris riches

Of golde, tresour, and rychesse,

1996　and goods

Grauntede him to han plente

¶ Iuno pr*im*o inci*p*it pro p*ar*te sua.

Of good witħ-out[e] skarsete,

Duryng hys lyf, for no myscħefe,

Yif he graunted hir in chefe

2000　if he'd give her the

The appul in possessio*n*,

Apple.

Witħ-oute more delacio*n*,

And ay in rychesse to haboun-de.

no*ta*

And **Pallas** tho, the secounde,

¶ Pallas propo*ni*t.　2004

Minerva promist him knowledge,

Whicħ is lady and maistresse

Of renou*n* and of higħ prowesse,

Of kon*n*yng also and pr*u*dence,

Of wisdam and of sapience,

2008　wisdom above all other men,

Grauntede him to be most sage

That ever was in eny age,

Mercury.	" And for to shyne most in glorie	
and victory over his foes,	Of conquest and of victorye,	2012
	And al hys enemyes pute dou*n*,	
if he'd ad-judge her the Apple.	Yif he, in conclusio*n*),	¶ Condicio*n.*
	Bothe of equyte and ryght',	
	Gaf hir the appul ano*n*) ryght'	2016
	Witħ-out[e] more in hir demeyne.	no*ta*
Venus	But Venus, witħ hir firy cheyne,	¶ Venus propon*it pro parte* sua.
	Which hatħ loue in gouernaunce,	
(who is Goddess of pleasure)	And goddesse is of al plesaunce,	2020
	Of lust, and flesħly appetyte,	
	And of voluptuous delyte,	
[leaf 230]	Wytħ hir[1] bronde to enspire,	[1] hir] his A.
	And folkys for to set a-fire,	2024
	In euery age, yong and olde,	
	T[h]at ther is noo*n*) so strong, nor bolde,	
	Nor so vprygħt', nor so lame	
	That she ka*n*) daunte and make tame,	2028
	Be he ryche or be he wys.	
promist Paris the loveliest living woman,	And she hatħ graunted to Paris,	
	To han in his possessio*n*)	
	The fairest lady of renou*n*	2032
	Of al this worlde, to rek*n*e echo*n*),	
	As fer as me*n*) ryde or go*n*),	
	To han hir knyt to him by bonde,	
	And borne also in grekys londe,	2036
Helen, as	Which that called ys heleyne ; ·	
	For whom) she shal also ordeyne	
	That [Dam] Paris shal in Ioye	
his wife in Troy, if he'd	Bringe hir hoom in-to Troye,	2040
	And the proude grekys dawnte,	
give her the Apple.	Yif he the Appul to hir graunte,	
	And to denye hyt be nat bolde.	
	And wha*n*) they had her talys tolde	2044
	To for*n*) her Iuge, Dame Paris,	
	He lyst no lenger take avys,	
	Nouther by wysdam nor prudence,	
Paris gives it her.	But in al hast[e] yaf sentence	2048
	That Venus, lyke as I ha tolde,	no*ta*
	Shal ha*n* thappul rounde of golde,	¶ Iudicium paridis.

" As she that was the goddesse

Most excellent in fairnesse. 2052

Thus dempte Paris, this no drede,

For which look vp and take good hede,

And by counsayl and rede of me,

Sith thou hauest lyberte, 2056

Considre wel in thy resoṅ

Of euerych the condicioṅ :

Rychesse and tresour of Iuno,

And how that Pallas eke also 2060

Ys in vertu most habounde,

And how Venus also ys founde

In love passyng debonayre,

And se, how al[le] thre be faire. 2064

Voyde fauour, and sey[e] ryght,

Lyke as the semeth in thy syght,

And thy wittes hool applie,

To deme lych thy fantasye, 2068

Wher that Paris, to thyn entent,

Gaf a ryghtful Iugement."

Mercury.

Think, now,

of Juno's riches,

[leaf 230, bk.] Minerva's valour, and

Venus's love,

and say whether Paris judged aright.

¶ How thauctour reherseth the ansuere[1] which he gaf to Mercurius.

The Author.

[1] ansuere] vnsuere F., A.

Whaṅ the god Mercurius

Hadde I-tolde hys tale thus,

Of euery thing, how that hyt stood,

And I the matere vnderstood,

I be-helde hem al[le] thre,

And gaṅ consyder and eke se

Her behestys by and by,

Of nooṅ avys, but lyght[e]ly,[2]

And dempte in sothe, as thoughte me,

That ther was nooṅ, as of beaute,

Half so fair as was Venus ;

For which I answerde thus

To mercure, in sentence,

Which is god of eloquence,

Declaringe myṅ oppinioṅ

With-oute more dilacioṅ,

Vaylle or wher yt vaylle nought,

¶ Per istam fallaciam trium deorum clare sig-*nificatur* quod Iuuenis cum venerit ad annos discrecionis *sibi* potest proponi triplex modus viuendi uel triplex vita *scilicet* contemplatiua actiua *et* voluptuosa de quibus potest eligere illam que sibi magis placuerit sua libera voluntate etc.

I gazed at the 3 Goddesses,

[2] lyght[e]ly] lytely A.

¶ Iuuenes autem quia sunt passionum inse-cutores eligunt vitam vt voluptuosam et hoc est quod poete volue-runt innuere per indi-cium paridis secundum veritatem.

saw that Venus was twice as lovely as the other two,

2084

As hyt stake ryght' in my thought':   2088

That the Iugement of Paris
Was even) lyke to my devys,
Touching thappul, ryche of golde,
Lyke to form) as I ha tolde,   2092
And that more ryght'ful Iugement
Myght' not be, to myn entent,
Nor more egal out of blame ;

" For I wolde ha do the same   2096
Of equyte and no fauour,
Yif I hadde be arbitrour ; [1]   [1] arbitrour] artribitour A.
For she semys, shortly for to telle,
Al the tother [2] doth excelle."   [2] tother] tether A. 2100
And with that word anoone ryght'

Mercure gan) to take hys flyght'
To the hevene, and that a-non),
Bet his winges and is gon),   2104
Spake no worde at his partyng,
Save he sayde concludyng :
" Al this worlde gooth the same trace
And stondeth in [the] selve case."   2108

And after **Pallas** and **Iuno**
Ben) departed bothe two,
With-outen any more arest,
What party that hem sempte best.   2112

But venus, as I kan) devise,
Kam) to me in curteys wise,
Took hir leve, or she wente,
And tolde first what she mente.   2116

¶ **How Venus, the goddesse, kam to thanke
thauctour of hys goodly Ansuere.**

" Myn) ovne frende," first, quod she,

" With al myn) hert I thanke the
Of the love and frendly-hede
That thou hast shewed me in dede,   2120
This ylke day, so feythfully,
To sustene my party,
And conferme hyt, in sentence,
In the noble, high presence   2124

" Of Mercurye, myn) allye,

Resemblyng in thy fantasye

Vnto **Paris** of Troy[e] toun,[1]

Which whilom), in conclusyon),

The Appul grauntede vnto me

Of Iust reson) and equyte ;

For I was fairest in his syght',

For which he gaf yt me of ryght',

Thogh **Iuno, Pallas** of envye

Ther ageyn[e]s gan) replye ;

For I dar seyn), in sothfastnesse,

Y excelle hem in fairenesse,

For they be nat resemblable

To my beaute nor[2] comparable ;

For I dar wel specifye

For to fynde on) my partye,

Hyt to sustene and that anoon),

A thousand peple ageyn) ther oon),

For which al folke, as y desserue,

Ben) euer bysy me to serue.

For in euery maner age,

Both of lowe and high parage,

I ha servantis foule and faire.

Vnnethis ys ther oon) contrayre,

In noon) estate, to myn) entent ;

For euery wight' ys diligent

Me tobeye eve and prime

And ha be, sith thilke tyme

That **Parys** of fre volunte

Gafe the Appul vn-to me

Which was broght' in by discorde.

And sith thou art eke of Acorde,

And hast eke demed feythfully

That I ther-to am most worthy,

Be ryght' sure that certenly

Thou hast wonen) enterely

My love al hool and that for evere,

Neuer pleynly to dyssevere,

And, for rewarde of thy sentence,

Conquered my benyvolence,

Venus.

1 Troy[e] toun] Troy of toun F., troye of ton A.

2128 She says that

2132 [leaf 231, bk.]

neither Juno nor Pallas

2136

2 nor] nor to F. A.   can be compared to her for beauty.

2140

All folk strive to serve her.

2144

2148

2152

2156 And as I have judged her the worthiest,

2160 I have won her love.

2164

" Wher-of thou shalt ha gret profyt
And in effect as gret delyt,

As she gave
Paris Helen,
the flower of
beauty,
[leaf 232]
As **Paris** hadde, in certeyn),
What tyme that he wan) El[e]yne,   2168
Which was callyd flour and welle
That al other dyd excelle,
In hir tyme, as of beaute.
But truste pleynly vn-to me   2172
Of al that euer y ha the tolde.

so she will
give me a
woman a
thousandfold
fairer,
Thou shalt han oon), a thousande folde
Fairer than she, to thy plesaunce,
To ben of thyn) aqueyntaunce,   2176
Yif thou tryste, in substaunce,
To stonden) at myn) ordynaunce.
For I haue in my demeyne,
Lacyd in my large cheyne,   2180

out of the
many thou-
sand lovely
ones she has
in her chain,
God wot many thousand payre
Of wommen), bothe fresh and faire,
Without[e] novmbre, to governe,
Of which, yf thou kanst discerne,   2184
Thou shalt' chese, and thou be wyse,
The fairest vn-to thy devyse,
Fynally, the for to plese,
Sette thyn) hert[e] best at ese,   2188
In al ioye the to assure.
And her vpon) I the ensure
At thyn) ovne comaundement':
Yif thou folowe myn) entent,   2192
I shal the holde iust covenant,
And conferme also by graunt
To yife her the for thy guerdon),

to keep in
hold,
To holde in thy possession)   2196
Hir that is fairest and mete,

and quiet my
heart.
To set thin hert[e] in quiete.
For thy decert thou maist trust yt,
That Pallas, for al hir wit,   2200
Nor **Iuno** vn-to thy fauour,
With al hir rychesse and tresour,
Ne may to the so moche avayle,
As I shal do, with-out[e] faile,   2204

"Yif thou thy purpose nat remewe
My tracys feythfully to sewe."

[leaf 232, bk.]
Venus.

¶ How thauctour ansuerd to Venus.

The Author.

And thus dependent in A were[1]   [1] A were] A where F., awhere A.

I gan lyften vp my chere   2208

And seyde : "o Venus, cheffe goddesse,   I tell Venus

Of love lady and maystresse,

For lyf and deth, as yt ys dywe,   I'll follow her

I shal folwen and pursywe   2212   in Life and Death,

Your pathis pleynly and doctryne

And from hem nothing[2] declyne ;   [2] nothing] nas F. A.

For in this worlde ther is no thing   as nothing is

More trewe, as to my levyng,   2216   truer than she is.

More credible, nor more stable,

Nor to me more agreable

To leve vpon, as in substaunce ;

And ther with al your contenaunce,[3]   2220

So ful of grace and of plesaunce,   [3] contenaunce] contenAunce F.

With euery maner circumstaunce

Conferme, as to my felyng,

That ther is in your menyng   2224

Nat but trouthe, as I assure,   ¶ id est confido.

Good chaunce, and happy auenture.

But so that yt be non offence

Vn-to your magnificence,   2228

I shal reherse to yow anoon,   Then I tell

How hit[4] fille, nat yore agoon,[5]   [4] hit] yit A.   [5] nat yore agoon] not longe agone A.   her, how I fell in love

Of verray hap and sodeyn chaunce,

For [me] to falle in dalyaunce,   2232

As yt cometh to my mynde,

With the cheff princesse of kynde,   with Lady Nature,

Which that called ys nature,

And did also hir bysy cure   2236

Benyng[e]ly me for to preche

And tenforme me and teche,

Chargyng me ful prudently,   [leaf 233]

That I sholde avysely   2240   who chargd me to

Be wel war, and euer among   avoid the wrong road.

The wey eschewe that went wrong,

" In no wyse my course to dresse

Vn-to no pathe of wylfulnesse   2244

Nor of sensualyte,   sensualyte [in the margin, in a late hand.]

But forth ryght, as she taughte me,

The trewe way, and nat declyne,

Whiche ys ryght as any lyne,   2248

As I hadde of hir conceyved.

And lyst that I be nat deceyved,

I am ful set nat to varye

To hir wil to be contrarye,   2252

In hope ther-by to amende.

And for that I am lothe toffende

To yowe or hir by displesaunce,

I hange as yet in ballaunce."   2256

¶ Her sheweth thauctour, how venus
repleyed ageyn.

" My frend," quod she, " I the ensure,

How that I and eke nature

Be so ful of oon accorde

That ther may be no discorde   2260

Fynally atwene vs two,

In no thing, what so we do,

For I am guyed by hir reyne,

And she as lady souereyne,   2264

And I mynistre hir to serve,

Fully her byddyng to ob[s]erve, .

Humble of port and eke of chere,

Louly as hir chamburere,   2268

By goddys disposicion

Ordeyned, by comyssion),

To be next hir, in special,

In hir paleys principal.   2272

And thus, by goddys ordynaunce,

Vnder natures obeysaunce,

I stonde hir lustes to obey,

And shal neuer dysobey   2276

To serven hir[e] to plesaunce.

And touching eke our aqueyntaunce,

Who that kan the trouth espye,

"We be bothe of oon̄ allye,   2280   *Venus*

Dyssendyd eke of oon̄ kynrede,

As men̄ may in bookys rede.

I take recorde of thise clerkys,

That the forge of al hir werkys,   2284   says that Nature's

Without[e] me, in certeyn̄,   forge, with-out her,

Was nat maked but in veyn̄,   would be in vain.

For but I put[te] to my cure

Hir forgyng myghte nat endure,   2288

To hyr I am so knyt by bonde

Necessarie to hir honde.

I make redy alle thing   She prepares all things for

Pertynent to hir forgyng,   2292   Nature's work.

And pleynly, lyke to hir desire,

In hir forge I make the fire,

Ordeyn for hamer and for stith̄ ;

For she hath noon̄ so crafty smyth̄,   2296

With̄-out[e] me, that forgeth ought̄.

For which̄, my frende, dred the nought̄   I may there-fore walk in

Euery hour and euery space   Venus's paths,

After my weyes for to trace ;   2300

For I kan̄ preven̄, in sentence,

By a maner consequence,

That nature And also I   as she and Nature are

Be conbyned so Iustly,   2304   one.

In al[le] weyes accordable,

That be in kynde resonable.

And sith̄ I make the this offre,

Be war refuse nat my profre,   2308   I must not refuse her

Sith that[1] I hit do the to queme,   1 that] *om.* A.   offer,

As thou maist thy selve deme ;

And profre made to thy delyt,   [leaf 234]

Which concludeth to thy profyt,   2312

Ne sholde nat, as semeth̄ me,

To oft[e] sythe rehersed be ;

For, by doctryne of the wyse,   as once is enough.

Oones ought̄ y-nowgh̄ suffise."   2316

F

¶ **How thauctour ansuerd, and yalde him self
holy to the seruise of Venus,** *and* **be-kam
hir man.**

"My lady," quod I,[1] "and maistresse,   [1] I] he F. A.

*I thank
Venus,*
    I thanke vnto your high noblesse
For of al that ye ha sayde,
I am ryght wonder wel apayde,   2320

*and become
her man.*
For which, in what that ever I kan,
With hert and al y am youre man.
Shortly, I may me nat restreyne,
And what that doth me so constreyne,   2324
I kan nat tel hyt in certeyn,
But wel I wote al hool and pleyn :

*My heart is
drawn to her.*
Myn hert[e], in ful sodeyn wise,
Is drawe al hool to your seruyse,   2328
And myn enclynacion
Is hool in your subieccion.
For, in reyne and eke in shours,
Douteth nat that I am yours ;   2332

*I pledge her
my faith,*
Hath her the feyth of my body,
Nat compelled, but frely,
To contune, for ioye or smert,
Fully acorded in myn hert   2336

*to be ruled
by her.*
To be rewled by your devis.
For me semeth in myn avis,
Inwardely in my conceyt,
That ther may be no deceyt,   2340
Engyn, nor fraude, on no syde,

*I ask her to
teach me,
how to obey
her.*
Beseching that ye wol provyde
To teche me and to concerne,
How that I shal me gouerne   2344
By the statutis of your law,
And what wey[e] I shal draw ;

[leaf 234, bk.]
For euere platly, to I deye,
To your wille I shal obeye,   2348
As ferforth as I ha konnyng
To fulfille your biddyng,

*I am her liege
man.*
Fro tyme that I first began
To bekome your lyge man."   2352

¶ **Venus.**

" In feitħ," quod she, " dred neuere a del,
Thy seruise shal be quyt rygħt' wel.
Yif thou perseuer lyke thy bonde,
I shal yive in-to thyn̄ honde   2356   She promises
                                                                me the fairest
A mayden̄ oon̄ the gentylest,
The fairest, and the goodlyest,
Botħ of shap and of visage,
And also oon̄ the most[e] sage   2360   and wisest
                                                                maiden,
That any man̄ may se or fynde,
Thogħ men̄ soughten̄ in-to ynde,
And but yonge and tendre of age,   young and
                                                                tender,
Whiche shal appesen̄ al thy rage   2364
That no man̄ koude wissħ a bet,
Thogħ al wer in his choys y-set.
And she shal be, as hyt ys skylle,
Fully accordyng to thy wille,   2368   who'll do all
                                                                my will.
And yet, or thou thy lust atteyn̄,
Thou shalt fele annoy and peyn̄,
But I wil first to the devise
How thow shalt werke in my servise.   2372

¶ How Venus thaught him what he shal doou*n*, And of hir .ij. sonys Deduyt and Cupido.

" I ha two sonys of higħ degre,   Venus has
                                                                two sons:
And gret of ther Auctoryte,
Botħe redy of entent
To doon̄ at my comandement,   2376
What so that me lyst devise
To acheve in my seruise,
Gentil, fre, and debonaire,
Whicħ shal be rygħt' necessaire   2380
Vn-to the and gret Refuit.   [leaf 235]
The toon̄ callyd ys Deduit,   ¶ Deduit filius veneris.   1. Pleasure,
Yong, fresħ, and lusty on̄ to se,
And rygħt' gentil in his degre,   2384
To al[le] folke benigne of port;
And of solace and dysport
He ys the god most auctorised,   the God of
                                                                Games.
And al[le] pley[e]s be deuysed   2388

Venus. " By his avys and his purchace ;

For ther kaɳ no maɳ, in no place,

Of vnkoutħ pleyes tel[le] nooɳ

But he kaɳ hem eue*r*ychoɳ :   2392

Her son Pleasure knows Harp, Touche be crafte, and nat be rote,

Harpe and lute, fythel and Rote,

Song, And synge songes of plesaunce,

Dance, Maisterly revel and Daunce,   2396

Pipe and floyte lustely.

And also eke ful konyngly

In al the crafte and melody

Music, Of musyke and of Armony,   2400

What tyme that hit shal be do,

He ys expert ; and eke also

At al[le] pleyes delytables :

Dice, At mereles, deeṡ, and tables   2404

He kaɳ pley[en] passyngly ;

But best and most specialy

Chess, At the Chesse he dootħ excelle   2407

That philomestor, sotħ to telle, ¶ Iste phi*lo*sophus secu*n*du*m* quosda*m* i*n*uenit ludum Scaccor*u*m.

For to make comparysoɳ),

Nc was nat lyke him of renouɳ,

That first founde this play notable,

With him to play[e] was not able.   2412

and the game of Arith-metic, And I ɒar also specefie,

The play he kaɳ of Ryghtmathye, ¶ Rihtmachia est ludus phi*lo*sophor*um* et consistit in ar*s*metrica et proporc*i*onib*us* nu-merorum.

Which dulle wittis dotħ encombre,

For thys play stant al by ɳovmbre,

And hatħ al his conclusions   2417

[leaf 235, bk.] Chefly in p*r*oporsions

By so sotil ordynaunce,

As hyt ys put in remembraunce   2420

By thise Philosophurs olde.

Also my sone, of whomɔ I tolde, ¶ id *est* Deduit.

and can an-swer ladies' questions Amonge ladyes honourable

Is, in sotħ, ryght¹ acceptable,   2424

Lycħ to her oppinions,

For tassoyle questions,

on the Art of Love. And demaundes oɳ eue*r*y part

That longen vn-to lowes art,   2428

" And sotiltees many oon),
That to answere vn-to echon)
Is noon), to rekne al[le] thing,   2431
Save he that hath therto[1] konnyng';   [1] that hath therto] that
                                          ther to hath A.
For ther ys nought', I dar wel say,   Her 1st son
That longeth vnto merthe and play,   Pleasure
                                          knows all
To reherse compendiously,   about Mirth
                                          and Games.
But that he kan) hyt perfytly.   2436

¶ Her reherseth Venus to thauctour of hir other sone callyd Cupido.

" I haue eke, on the tother syde,   Venus's 2nd
A sone that callyd is Cupyde,   son is Cupid,
Nat lasse of reputacion)
But passingly of gret renoun ;   2440
Which, throgh his myghty gouernance,
Hath al vnder his obeysaunce,
And in the See, wher he is stallyd,
He is the god of love callyd.   2444   the God of
                                          Love.
For he lordshyppeth, and hath cure   He is Lord
Of euery maner creature,   of every
                                          creature.
For rude folkys and eke sage
He hath bounde in his servage.   2448
No man) kan) no resistence   No one can
Ageyn) hys myght', by no diffence,   resist him,
For poetis specifye
That goddys of her surquedye   2452   not even the
Purposede of presumpsion)   Gods.
To wrastle with this Champyon),   ¶ *id est* cum cupidine.   [leaf 236]
But he, in A lytel throwe,
Cast hem to the erthe lowe,   2456
Vnder daunger kept hem evere[2]   [2] evere] were F. A.
That they myghte nat dissevere.
Phebus eke, that was so sage,   He subdued
He attamede with his rage,   ¶ Amor omnia domat. 2460   Apollo.
Made him throgh his myght' alsoo
In servitute, sorwe, and woo,
Vnder hys yokke to be bounde,
And yaf to him so large a wounde,   2464
Mortal and perilouse many folde,

" With his dredful arwe of golde,
For love of daphne, I dar say,
That he was in poynt to dey.   2468

For ay the more he gan to prey,
The more she dide dysobey
To his desire, on euery side,
He siweth, but she nolde abyde ;   2472
For the more he dyd hys myght,

The more she fledde out of hys syght ;
But suche pursuyt he gan make
That he shulde haue ouertake   2476
Hyr, that was most faire to se,

Tyl Goddys gan to han pite
On hir youthe and tendernesse,
And on hir excellent fayrenesse,   2480

To conserve hir virgynite
Tourned hir to a laurer tre,
Closed vnder bark and rynde,

For which Phebus, as I fynde,   2484
Loste al worldly plesaunce
Throgh Cupidys high vengeaunce.
      " And thus my sonys boothe twoo,

First Deduit and Cupido,   2488
Lyke as I haue declared the,
Ordeyned ben to serve me,

As I serve vnto nature
In furthering of myn Auenture.

So is ther lust and ther plesaunce,   2493
By diligent attendaunce,
To A-wayte on me euery tyde,
Bothe Deduit and eke Cupide.   2496

      " And her-vpon I wol the telle
In what place that they duelle,
That thou mayst[1] vn-to hem drawe,

The gouerne by her lawe ;   2500
And ther-vpon do thy peyne
To gete frendshippe of thise tweyne.
For elles thou ne mayst nat chese,   2503
But thow shalt thy tyme lese ;

For they hir han in gouernaunce

"That may to the do best plesaunce.

And alder first thou shalt lere,

Love and Deduit duelle y-fere ;

And, trewly, elles yt wer wonder,

For they kan nat be assonder.

For trust[e] wel that of reson)

Her bothe conversacion)

Gladly drawe by oo lyne,

And love of ryght‘ doth Ay enclyne,

Wher he be, in any place,

To siwe play and eke solace,

For love myghte nat endure,

But Deduit dyde hys [busy] cure

Him to support[e] with gladnesse,

For he may with noon) heuynesse ;

For which as brethre in eche place

Eueryche other dooth embrace ;

That, to conclude at oo worde,

Deduit serveth and love ys lorde,

So nyghe borne of oon) allye

That, fynally, her companye

Ne seuereth nat, but y-fere

Eche ys to other so entere.

For Deduit, I warne the,

Hadde lever exilled be

Than) to twynne on any syde

From presence of Cupide ;

For whiche thinge, as hyt ys dywe,

Be diligent to pursiwe,

With al thin) hool[e] besynesse,

Lyne ryght‘ thy cours to dresse

To thilke[1] path[e], thus I mene,   [1] thilke] the same A.

That ledeth to the Erber grene,

Wher that Deduit ys lorde of ryght‘,

To plese love with al hys myght‘ ;

For ther they tweyn), of oon) assent,

Soiourne ay with her covent.

2508

2512

2516

2520

2524

2528

2532

2536

2540

Venus.

Love and Pleasure dwell together.

Love could not last without Pleasure.

Pleasure had rather be exiled than part from Cupid.

[leaf 237]

I am therefore to line my course to the Arbour or Garden of Pleasure and Love.

¶ Here Venus discryveth to thauctour the gardyne of Deduit.

Venus.
Pleasure's garden is as beautiful

"This lusty Erber most notable
    So plesaunt ys and agréable,
The which, yif trouthe be nat spared,
May of beaute be compared,
Of lustynesse and of delys, 2544

as Paradise.

Werreyly to paradys. 2548
And, as to myn entencion,
That heuenly habitacion
So excelleth in beaute
That hit may nat descrived be, 2552
Nouther by worde nor by wryting ;
For to remembren euery thing,
Of lustynesse and of plesaunce
It hath so moche suffisaunce, 2556
In dede and nat in apparence,
Foundyd by the diligence

Pleasure made it, and daily tends it.

Of Deduit, which day by day
Ful besy is with nyw aray 2560
To conserve hyt, and to Raylle
With fresh and lusty apparaylle,
To kepe yt, that by violence
No man do ther-to offence. 2564
Euer y-lyche fressh of hewe
He yt preserveth, new and newe,

[leaf 237, bk.]

Ful of suetnesse and of grace.

It is Cupid's playing place,

For hyt ys the playing place 2568
Vn-to the myghty god Cupide,
Wher Deduit doth ay provyde
For his solace and hys disport,
Wher love hath euer most comfort. 2572
For he pleynly of entent
Selde doth him self absent,
But gladly euer ys ther present.
For the chefe of his entent 2576

where, in play, he spends his life.

Ys noght but study, nyght and day,
Vnto solace and to play,
Therin he haunteth al his lyf.

" For al debat, contek, and stryf,   2580   *Venus.*

Pompe, pride, and surquedye,   In Pleasure's Garden is no strife or sorrow,

Malys, rancour, and envye,

Angwyssħ, sorowe, and hevynesse,

Pensyfhede, nor tristesse   2584

May nat ther, for foul nor fair,

Soiourne ther nor ha repair ;

For hyt voydeth al distresse,

That no thing but glad[e]nesse   2588   but only joy.

Abydeth ther, yt is no doute ;

For al raskayl ys put oute,

For which this place most entere

Of glad[e]nesse hath noo pere.   2592

¶ The conclusioun of Venus.

" And in this lusty, freshe place,   In it dwells Pleasure ;

So ful of beaute and of grace,

Duelleth Deduit, as made ys mynde,

In the whiche thou shalt fynde   2596   and in it I shall find the lovely Maiden

The mayde of most excellence,

Which ys, in verray existence,

Rote of beaute and womanhede,

And Merour[1] eke of goodlyhede.   [1] Merour] Mercur F. mercure A.   2600

Whom that Deduit, by my byddyng,   whom Pleasure is keeping for me.

Hath the charge of hir keping,

For to my lust I dar wel seyn)   [leaf 238]

He is trewest and best wardeyn) ;   2604

To whom thou shalt the fast[e] hye

For to fynde companye.

   " And first, thy self best to avaunce,

Thou must geten aqueyntaunce   2608   But I must

Of Deduit and of Cupyde,

But yet aforn) thow must provyde

For to [do] thy besynesse

To a-queynte the with ydelnesse,   2612   first know Idleness,

Necessarie to thy purpose,

For of the gardyn) and the close   the head Portress of the Garden.

She is the chefe porteresse,

Of the entre lady and maistresse.   2616

Who that cometh, erly or late,

"She ys redy at the gate
To let him in, that is hir charge,
At the Gatys brood and large,　　　　　　　2620

For she hir self bereth the key.
And best of alle may the convey
To expleyte thy viage,
For ther ys noon herbergage　　　　　　　2624
But at hir delyueraunce
In the gardyn of plesaunce.
For which, by the rede of me,
Gete aqueyntaunce[1] of thise thre :　　　　2628

Deduit, Cupide, and ydilnesse,　　[1] aqueyntaunce] aqueytance F.
And I shal do my besynesse,
With help of hem, the to avaunce
With euery maner circumstaunce,　　　　　2632
To thy desir that may avayle ;

And alder first I shal nat fayle
To be present, and to spede
And further the in al thy nede."　　　　　2636

¶ How thauctour ansuerd to Venus.

"Madame," quod I,[2] "for goddys sake,　　[2] I] he F. A.
Short processe for to make,

Wyth-oute any more taryingᵗ

Enformeth me of the duellyngᵗ　　　　　2640
Of Deduit and of Cupide ;
And that ye wolde[3] be my gyde,　　[3] wolde] wyl A.
For I stonde in grete fere,　　　　　　　2644
How I shal euer kome there."

¶ Venus.

"Towarde the gardyn and the place
Of Deduit and of solace,
Yif thou make no delay,

Thow art wel onwarde on thy way,　　　　2648
Yif thou be stable and contune.
And I shal make thy fortune
Happy to the, the thar nat charge
The wey[e] also brood and large,　　　　　2652
Nygh at thyn hande and nat ferre,

" That, but thou wylt, thou maist nat erre ;

Venus.

For the crestys enbataylled

That stonde yonde, so higħ entaylled,   2656

In the embattled Castle, a mile off,

Shal to the casteħ bringe the,

Wher they duellen all*e* thre.

dwell Pleasure, Cupid, Idleness.

Hyt is fro henys but a myle,

Thou shalt be ther in a while,   2660

Where that love, as I ha tolde,

Stately holdetħ his housholde

Witħ his meyne in gladnesse.

" For ther is nooɴ hevynesse   2664

But Ioy and merthe among hem aħ

Mirth is ever with them.

Witħ-outeɴ any intervaħ,

That, whaɴ thou comest at the gate,

So fortunat shal be thy fate,   2668

Thou shalt fynde no diffence

To make ageyɴ the resistence ;

For Idelnesse ys porter,

Idleness will let me in.

And she wol make no Daunger   2672

To lete the in[1] wythyɴ a throwe,   [1] the in] them A.

Yif so be thou bere the lowe.

For she ys curteys, large, and fre,

[leaf 239]

For to opeɴ and yive entre   2676

To al[le] folkys that be digne,

Amyable, and eke benigne,

And kaɴ not make no daunger,

Iu countynaunce nor in cher,   2680

And she shal p*er*forme vp of ryght⁏

Al that euer I haue behight⁏.

" For, short[e]ly, I the ensure

Thou mayst cleymen of nature,   2684

I have a natural right to enter there,

Wel fortunat oɴ eu*er*y syde,

In the gardyɴ to a-byde,

Euer mor ther to soiourne,

And ha no cause for to mourne.   2688

For, sith*e* tyme thou wer borne,

Thou were neuer so glad aforne,

For þou shalt han a priuelege

and join the College of Lovers.

For to be of my college,   2692

Amonge folkys amerouse

Venus.
" That be professed in myn̄ house,
After thyn̄ in-clynacion̄
To kepe the religion̄.   2696
Thinke her-vpon̄, and varie nought̄,

She bids me
remember
her words,
and goes.
And remembre in thy thought̄
Of al that I ha sayede to the,
For now thou gettest no mor̄ of me."   2700

The Author.
¶ How venus departed, and of the Forest wher Dyane mette wyth him.

Tho Venus, shortly, thus yt stood,
    Departed ys and I abood,
Lefte al sool fro my maistresse,

I go towards
Pleasure's
Garden,
And in al hast[e] gan me dresse   2704
Toward the gardyn̄ of disport,
Ther to fynde some comfort
By the byddyng of Venus.
For, Douteles, I thoughte thus :   2708

[leaf 239, bk.]
as I wouldn't
disobey
Venus for all
the King of
Denmark's
pounds and
marks.
I wolde, for noon̄ erthely thinḡ,
Do contrary of hir byddynḡ
To wynnen̄ euery pounde and marke
That the kyng hath of Denmarke,   2712
Hir preceptis to dysobeye ;
Me wer in soothe lever deye,
Apparceyvyng by hir techinḡ
That nature in euery thing   2716
From̄ hir lesson̄ doth nat varie ;
And as tho me lyst nat tarye,
For to make noon̄ areste

I enter a
forest,
Entrede in-to a gret forest,   2720
Large as I reherse kan̄,
And, sothly, ther my wey[e] gan̄,
The whiche, shortly to devyde,

and take the
right-hand
path.
Strechched toward the ryghte syde,   2724
For other geyn̄ path was ther noon̄
By the which I myghte goon̄.
And this forest ryght̄ notable
Was wonder fair and delytable,   2728
Ful of trees, the which of sight̄
Massiffe and grete and evene vpryght̄

As any lyne vp to the toppys,
As compas rounde the fresshe croppis,   2732
That yaf good air with gret suetnesse,
Whos fressħ beaute and grenesse   The trees are
Ne fade neuer in hoote ne colde,   evergreens,
Nouther Sere, nor wexen olde,   2736
No wynter frost may hem constreyn,
Thogħ hit Snowe, haylle, or reyn.
The levis be so perdurable,
Yliche grene, nat chaungeable,   2740
Of naturel condicion;
For ther' may no corrupcion   and never
Damage nouther crop nor rote,   rot.
Nor the holsom fruytes sote   2744
Corupte neuer, nor apayre,
But ylyche fressħ and faire   [leaf 240]
Throgħ the vertu vegetatyve,   ¶ Virtus vegetatiua in herbis
                                        et arboribus.
Passyngly restoratyve,   2748
Holsom to norissħ and to restore.

And ther be treen eke lesse and more,   Some of the
In that vnkouthe lusty holde,   trees bear
That bere Appuls rounde of golde,   Apples of
                                                Gold.
                                                2752
As whilom in the gardyn was
Which longed to the strong Athlas,
And also eke to hercules,
That was of streng[t]ħe pereles,   2756
Rounde, and square, and of gret height',
The whiche, by his whily sleygħt',
Bar away the ryche fruyt,
Quyk and fre from al pursuyt,   2760
Fro the horible fers Dragon.
He was so sterne a champion,
That eche man had of him doute.
And in the lannde rounde aboute   2764 The open
Of this forest, in certeyn,   ground is
Tapited al the large pleyn   carpeted with
Of herbys and of fresshe flours,   flowers that
                                                      never fade.
That fade witħ no wynter shours,   2768
But lyche new in eche seson
Preserved fro corrupcion;

The Author. They be so noble of ther kynde,
Who that preveth, shal hyt fynde.   2772

The forest
is long and
narrow. This forest was eke wonder longe,
Ryght' as lyne and no thing wronge,
Eke wonder streyght', and narwh also,
For which but fewe folkys go   2776
Nor passe throgh for streytnesse,
For drede oonly of werynesse.

¶ How he sawgh ther Diane the goddesse.

Whaɳ I had this forest seyɳ,
Passing of beaute, in certeyɳ,   2780
[leaf 240, bk.] As ye to forɳ haue herd me telle,
I caste ther no lenger duelle,
For I hadde othre thing adoo,
And I dar afferme also   2784
That my thought was elles-where,
For which I boode no lenger there,
But furth the ryghte wey I took.
And ryght' as I cast vp my look,   2788

Under an
ebony-tree I
see a lady, I sawgh vnder aɳ Eban tre
A lady sytte of high degre,
And y had[de] gret talent
For to knowe in myɳ entent,
What she was that sat so there,
And thoghte that I wolde enquere
The cause, without more a-doo,
Why that she sat allone soo.   2796
And by the ryghtest wey anooɳ
and go to her. Towarde hir I gaɳ to gooɳ,
And hir presence dyde atteyɳ,
And certys, yif I shal nat feyɳ,   2800
I dar afferme with-out[e] fage :
Of body, shappe, and of visage,
Of plesaunce, and of symplesse,
And by al other lyklynesse,   2804
No fairer was
ever born, Ther was no fairer borne a-lyve,
Who so euer ageyɳ hyt stryve,
or more
gracious. Ther was nooɳ erthely creature
More perfyt, as by nature,   2808

¶ Ebenus *secundu*m plinium[1] est
arbor preciosissima auro et
ebori compar*a*bilis *et* ha*n*c arborem soleba*n*t ethiopes offerre
imperatoribu*s* pro tributo et
legitur *quod* Regina Saba dedit talia ligna salamoni et i*n*-
tud lignum *conser*vat mu*n*di-
ciam *et* ideo *est* consecrata
*secundu*m quosdam.

[1] plinium] plunium F.

More plesaunt,[1] nor more gracious, [1] plesaunt] plesaunce A. *The Author.*

Hyr clothing⹁ rych and precious,   Her clothing
                        is rich,

That I ha no konnyng dywe

To declare the walywe   2812

So ryche of stonys and tresour.

But as touching the colour,

Hyt excelled, I dar expresse,

Al erthely thing in w[h]ittenesse,   2816 and dazzling-
                        ly white.

That outerly, and thus I mene,

That I myghte nat sustene   [leaf 241]

Myn eyen clerely to vnfolde,

Ther-vpon for to beholde,   2820

That, yif trouthe be nat spared,

Ther may no w[h]itenesse be compared

To that w[h]ittenesse, I dar telle,

For al w[h]itenesse yt dyd excelle,   2824

The cloth in whiche she was lacyd,   Her kirtle
                       is tight-laced.

In a kyrtel streyt enbracyd,

That ther was no thing to blame.

A-bove A mantel of the same,   2828 Her mantle
                        open in front;

Open to forn, of good entaylle,

The whiche also, this no faylle,

Closed hir body nat in veyn

That of hir shap was no thing seyn.[2] [2] seyn] sene A. 2832

The whiche mantel also shoon

Clerer than any maner stoon,

Of which the forour was more fyn   finely furd,

Than menyver outher ermyn,   2836

Wympled but in symple guyse,

Yet neuer the lesse to devyse,

Who consydred euerydell,

Hyt bekam hir wonder well.   2840 and becomes
                        her well.

And by sygnes dyde seme,

As ferforth as I koude deme,

Be lyklyhede and of reson,

She was of somme religion.   2844

Vpon hir hed of gold a crovne,   On her head
                       is a crown

The whiche dyde envirovne   of gold.

Hyr wymple whyt[3] more to delyte, [3] whyt] whyit F.

Ful of grete pereles whyte: 2848

The Author.
Rycher no man) koude knowe.

Diana has an ivory bow, and arrows,
And in hir hande she had a bowe
Of white yvere, pulshed clene,
And arwes, forged sharpe and kene,　　　　2852
Of yvere eke, for hir emprise,

[leaf 241, bk.]
Made in the most[e] crafty wyse

to shoot wild beasts,
At wylde bestis for to shete,
Wher so that she doth hem mete,　　　　2856
Whan) she seeth hem to savage,
Hygh of gres, or to Ramage.
And, specialy, she hath solace
With hir arwes for to chace,　　　　2860
With alle hir hool[e] bysynesse,　　　*Nota*
For to shete at ydelnesse,
To avoyde hir oute of hyr Forest,
Therin) to make noon) arest;　　　　2864
For of entent, with al hir myght,

She hunts both day and night.
She chaceth hir, both day and nyght,
For that ys hooly hir delyte;
She hath hir in so gret despite,　　　　2868
And hateth, shortly, no thing[1] more.　　　[1] shortly no thing] nothinge shortly A.
For by the holtys gray and hore
And by the dalys depe and lowe
To hunten hir she bereth a bowe　　　　2872
Most specialy, as ye shal here.
And whan) I gan) to negh hir nere,

I salute and greet her.
I gan Saluen) and enclyne
To that lady most devyne,　　　　2876
And seyde: "honour and reuerence
Be vnto your excellence!"

Diana.
¶ How Diane ansuerde.

"My sone," quod she, "good auenture
Be vnto the and ryght good ewre,　　　　2880
Myn) honour safe, and my renoun,
For I ne ought, of Iust reson),
Nat the salue nor taken) hede
To shew[e] the no frendelyhede;　　　　2884

She says I'm not worthy of her notice.
For I the telle outerly:
Thou art ther-to no thing worthy."

¶ How thauctour ansuerde.

Whan I herd that goodly faire,
Benigne, and ryght*e* debonayre,   2888
Seyn) so to me witħout[e] more,

Diana's re-
buke abashes
me.

I was a-basshed wonder sore,
Sytħ I dempte, as in my thought,
Pleynly that she knyw me nought,   2892
Musyng, what hyt myghte be
That she so straungely spake to me,
Whicħ neuer aforn), in no place,
I hadde doon) no trespace   2896
Ageyn[e]s hir, by my wetyng,
Nor hir offended in no thing.
And thus I stood al in a rage
Witħ look cast fix in hir visage,   2900   I look at her,
Wavering as in a were,
And parceyved by hir chere
That she, so as I koude gesse,
Bare to me som*m*e hevynesse,   2904
Til at the last[e] out I brake,
And evene thus to hir I spake :   and tell her
" Madame," quod y, " with al my myght
I wolde your honour and your ryght   2908
Were safe in al[le] maner wyse,
As your selfe kan) best devyse,
For so wyssly god me amende,   I wouldn't
wrong or
To doon) yow wrong or to offende   2912   offend her,
Ys my wylle high nor lowe.
But for desire[1] I ha to knowe,   [1] for desire] for to desire F.   but only want
                                      for to desyre A.   to know who
                                                              she is,
What that ye ben), thus her syttyng,
Is the cause of my komyng,   2916
Ful humb[e]ly, without offence,
Requering with al reue*r*ence,
As I dar without[e] blame,
To reherse me your name ;   2920
And eke the cause, why that ye   and why she's
                                                              displeasd
Ben displesed so wyth me ;   with me.
And fynaly (cause) of your grevaunce ;
For I ha no remembraunce,   2924

" Sithe tyme that I was borne,
That euere I saugħ yow her to forne.

[leaf 242, bk.]
I also tell
Diana I'll
amend any
wrong I've
done,
Yet neuere-theles, as hyt ys skylle,
I am in purpose and ful wille   2928
Holy to amende in .hert and thought',
Yif any thing I ha myswrought',
To ouer more to my konnyng',
As I best kaṇ, in any thing'   2932
That myghte plese your highnesse,

I wolde do my besynesse
Yow to quemen and to plese,
And your trouble to apese."   2936

              ¶ **Diane.**

" In good feyth, my childe," quod she,
    " As now hyt longeth nat to the,

Thow art in *party* out of Ioynt,
But yif thou stood in swiche poynt,   2940
And wer as now so fortunat,
So clere and hool in thyṇ estat,
And acceptable also to me

'Twould be
better if I
were of her
counsel.
Of my counsayle for to be,   2944
Yt wer wel bet vn-to thy prowe,
I dar wel seyṇ, thaṇ yt is nowe.
For, pleynly, thin entencioṇ,
Wil, and inclynacioṇ,   2948
I dar afferme, and knowe hyt wel,
Ymagynacioṇ, and echedel,
Hyt ys no drede, thou art so in,
They hangen by another pyṇ ;   2952
But for al that me lyst nat lye,

She will tell
me who she
is,
I shal shortly specefye,
What that I am, and nat faylle ;
Al be I lese my travaylle   2956
The to enfourmeṇ or to preche,
Yet at' the lest I shal the teche,
That thou mayst haue yt bet in mynde,

And eke of hap that thou maist fynde   2960
The verray trouth, and takeṇ hede
For to repent, or thow be dede,

" The wrong and errour thou art ynne, [leaf 243]
And ryght anoon) I wol begynne.   2964   *Diana.*

¶ Her Diane declareth her entencion).

" Myn) ovne frend, in soth.," quod she,   She says her
" Folkys whiche that knowe me,
Bothe here and be-yonde se,
Throgh the worlde in ech contre,   2968
Thys no les, bothe oon) and alle,   *nota*
Dyane of custom) they me calle,   name is
                                   Diana.
Which, as poetys specyfye,
Am goddesse of venerye   2972   She is the
                                    Goddess of
And of Bestis[1] eke savage ;   1 Bestis] best A.   Hunting,
Touchynge also my lynage,
Iovis doghtre by dyscent,   daughter of
                                    Jupiter,
Most myghty in the firmament,   2976
Whiche throgh his pover eterne
Hevene and erthe doth gouerne
Of hys hygh Magnificence.   *nota*
And Phebus eke, god of prudence,   ¶ Diana est soror Phebi.   sister of
                                    Apollo,
My brother is sothely in dede ;   2981
And as touching my kynrede,
That oughte y-nogh to the suffyse,
But myn) office, and my fraunchise,   2984
Fredam), and Iurisdiccion),
Which I haue by commyssion)
By the goddys to me committed,
Which, in soth, may nat be flytted,   2988
For alle the court celestial
Han made me lady princepal
And goddesse of venerye,
Wode and Forest for to guye,   2992   ruler of
                                    woods and
Of chace also and of huntyng.   forests.
And for this skylle, in my walkyng,
As she that hath most maistry,
I bere thys bowe of yvory,   2996
For my play and for solace,
Wylde bestis for to chace.   [leaf 243, bk.]
                                    Hunting is
This my crafte, in soth[e]nesse,   her craft, to
                                    avoid idle-
To eschewen) ydelnesse,   ¶ Ad fugandum ocium. 3000   ness.

Diana.

"Which is to me most noyouse,
Loth-som), and most odyouse,

To shun idle-ness,

Whom) to avoyde, in special,
I ha my duellyng principal 3004
And myn) habitacion),

Diana roams the forest

To walke and romen) vp and doun,
In the forest most notable,
Of beaute incomparable, 3008
Chefe close vnto my resort,

to have her sport.

Therin to haue my dysport,
Wher I may lyve in Ioye and play,
In fraunchise from) al affray, 3012
Perpetuelly in gladnesse,
Without envyous heuynesse,

But she's out of joint in one point.

Except, surely, that in oo poynt
I stond in partye out of Ioynt, 3016
Which troubleth me with swich distresse
I may nat lyven) in gladnesse."

The Author.

¶ **The auctour.**

"Madame," quod I,[1] "I yow besech   [1] I] he F. A.
    Goodly that ye wil me tech, 3020

I ask her what that is.

What poynt is that, and me to lere,
And humb[e]ly I shal yow here."

Diana.

¶ **How Diane repreued hys purpose and compleyned vpon Venus.**

She says that of old she was full of mirth,

"I was wont whilom," quod she,
    "Yn tyme of olde antiquyte, 3024
In ioy and myrthe to habounde,
Glad of hert and ful Iocunde,
And had gret prosperyte,
Worshipped eke of ech degre 3028

and every one honourd her.

And welkome in euery place,
Most accepted vnto grace   ¶ Castitas quondam fuit
Of al goddesses[2] high and lowe,   magne reputacionis
                                      ab omnibus accepta et
                                      honorata.

[leaf 244]

Whan) they wern) echon) arowe ; [2] goddesses] goddesse A. 3032
For tho had euery wight plesaunce
Of me to taken) aqueyntaunce,
Frend-shippe, and benevolence,

"And wer wel payed of my presence;   3036
And with high and lough degrees
I was with-holden, and, of Fees,
Eche man redy me to serve,   3039
Oonly my grace to[1] dysserve,   [1] grace to] grace and to F.,
                                              grace and A.
Bothe at borde and eke at table;
For thise folkes honourable,   Folk of hon-
                                                     our come to
Grete plente, both nyght and day,   the forest to
                                                     stay with
Kam to this forest for to play,   3044   me;
Of entent with me to abyde,
Gret novmbre vpon euery syde;
But now I see her purpose chaunge,   but now they
And how that folke ar wexe straunge;   3048
For euery wyght in his degre
Fleeth and draweth now fro me,   all keep away.
And maketh sothly no pursuit,
For which, withouten al refuit,   3052
I stonde allone desolat,   I am left
                                                     alone,
As she that is disconsolat
Of al ioye and al comfort,
So ful I am of discomfort,   3056
With sodeyn newe oppression,
And of no reputacion,   and am of no
                                                     account.
Fro day to day most ful of moone,
Solytarye, and allone,   3060
As a woman in gret wer,
Which in thys forest that ys her
Abyde without companye.
And cause of al, as y espye,   3064   And the sole
                                                     cause of this
That I am left allone thus,   is Venus,
Is myn enmy, Dame Venus,
That regneth with hir companye,
And pleynly hath the regalye   3068
Throgh the worlde on euery syde,   [leaf 244, bk.]
So pompose and so ful of pride
That hir domynacion   who rules
                                                     everywhere.
Ys nowe in euery region,   3072
For in delys she so haboundeth
That many folkys she confoundeth
With lustys that she dooth present,

Diana.   " For which with al ther hool entent   3076
               They folwen) hir, and me forsake,
               For which I may my compleynt make
Venus reigns. That she regneth in hir estat,
Diana is deso- And I stonde al desolat,   3080
late.
               Muet as hyt wer a stoon).
               And this myschef of yore agoon),
The mischief   As cause first of my mournyng',
began, when
Jupiter de-   Be-gan), whan) Iubiter was kyng'   3084
throned
Saturn.   By violent oppression),
               Whan) he caste hys Fader doun,
               Satourne fro his Royal see,
               And made him also for to flee   3088
               That he durst[e] nat abyde
               In hys kyndham on) no syde ;
               For he was courbed, gray, and olde.   3091
In Saturn's   The worlde whos tyme was of golde—   ¶ *Tempore saturni
golden time,   secula fuerunt
was plenty.   Ther was swich plente, in sothnesse,   aurea.*
               Bothe of tresor and of rychesse ;
               But al is turned vp so doun,
               For the dominacion)   3096
Now Jupiter   Iubiter, on) se and londe,
               Hath sesed now in-to hys honde.
has made   For siluer now, that first was golde,
silver equal
to gold.   Of as high pris ys bought' and solde   3100
               Both[1] at market and at Feyre,   [1] Both] But F. A.
               And thus ech thing doth appeyre,[2]   [2] appeyre] appeare A.
               Syth Satourne with his siluer berde
               Of Iubiter was made afferde.   3104
               And syth hys exil was purchasyd,
[leaf 245]   Al vertu hath be dyffasid ;
Virtue is
defaced.   For with Satourne, and that is routhe,
               Ryght'wissnesse, honour, and trouthe,   3108
               Good feyth, and al honeste,
Purity is   Clennesse eke, and chastite
banisht.   Exiled wern), shortly to tell,
               With vs no lenger for to duell,   3112
               As hyt had be for the nonys,
               With him they fledden) al attones,
               That now allas, this the fyn),

" Al the worlde gooth to declyn),   3116   *Diana.*

And ys peruerted with Satourne.   The world is going to the

For no man) lyst now to tourne   bad.

To Vertu nor to perfytenesse,   Virtue, Faith, and Trust are

But to delyt and ydelnesse ;   3120 lost in Lust.

Ther is no feyth, ther is no trust.

For the girdel of fals lust

With bokel and thong hath so enlacyd,

And the worlde so streyt enbracyd,   3124

That euery wyght, in certeyn),

Both gentil and eke vileyn),

Wher so that a man) repaire,

And ladyes, boothe foul and faire,   3128 Ladies and girls

And maydenes tender of age,

Born) of lowh and high parage,

Pore and ryche, to rekne echon),

That vnnethe ther is noon),   3132

But that they be, who lyst to se,

Mortal foon) to chastite,   hate chastity.

And lust ha noon) now to enclyne

To the ryw[l]e of my doctryne.   3136

For which, allas, sool and allone   ¶ Quomodo Diana plangit de muta-

I may sigh and make moone ;   bilitate mulir erum.

For trouthe and feyth ben) al agoo,

Yt was not wont for to be soo   3140 It wasn't so in King

In tyme of the kyng Arthour,   Arthur's day.

The noble, worthy conquerour,   [leaf 245, bk.]

Whom honour lyst so magnyfye,

For of fredam and curtesye,   3144

Of bounte, and of largesse,

Of manhode, and [of] high prowesse,

To remembre all[e] thinges,

He passyde al other kynges.   3148 He surpast all other kings:

He was so prudent and so wis,

In gouernaunce of so gret pris,

Whos high renoun to descryve,

Al[le] tho that wern) a-lyve   3152

He surmountede[1] of his degre ;   [1] surmountede] surmont toke A.

For honour and prosperyte   God prosperd him,

God and fortune lyst him graunte.

" In whos tyme, y[1] dar avaunte,

I had of frendes gret plente,

Wel willed for to serve me,

And to honoure my partye,

And diligent, for to applie   3160

Hooly her wittes in ech place,

To perseuer in my grace

And to ben) of myn) allye ;   3163

Wher-of Venus had envye,

Whan) she sawgh and knyw certeyn)

That she was had but in[2] disdeyn) ;

For love was tho so pure and fre,

Grounded on) al honeste   3168

Withoute engyn of fals werkyng

Or any spot of evel menyng,

Which gaf to knyghtes hardynesse,

And amended her noblesse,   3172

And made hem to be vertuous,

And, as the story telleth vs,

Which the trouthe lyst nat feyne,

How the knyghtes of Breteyne,   3176

Most renomyd and most notable,

With Arthour of the rounde table,

The myghty famous werriours,

Lovede the dayes paramours,   3180

Gentilwymmen of high degre,

Nat but for trouthe and honeste,

And hem self to magnyfye

Put her lyf in Iupartye   3184

In many vnkouth straunge place,

For to stonde more in grace

Of ladyes, for ther high empryse.

And al they mente in honest wyse,   3188

Vnleful lust was set a-syde.

[3]Women) thanne koude abyde,[3]

And loveden hem as wel ageyn)

Of feythful hert[e] hool and pleyn),   3192

Vnder the yok of honeste,

In clennesse and chastite,

So hool that Venus, the goddesse,

"Hadde tho noon) Interesse.   3196   *Diana.*
That wer so feythful and so stable
To knyghtis that wer honourable,
Chose out for her ovne stoor   In Arthur's
                                                     days, ladies
To love hem best for euer moor ;   3200   chose their
                                                     lovers
Wher so as her sort was set,
The knot never was vnknet.
Their choys was nat for lustynesse,
But for troutħ and Worthynesse,   3204   for truth
                                                     and worth.
Nor for no transitorie chaunce
Nor, shortly, for no fals plesaunce,
How ofte that they wer requered ;
Of my scole they wer so lered   3208   Diana taught
                                                     them so ;
To love hem that wer preved best,
And in armys worthyest,
Many sithe and nat oonys,
That wer chose out for the nonys   3212
In higħ prowesse hem self to avaunce
Throgħ her long contynywaunce.
That tyme was my name raysed,   and then was
                                                     honourd,
And loue worthy to be preysed.   3216
Wher so Venus wer lef or lotħ,   [leaf 246, bk.]
                                                     Venus
They gaf no fors, thogħ she wer wrotħ,   thought no-
                                                     thing of.
Be-cause oonly she was put vnder.
But certes now it ys no wonder,   3220   But now
Thogħ I compleyn) and sigħe ofte,
Sytħ I am doun and she alofte   Venus is up,
                                                     Diana down.
And is enhaunced newe ageyn),
And my partye is but in veyn),   3224
So sengle that I stonde in doute ;
For Venus hath so gret a route
Ageyn[e]s me on) hir partye
That, to holde chaunpartye   3228
Ageyn[e]s hyr, I am nat strong ;
For love, allas, and that is wrong,
Hath now no lust nor appetyte
But in thinges for delyte.   3232
Thus by constreynt of hir lawe   ¶ Sunt verba Diane.
Venus al the world dotħ drawe,   Venus draws
                                                     all the world.
For eche empire and region)

Diana.

"Is now in hir subieccion),   3236
For she with strong and myghty honde
Regneth now in euery londe,
And eche man) foloweth hir in sothe,
Honour and worshippe to hir dothe.   3240

Not only do men follow Venus, but all the Gods do too.

Nat oonly men) in generall
But al the goddis celestiall,
Gret and smal, hir lust obey,
For ther is noon) that dar with-sey   3244
To serven) hir with grete delyte,
As hyt wer doon) in my despite
And in contempt of my renoun.
Maydens of my relygion),   3248
Ladyes of high and low degre,
Which sholde of ryght stonden) with me,
Ben tourned shortely fro my lore,
And therof ne wil no more,   3252
But of Freel condicion)

[leaf 247] And wylfull dissolucion)   [This line in the margin.]
Davnce on) hir ryng ful nygh echon) ;

Jupiter

For Iubiter ful many oon)   3256
Ravysshed hath of force and myght
By fals outrage ageyn) al ryght :

ravisht Europa

He took Europe vn-to his stoor,   ¶ Europa fuit filia regis agenoris rapta per Iovem.
The Doghter of kynge Agenor ;
And in Ouide as hyt is tolde,   3261
He ravissede in a clode of golde   ¶ Rapuit eciam Danaen per ymbrem aureum.

and Danae.

Danne, as bookes lyst expresse,
For hir excellent fairenesse.   3264

Apollo attempted Daphne.

And my brother eke Phebus
Stood vnder daunger of Venus
For dafhne aforne, as hyt is tolde.   3267

All the Gods

And alle the goddys yonge and olde[1]   [1] olde] yolde F. A.
And in this worlde nygh euery man),
As ferforth as I reken) kan),
Ben) euerychon) of oon) accorde
With me to stonden) at discorde,   3272
And my servise hool forsake,
Of assent they han) hem take

serve Venus.

To the servise of Venus.

" I se ryght^t wel that it is thus,   3276

The sleyghtis eke I ha conceyved,

How the world hath hem deceyved

With fals delytys temporal.

And thou thy self, in special,   3280

Art oon of hem bekome of late ;

The tyme I know and [eke] the date,

Thyn errour so I haue espyed,

How thou art of new allyed,   3284

Vnder hir yokke y-bonde the,

Which may nat lyghtly broke be ;

For by othe and assuraunce

Thou art knet, by alygiavnce,   3288

To hir seruise throgh thy rage,

And ther-vpon do thyn homage,

And thus bekome hir man at al

To holde of¹ hir in special.   ¹ of] of of F. 3292

I know the maner euerydel,

And haue espyed eke ful wel,

How of slyper conscience

Thow yaf a doom and A sentence   3296

To hastely of wronge entent,

To conferme the Iugement^t

Whilom yoven of Paris,

And took ther-on but short avys,   3300

Touching the appul mervelous

Which he graunted to Venus,

Seydyst, with-out[e] more abood,

That his Iugement^t was good,   3304

Al be that hasty Iugement

Was neuer good to myn entent^t."

¶ The auctour.

" Madame," quod I, " it is certeyn :

I dempt[e] pleynly as ye seyn.   3308

And yet me semeth in my syght^t

That his Iugement was ryght^t ;

For errour noon, to my semyng,

Was noon founde in his demyng,   3312

And yet, in myn oppinion,

Diana.

Venus has deceiv'd all with earthly pleasures.

I too, the poet, says Diana,

am under Venus's yoke,

[leaf 247, bk.] and have become her man ;

for I've confirm'd the Judgment of Paris.

The Author.

I confess that I still think Paris right.

"I conferme yt of reson)."

¶ **How Diane ansuerd blamyng Venus.**

"My faire frende, in soth[e]nesse,
Thou gaf thy doom) of wilfulnesse,   3316
Ouer lyghtly, and al in hast;
Thy sentence was soone past,
And hasty domys ever among
Ben oft[e] sithe meynt witȟ wrong,   3320
And who that haueth noon) insight'
Demeth alday ageyn) ryght':
And so destow, I dar afferme,
And notably hyt conferme;   3324

For thou took, yt is no doute,
The worst of al the hool[e] route,
And yaf thy Iugement by graunte
To the lest[e] suffisaunte   3328
Of al[le] thre, so she[1] the blent,   [1] venus is added above the line
                                                in F., to explain 'she.'
Wherof, in sooth, thou shalt repent;
For thou shalt knowen in certeyn,
How that of the tother tweyn)   3332
Kometh worshippe and noblesse:

For **Iuno,** lady of rychesse,
Graunteth tresour and gold also
Fulsomly to alle tho   3336
That drawen) vn-to hir servise,
Maketh hem ryche in sondry wise
Of worldly goodys and dispence;

And Pallas, goddesse of science,   3340
Causeth folke to be prudent
And in worshippe excellent,
Whiche ar two thinges ful notable
And in this worlde ryght' profitable   3344
And passyngly of gret renoun.

But Venus, in conclusion),
By in-fluence of hir mevyng,

Yiveth to man) no maner thing   3348
Of profyt that may avaylle.
For she of custom) doth assaylle

With gret plente of flesȟly lust,

" In which ther is but lytel trust ;   3352

For al hir gyftes ar gynnyng   All Venus's gifts lead to grief.

Of myschef, sorowe, and wepyng,

Of compleynt and mysaventure,

Importable to endure,   3356

Whos lustys be so deceyvable,

So vnsure and variable,

Farsed ful of sorwe and dool,

That he may be cleppyd[1] a fool   [1] cleppyd] called A.   3360   He is a fool who trusts them.

That trusteth on) hem any tyme,

Outher at even) or at prime.

For the fyn) of hir swetnesse   [leaf 248, bk.]

Concludeth ay[2] with bitternesse,   [2] concludeth ay] conclude thai F. A.

And wyth myschef dooth manace,   3365

Thogh she be soote att prime face,

The sugre of hir drynkes all   The sugar of her drinks turns to gall.

At[3] the ende ys meynt with gall :   [3] At] That F. A.   3368

Experience shal the lere.

She may be lykned to chymere,   ¶ Vnde valerius ad Rufinum : chimeram nescis esse quam petis / sed eciam scire devoves quod triforme illud monstrum insignis venustetur capite leonis / olentis maculetur ventre capri virulente armetur cauda vipere.   She is like the beast Chimera,

Whiche ys a best[e] Monstruous,

Ryght' wonderful and mervelous,

Hedyd as a stronge lyon),

And even) lych a scorpion) ;

Hyr tayl ys werray serpentyne,   with a serpent's tail,

And hir bely eke Capryne,   3376   and a goat's belly, full of lust.

This ys to seyn), when she is hoot,

Rammysh taraged as a goot :

So stronge and vnkouthe of nature

Is hir mervelous figure   3380

That swich a best[e] now a-lyve

Is no man) that kan) descryve.

And swich on[4] pleynly is Venus,   ¶ Nota quomodo Diana dea castitatis describit venerem deam voluptatis.

That foolis kan) deceyven thus,   [4] on] wone A.

Whos name for to specyfie

Aftir ethymologye,

Venus, by exposicion),   Venus's name means

Is seyde of venym) and poysovne ;   3388   'venom.'

And of venym), this the fame,

Venus pleynly took her name.

For she venemyth many wyse   She poisons all who serve her.

Diana.

" Al that doon to hir servise,   3392
This her guerdon day and nyght'.
For she skorneth euery wyght',
Swiche as she dooth governe ;

When folk come to Venus's tavern, she gives 'em delicious drinks.

And whan they come to hir taverne,   3396
She serveth hem first, of entent,
With ypocras and with pyment,
Ryght' soote and ryght' delycious
To folkys that ben amerous ;   3400
But hir confeccioun[e]s alle

[leaf 249]
But they're mixt with aloes and gall,

With alloes and bitter galle
Ben ymaked and y-tempryd,
That make a man gretly distemprid.   3404
They be so venymous at al,
So to be drad and so mortal,
A-bove y-cured with suetnesse
That no man the treson gesse ;   3408
Hyt is so dredful and pervers,
So perilouse sothly and dyvers,

and cause death.

Causyng so gret mortalyte
That non may recuryd be   3412
Ageyn[e]s deth, by noon obstacle,
By herbe, stoon, nor [by] triacle ;
So ferful is that maladye,

Flight is the only remedy.

Save flyght' ther is no remedye,   3416
As seyn clerkes that be sage ;
For this mortal beverage
So noyous ys and so doutable,
First soot and after deceyvable.   3420

Such was Circes's drink which turnd Ulysses's folk

This the beverage of Circes,   ¶ Circes fuit maxima incantatrix.
With which the folke of Vlixes,
As Auctour[e]s lyst expresse,
Ytourned wer[e]n to lyknesse   3424
Of bestys and, maked bestial,
Lost hir reson natural.
Thynke wel theron, this was the fyn,

into asses, swine, foxes,

Somme wer asses, somme swyn,   3428
To foxes fals and engynovs,

wolves.

And to wolves ravynouse,
And yet wel wors peraventure.

" For thys the drynk, I the ensure,　　　　3432　*Diana.*

Most ynly soote, cler, and fyn͡,　　　　　　Circes's
　　　　　　　　　　　　　　　　　　　　　　　　drink

And in tast fressher than͡ wyn͡,

But in werkyng dedely felle,

Which the mynystres of babel　　　　　　3436

Maden falsly of envye,

And gaf hyt to kyng Sedechye,　　　　　was given to
　　　　　　　　　　　　　　　　　　　　　　　Zedekiah,

Wher-thorgh he had A laxatyf　　　　　[leaf 249, bk.]

That he shortly lost hys lyf,　　　　　3440　and kild him,

Ageyn[e]s which ther was no bote ;

But first he foun͡de hyt wonder sote,

Tyl aftir-warde he hath parceved,

How fals[e]ly he was deceyved :　　　　3444

Of the Drynke he dyd attame,

Deyede anoon͡ for verray shame.

And yet the pyment of Venus　　　　　Venus's is
　　　　　　　　　　　　　　　　　　　　　　worse.

Is wors and more malycious,　　　　　　3448

With which so moche folke ar blent.

And ther-of drinketh[1] the covent　　[1] ther of drinketh] drinketh
　　　　　　　　　　　　　　　　　　　　　　ther of A.

Professid in hir Relygion͡

Throgh fraude and fals decepcion͡.　　3452

And so shalt thow deceyved be,

Ther is noon͡ help[e] but to fle　　　My only
　　　　　　　　　　　　　　　　　　　　chance is to

With al thy myght' and al thy peyne,　　flee from her.

And from͡ hir Daunger the restreyne ;　3456

Noon͡ other helpe ys in the case

But for to flen͡ a ryght' gret pase."

¶ How the auctour ansuerde.　　　　*The Author.*

" Madame," quod I,[2] " I kan͡ nat se,　[2] I] he F. A.　I say I don't
　　　　　　　　　　　　　　　　　　　　　　　　　　see it,

Wher any perel sholde be.　　　　　3460

I wold[e] knowe and apparceyve,

How she myghte me deceyve,

For I kan͡ no deceyt espye,

For, pleynly, to my fantasye　　　　3464

She is benigne, curteys, and fre,　　　as Venus was
　　　　　　　　　　　　　　　　　　　　　　kind to me.

And shewed hir goodly vn-to me,

And with al bounte doth habounde ;

For I ha preved and y-founde　　　　3468

Fredam͡ in hir and gentilesse,

"And is also my cheffe goddesse, [This line added in the margin.]
Whom I shal serve in colde and hete ;

As I've vowd to serve Venus, She hath me made by-hestys grete   3472
That, yif I may hem ful acheve,
Ther is no thing shal me greve
Nor happe amysse to myn) entent,

[leaf 250] For which, with ful awysement   3476
And without[e] doublenesse,
For sorwe, myschef, or gladnesse,

I'll not leave her. This a-vowe to hir y make :
I wil hir servese nat for-sake."   3480

¶ **How Diane shewed [and] declarede**
him the pereills of Venus.

"My faire frende, yif thou lyst lere,
tells me   Somwhat of Venus thou shalt here.
For god so wisly yive me blysse,
And the also, so iustly wisse,   3484
And yive the grace be good avys
To be so prudent and so wis,
Of entent thou maist declyne
Fer away from hir doctryne,   3488
For yif thou knywe the damage,
that I'm in great danger, The grete pereill, and the rage,
And the myschef thou art ynne,
I wot ryght' wel, thou woldest twynne   3492
And fle from hir in euery part,
As doth an hare the lyppart.
For thou hast noon) experience
Of hir large conscience,   3496
Nor of the grete aduersyte
Which lykly is to come to the,
And of the grete high myschaunce,
and that, unless I repent, But thou in hast ha repentaunce ;   3500
For shortly elles, this no nay,
I shall curse the day I ever saw Venus. Thow shalt curse thilke day,
Wepe and be-waylle many wyse
That euer thou kam in hir seruise,   3504
Or hir presence dist atteyne,
And I my silf also compleyne,

" Whan I considre of reson,

How thy disposicion   3508

Ordeyned had the table

By lyklyhede of high degre

And of estate ful worshipat le.

But gery Venus, euer vnstable,   3512 [leaf 250, bk.]

Hath with hir perilouse face double

Put the abak in ful gret trouble,   So great is
                my danger

That I kan nat by-thynk[e] me,   from
                Venus,—

How hyt may remedyed be,   3516

The tescape out of hir lace.

For, fynaly, thus stant the cace :

Geyn is ther noon teschew[e] blame,

But oonly deth or elles shame.   3520

¶ Her declareth Diane the pereils by exaumple.

" In good feyth, I dar assure,

Thou stondest in wors aventure[1] 1 aventure] aventurne F.

And more perilouse condicion

Than whilon dyde Duke Iason,   3524 worse than
                Jason's,

In-to Colchos whan he went   when he went
                to win the

Ther to conquere of entent,   Fleece of
                Gold,—

In-to that Ile famous and olde,

The Ram that bar the flees of golde, 3528

And passede the grete see.

Thow standest in more pereil than[1] he, 1 than] that F.

Which hast, as I kan deuyse,

Take on the so gret emprise   3532

To entre the gardyn of pleying,   that, if I enter
                the Garden

Wher Deduit hath his duellyng   of Pleasure,

And his Brother by his syde,

Which that callyd is Cupide,   3536

Ther to pley hem and solace,

In that freshe lusty place,

They with many another mo,

And thy self art oon of tho   3540 I shall go to
                my confu-

Of new to thy confusyon,   sion.

That, as I seyde, Duk Iason,

Which was so hardy and so bolde,

H

Diana.	" Wham he wam the flees of golde,	3544
The Golden Fleece was	That was kept by the high prudence	
	And by the gret[e] diligence	
	Of myghty Mars, the god of Werre,	
[leaf 251]	The which ys spoken of so ferre	3548
	From est in-to the occydent,	
kept by big Bulls snorting flame,	And was kept by enchauntement	
	With huge boolys of metal,	
	With flavme dredful and mortal,	3552
	Which yssed out at nasse and mouthe,	
	Spredyng abrood[e] west and southe,	
which burnt every one,	Brent[en] al that kam be-syde :	
	Ther koude no man hym provyde	3556
	To save him that he was brent.	
and by a great Serpent.	Ther was also a gret serpent,	
	Passing cruel and horrible,	
	That hyt sempte an Impossible,	3560
	In that dedely mortal stryve,	
	A man to eskape with his lyve.	
But my danger (says Diana) is more than Jason's,	But thy meschef, who loke wel,	
	Is more perilouse a thousand del.	3564
	For Iason, throgh his hardynesse,	
	Throgh his force, and high prowesse,	
	And also throgh his sotyltee,	
	And by the helpyng of Medee,	3568
	And by his swerde so sharpe and kene,	
	Fortunyd was for to sustene	
	Al the pereils oon by oon,	
for he won;	And ouer-kam hem euerychon ;	3572
he made the Bulls plough,	Made the boolys wyth strong honde	
	Vp and doun to ere¹ the londe,	¹ ere] here F. A.
and he kild the Serpent, and sowd his teeth, which came up Knights,	The serpent slough, as hit ys knowe,	
	Took out his teth and gan hem sowe,	3576
	The which, to euery mannys syght,	
	Euery tothe Roos vp a Knyght,	
	The whiche fersly in bataylle	
	Ech gan other to assaylle,	3580
	Al the while hem lasteth breth :	
who kild one another.	And thus the fyn of hem was deth,	
	And so Iason, this knyghtly man,	

" The flees of golde by man-hode wan), 3584 *Diana.*
Which was so noble and so ryche.

So Jason
won the
Golden
Fleece:

But thyn) emprise ys nat lyche,
Who lyst take hede vnto the fyne,
Yif thou entre the gardyn). 3588 but if I enter
Pleasure's
Garden,
no wit or
strength

For nouther wyt, nor worthynesse,
Manhode, force, nor noblesse,
Enchauntement, nor sorcerye
In this perilouse Iupartye 3592
Avaylle may, me lyst nat glose, 'll be worth
a rosebud
to me.

Nat the boton) of A rose ;
For fro thens no man) retourneth No man who
goes into it
ever returns.

That any while ther soiourneth. 3596
A man) may entre wel certeyn),
But he shal neuer resorte ageyn).
For the treynes that be there
Be more to drede, and ful of fere, 3600
And more perylouse of to telle
Than) the snarys depe in helle,
Wherin) ys trapped tantalus,
For this the house of Dedalus 3604 It is the
house of
Dædalus.

Wyth the clowthy and the threde,
Dedly perilouse, who taketh hede.
It is so wrynkled to and froo
That man) not,[1] how he shal goo, ¹ not] wot F. A. 3608
For who hath onys ther entre, No enterer
comes out
of it.

To come ageyn) yt wil nat be.

¶ Her declareth Diane the perils that ben in the gardyn and the herber of Deduit.

" In this gardyn amerouse,
Most woful and most dolerouse, 3612
Ther is of sorwe so gret novmbre It is full of
sorrowing
folk.

That they wil a man) encombre.
It is so ynly deceyvable
That thou woldest holde a fable, 3616
Yif I sholde hem oon) by oon)
Rekne hem to the euerychon),
Al the pereils as they ben) :

"For ther thou shalt syrenes sen),

Crestyd[1] as a gret Dragon),

Feller than) any scorpion),

Of which in ysidre ye may se,

Specialy, how ther be thre,

Halfe brid and fissh the navele doun,

And vpward of inspeccion),

Who that a-ryght beholde kan),

Eche hath an hede of a woman),

And euerych hath a mayde face

Of syghte lusty to enbrace,

Her nayles kene and wonder sharpe.

The ton) pleyeth on) an harpe   3632

Myd of the see, fer fro the londe,

The seconde toucheth with hir honde

On) a sawtre delytable,

The thirdde also, most agreable,   3636

Aungelyke of melodye,

Ful of soote armonye,

Syngeth songes Amerouse,

Wonderly delyciouse.   3640

And of hir hedes thise Sirenes

Arrayed fressh as any quenys,

Toward the tayl siluer shene

With scalis rede, blew, and grene,   3644

And disgesely arrayed,

With wynges large, brood displayed ;

And thus, as bokys maken) mynde,

Monstres of a treble kynde,   3648

Fyssh and foule, but hede and face

Meke as a mayde ful of grace,

But venym) in the tayl behynde,

Who that preveth shal hyt fynde,   3652

Crawmped as a gret gryffon)

Of nature and condicion).

Whan) they harpe, pley, and synge,

The noyse is so ravysshynge   3656

That shippes, seyling by the see,

With her songe so fonned bee,

So supprysed, and y-blent,

Sidenotes:

[leaf 252]
Diana.

In Pleasure's Garden are Syrens, worse than scorpions,

with women's heads,

who play on harps

and psalteries,

sing delightful songs,

have scaly tails and

wide wings,

with poison in their tails.

[leaf 252, bk.] Their song

deceives sailors.

¶ *Dicit Isidorus tres fuisse sirenes ex parte virgines / et ex parte volucres et pisces / vngulas et alas[1] habentes quarum vna voce / altera tubea / tercia lira canebat que illectos nauigantes sub specie cantus ad naufragium per trahunt / secundum veritatem / Meretrices fuerunt que transeuntes ad egestatem ducebant etc.*

¶ Sirenes.

---

[1] Crestyd] Cressyd A.

[1] alas] alias F. A.

" That they be werrey necligent   3660   *Diana.*

Of gou*er*naylle in ther passage,

Tyl, amonge the floodys rage,   The seamen are swallowd

Ther ys no thing that hem socoureth,   by Charybdis.

Tyl caribd*es* hem deuovreth,   [This line added in the margin.] 3664

The pereyl ys so mortal strong.

Lo ! this the fyn of al her song,

Lo ! thus concludeth her delyte,

And thou shalt ben in wors[e] plyte,   3668 And I shall be in worse

As shal preven) at the ende,   plight, if I go to Pleasure's

Yif thou in-to the gardyn) wende,   Garden,

And ley the Ere for to here   hear the Sirens of

Sirenes with her notys clere,   3672 Venus,

Ful lusty and melodious,

Whiche, in the chapel of Venus,

Day and nyght' do ther *ser*vise.

And as I shal to the deuyse,   3676

In this gardyn) ouermore

Ther is ful many wilde bore,   and am at-tackt by wild

Lyons proude in ther rage,   boars,

And many beste[1] ful Savage,   [1] beste] best*es* A. 3680

To annoye, whan) they be furious,

To[2] folkys that ben) amerous,   [2] To] The A.

Professed in Venus covent,

Ofte devoured and to-rent :   3684

As whilom) was Adonydes,   ¶ Adonydes fuit amasius veneris vnde in sacra as Adonis was in the

Yong, lusty, fresh, and pereles, scriptura / Mulieres sedentes in theatro

Of hardynesse and fers[3] corage, planxerunt adonidem.

Fairer eke of his visage   [3] fers] freshe A. 3688

Than) euer, in soth, was Absolon) ;

In the forest of cytheron)   forest of Cytheron,

Thys yong[e] knyght'[4], by cruel fate, [4] knyght] knyte A.

Was slay[e]n), for him lyst debate   3692

Wyth wylde bores in ther rage   [leaf 253]

In that forest most savage.

At a boor as he gan chace,   when he tried to spear

And with a spere him manace   3696 a boar.

With strong and myghty violence,

. The boor stondyng at diffence·

With foomy mouth and tusshes kene

Diana.   " Vnder a cedre fressħ and grene,   3700

Witħ grete noyse and gret affray

The Boar kild Adonis,   Stondyng at a mortaɫ Bay,

Whaɲ he myghtᵗ him nat with-drawe,

Hatħ thys yonge knyghtᵗ[1] y-slawe,   [1] knyght] knyt A.   3704

Who so ther witħ was lefe or lotħ.

and made Venus angry.   For whos detħ Venus was wrotħ,

Al be that ther was no socour,

By-cause he was hir paramour,   3708

And, for the beaute of his face,

Gretly accepted to hir[2] grace.   [2] ħir] his F. A.

But yt ne[3] myghte be amendyd,   [3] ne] me F.

Al be that she had him diffendyd   3712

She told him to avoid wild beasts,   And y-taughtᵗ him, as she koude,

Teschewe bestys that be proude :

As boors, lippardys, and lyouns,

That[4] Fray and rore in ther souns,   [4] That] And A.   3716

Fel and mortal to assaylle ;

and hunt   To hunte at hem yt may nat vaylle,

But at other bestys smale,

Bothe oɲ[5] hille and in vale,   [5] on] in A.   3720

To chasen hem she bad nat spare,

only rabbits, hares,   As the konyɲ and the hare,

Whicħ ay be redy to the flyghtᵗ ;

She bad at hem to doon hys myghtᵗ,   3724

Wher so that he may hem knowe,

To chase at hem and hornes blowe,

and deer.   Hert, and hynde, buk, and doo,

[leaf 253, bk.]   At reyndere and the dredful roo ;   3728

For they kaɲ no resistence

For to sto[n]deɲ at dyffence.

But Adonis was a fool like I am,   But for thys[6] yong Adonydes   [6] thys] thy A.

Was necligent and Rekkeles   3732

And a fool lyke as artowe.

Al that she taugh̄t him for his prowe

Was voyde out of hys retentyf,

and so lost his life thru knowing Venus.   For whicħ, in sootħ, he loste hys lyf,   3736

Throgħ hys vnhappy mortal chaunce,

Caused by the Aqueyntaunce

Whicħ he hadde witħ Venus,

"Wher-throgh he made an ende thus   3740
Throgh the bores[1] cruelte,   [1] bores] boors F.
That bet to him yt hadde be   Adonis had better have
Ta kepte him cloos out of his[2] syght',   [2] his] hyr A.   kept at home
But he may curse of verray ryght'   3744
That ever he kam in her forest
With-out[e] wisdam or arest
Or for lak of discrecion),
To hunte at Boor or at lyon)   3748   and not hunted boars.
In wode, forest, holt, or hethe,
Wher-through, in sooth, he caught' hys deth.

¶ Of moo pereils that Diane reherseth.

"In this gardyn) eke also,   In Pleasure's Garden
      Who that kan take hede ther-to,   3752   are beds worse than Lancelot's,
Therin) be beddes perilouse,
More dyuers and more mervelouse
Than) was the bed of launcelet,
With gold enbrowde and stonys fret,   3756
And maked by enchauntement,
With whiche he was al-most y-shent,
Of rychesse thogh yt dyde excelle.
But this bed of which I telle,   3760
Ys wors, and thou shalt fynde yt thus,   no*ta*
Than) the bed of Vulcanus,   or Vulcan's,
Al with cheynes rounde enbracyd,   [leaf 254]
In the which he hath y-lacyd   3764   in which he caught Venus and Mars,
Hys wyf Venus and Mars y-fere,
Whan) Phebus with hys bemys clere
Discurede and be-wreyed al,
And al the goddys celestial   3768   so that the Gods mockt them.
Of scorne and of derision)
Made a congregacion),
To wonder on) hem, wher as they lay
Asshamed and in gret affray,   3772
By fals compas of V[u]lcanus
Most Ialousse and suspecious,
Wich hath a bed contreved so,
That they wer take bothe two   3776
Al vnwar, whan) they lest wende,

Diana.   " That they koude hem nat diffende,

Whaṇ Vulcanus dyde hem assayle ;

Mars was beaten   For Mars, that god was of batayle,   3780

For al his knyghtly excellence

Ne koude tho[1] no resistence,   [1] A. inserts ' make ' after ' tho.'

Oonly to avoydeṇ his diffame,

and shamed by Vulcan.   Which tourned him to gret[e] shame,   3784

Whaṇ al the goddys in his face

Rebukede him of his trespace.

But Venus didn't care,   But Venus was ryght' noght' ashamed

Of no thing that Mars was blamed,   3788

for she hated smutty Vulcan,   Be-cause oonly that Vulcanus

Was to hir so odious,

For his smotry, swarte face

He stood clene out of hir *grace* ;   3792

and lovd brave young Mars.   But Mars was· yong, and eke lusty,

Gentil, manful, and hardy,

And eke with bysy Attendaunce

Redy to do to hir plesaunce,   3796

Wher Vulcanus, to conclude,

Had[de] many tachchis rude,

[leaf 254, bk.]   A cowarde and of no renouṇ,

And vileyns of condicioṇ,   3800

That she wolde, in her entent,

In wilde fire that he were brent.

¶ Here Diane reherseth mo pereils.

In Pleasure's Garden are poisonous springs,   " In that gardyṇ eke be wellys,

Springyng oṇ roches out of hellis,   3804

Which, of disposicioṇ,

Be ful of venyṃ and poysoṇ,

Which outwarde to a manṇys[2] sight'   [2] manṇys] mans A.

bright and clear.   Beṇ cler, ageyṇ the sonṇe bryght',   3808

As any cristall to be-holde ;

The stremys eke most fresh and colde

Vpoṇ the tonge, this no fage,

Wonder lusty of tarage,   3812

That neuer, sithe thou wer borṇ,

Thou saugh neuer nooṇ to forṇ

No welle vnto thy plesaunce

"Havyng so moche suffisaunce   3816   *Diana.*
Outwarde as in apparence,
But, verrayly, in existence,   But these
                                       springs
To make a breue conclusio⁊),
Ful of fals Illusio⁊),   3820
Who that ka⁊) of ryght¹ conceyve,¹   ¹ conceyve] reseyve A.
Oonly ordeyned to deceyve
A ma⁊), to drynk out of mesure,
Neuer after to recure.   3824
They be so ful of sorwe and dool,   are so danger-
                                      ous that they
That he mot dye or be [a] fool   kill or fool
                                      men.
That drynketh any quantyte,
For yt mot sywe, he may nat fle,   3828
The more he drinke to staunche his thrust,
The more shal ay encresse his lust;
And who that lyst[e] to be-holde,
To look vpo⁊) the watrys colde   3832   And in some
Of so*m*me wellys that ther be,
Hys ovne face he shal se,   a man can
                               see his own
By diligent inspeccio⁊),   face,
And by clere refleccio⁊)   3836
In the watir of his face,
The whiche, soothly, to enbrace   [leaf 255]
He shal so ravisshed be,   and get so
                               ravisht by it
For the excellent beaute,   3840
Which in the welle dooth appere
Among the cristal stremys clere,
Of hys shadwe this figure;
Love him shal so dysfigure,   3844
To doo⁊) hys besy myght¹ and pey⁊)
Hys ovne vmbre to restrey⁊).
By recorde of Ouidius,²   ² Ouidius] ovidus A.
As whilom dyde Narcisus,   3848   that, like
                                    Narcissus,
For hys shadwe fille a-swovne,   he'll drown,
Wha⁊) he dyde in the water drovne
For love, and fonde no bet socour,
Tyl he was tournyd to a flour: 3852   and be turnd
                                    into a flower.
The levys white,³ the greyne cytryne;   ³ white] whis A.
And thus Narcisus dyde fyne,
Wha⁊) he hys shadwe dyde se.

"Yt was so passynge of beaute   3856
By apparence vn-to hys syght'
That he was drowned anoon ryght',
As thou to forne hast herd me telle.

"But yet ther ys another welle,   3860
More perilouse a thousand folde
Than) this of which I ha the tolde,
In the gardyn) of Cupide,
As thou shalt seen, yf thou abyde,   3864
And cesse nat in thy pursuyt.
In this Erber of Deduit
Ther ys a welle wonderful,
That, who drynketh hys bely ful   3868
And ys bathed therin oonys,
Among the colde cristal stonys,
The nature shal him enclyne
To be-come Femynyne,   3872
And ouer, yif I shal not feyne,
Departed in-to kyndes tweyne,
Double of nature and yet al oon),
Neuer a-sonder for to goon),   3876
Resemblynge, as I kan) endyte,
Vnto an hermofrodyte,
Which, as poetys bere witnesse,
Hath a maner doublenesse ;   3880
For he hath partye both of man)
And party also of woman).
And yif he ther abyde longe,
The watrys ben) so ynly stronge   3884
That no wyght' may hym selven) kepe,
Yif he him bathe therin to depe,
It is so dyuers and so trouble,
Of nature he shal be double.   3888
But prudent folkys that be sage
Eschewe of wisdam) the passage,
Wher Cupide hath most hys hawnte
And is of custom) conuersaunte.   3892
The place yt is so perilouse,
So dredful and contagiouse,
Ful of treson) and of gyle,

In another well,

if a man bathes,

he becomes half woman,

[leaf 255, bk.]

hermaphro-dite.

So prudent folk avoid this Cupid's Garden of Pleasure.

"Of which I shal be stille a while.　　　　3896　　*Diana.*

¶ Here declareth Diane of the kynde and the natures of the trees in the gardyn of Cupyde.

"Eke in this gardyñ of Deduit　　　　¶ *id est* of play　　Also in the
Garden of
Pleasure,

The tren of kynde ber no fruit,

Thogħ nature hem sustene,

Ay tendre, fresħ, and grene,　　　　3900　　the trees, tho'
green and
leavd,

Ageyñ thassaut of al[le] shours

Both of levys and of flours.

Yet, verrayly, in existence,

Ther is but fals apparence　　　　3904

Fresħ to be-holde at prime face,

Lyghtly sone for to pase,

Holwgħ witħ-in, yt is no drede,　　　　¶ Hoc ad *literam dicitur*
de salicibus.　　are hollow,

And ful also, who taketħ hede,　　　　3908

Of fraude and of decepcions,

Ful of serpentys and Dragou*ns*,　　　　and full of
dragons.

Folke to deceyveñ and begile ;

And who abyt ther eny while,　　　　3912　　[leaf 256]

He shal haue experyence

Of ther cruel violence.

"Of trees ther beñ eke many paire

That ber applys gret and faire,　　　　3916　　Their apples

Delytable in shewyng,　　　　¶ Tales arbores habu*n*dare
dicu*n*tur *super* ripas

But wonder bitter in tastyng,　　　　maris mortui in loco vbi
sodoma et alie ciuitates　　are bitter,

Ful of pouder corruptible　　　　fueru*n*t di*u*i*n*it*u*s igne
et sulphur[e] destructe.　　rotten,

And asshes lothsoñ and odible,　　　　3920

In wirkyng wonder venymous,　　　　poisonous,

Stynkyng and contagious,

The heyre is so abhominable,

Faire witħ-oute, but coru*m*pable　　　　3924

They be wytħ-iñ, who taste aryghť,

Contrarye eveñ to the syghť,

Fresħ by demonstracioñ,

But ful of fals corrupcioñ　　　　3928　　full of cor-
ruption.

They be stuffed by the kore.

Euery mañ be war therfore

That he eschewe the tarage,

Lyst yt tourne him to damage.　　　　3932

Diana.
" And in this gardyn) eke also

In Pleasure's Garden,
Ther be many other frutys mo,

Of nature wonder straunge,

fruits often change colour
So ofte sithe a day they chaunge   3936

Both of colour and of hewe :

Somwhiles olde and somwhile newe,

And also eke, who taketh hede,

Sommtyme grene, somtime rede,   3940

Sommtyme white as cloth of lake,

And sodeynly they wex[en] blake,

Swich is the tarage of the roote,

and taste;
Somtyme as any sugre soote,   3944

And bitter sodeynly as galle,

Swich wonder chaunge doth on) hem falle ;

For what fruit blakkest now is seyn)

Vnwarly wexeth white ageyn).   3948

[leaf 256, bk.]
Swich ys the custom) in that place :

are first sweet, but bitter at last.
Soote alwey at prime face,

But bitternesse ay concludeth.

The fruit so falsly men) delludeth,   3952

Causyng among men) to be Murye,

The Mulberry, white at first, was turnd black
As whilom) dide the Molberye,

¶ *Fructus illius arboris secundum dicta poetarum fuit mutatus[1] de albedine in nigredinem.*

Whos fruit was turned to blaknesse

From his colour of whitenesse,

Poetys make mencyon),   [1] mutatus] mutata F. A.   3957

Oonly by the occasyon)

for the death of Pyramus and Thisbe.
Of thilke[2] woful deth noyous,   [2] thilke] the same A.

Ryght' wonderful and ryght' pitous   3960

Of piram*us* and of Thesbe,   no*ta*

Both y-borne in oo Cyte.

For love thise yong[e] folkys two

Had so moche sorwe and wo,   3964

Lych as Ovide kan) wel telle ;

When they met,
Whan) they metten) at the welle,

This Thesbe first of sodeyn) drede

Abasshed oonly of woman-hede,   3968

The whiche[3] made hir almost rave,

Thisbe, frightend by a lion, ran into a Cave.
Whan) she ranne in-to the kave,   [3] The whiche] Which almost F.

Causyd by the occasyon)

Of koun*n*yng of a fers lyon),   3972

" Which wolde have dronken) of the welle ;   *Diana.*

But al to longe she dyde duelle

In the kave, allas, the while,

Of drede oonly and nat of gyle,   3976

Sodeyn) fere so made hir quake

That vnwarly, for hir sake,

Piramus, for sorwe and smerte,   Pyramus stabd him-

Roof him self vnto the herte,   3980 self,

Wenyng playnly, how that she   thinking the lion had eaten

Hadde aforne deuoured be   Thisbe.

Of the lyon) in his rage,

Which was allone to gret Damage.   3984

For when that he hir wymple founde,

Anoon) ryght' with his ovne honde   [leaf 257]

Slough him self, yt was gret routhe,

Caused for hys ovne slouthe :   3988

That she was ther so long aforne,

For whiche bothe two were lorne.

For after she, no thing afferde,   Then Thisbe

With[1] the selve same suerde,   [1] with] whiche F. A. 3992

For gret constreynt of hir peyn),

Karf hyr hert even) atweyn),   cut her heart in two, to die

She wolde algate with him wende ;   with Pyra-mus.

Allas, thys was a pitouse ende.   3996

And for the dool and grete pite   And so the white Mul-

The fruit of thys Ilke tre,   berry was turnd black.

Which that I to forn) of spake,

Sodeynly was torned to blake,   4000

And his beries euerychon).

   " And swiche trees be many oon),

Growyng vpon) euery syde

In the gardyn) of Cupide,   4004

The which, in soth, I the behete,

Fruitys beren) that first be swete

And after ful of bitternesse.

And also, as I dar expresse,   4008

Ther ben) other trees mo   The shadows of other trees

Which ar cause of myche wo ;   in Pleasure's Garden kill

For ther shadwe, this no lye,   ¶ Hoc *dicitur* de taxo et de men.

Wyl make a man) vnwarly dye.   nuce magna. 4012

Diana.   "Ther mortal operacioṇ
Is of swicħ condicioṇ.

¶ Her declareth Diane of the perilouse erbys groving in the gardyn of the god of love.

In Pleasure's
Garden are
gay herbs;

"And in thys delytable place,
Ful of merthe and of solace,   4016
The sothe shal to the be sene,
Ther beṇ erbys white, and grene,

[leaf 257, bk.]
Yelwe, rede, ynde, and pers,
Of ther kynde ful dyuers,   4020
Fair to sygħt of ther colours.

but under
their flowers,
serpents lurk.
But lowħ vnder the freshe flours
Ful covertly, who kaṇ declare,
Many serpent ther doth dare,   4024
Many hadder, and many snake,
Whicħ day and nyght' espye and wake
Tyme and leyser for to stynge,
Dedly and mortal of werkynge ;   4028
For they her venyṃ euery syde
Vnder flour[e]s close and hyde,
That no maṇ hatħ inspeccioṇ
Of ther covert fals tresoṇ.   4032
For lyke, in sootħ, as thou shalt lere,

The flowers
too
The flour[e]s outward faire appere
And shew hem also fresħ and soote,
The venyṃ closed in the roote,   4036
Oṇ ther stalkys blosome and shyne,

hold poison,
But the venyṃ serpentyne,
Whicħ is kept cloos, both eve and morwe,
Concludetħ ay witħ dool and sorwe   4040
Throgħ hys dredful violence,
Whos beaute ys but apparence
Made to deceyve, or meṇ take hede :

and are dan-
gerous.
And yt is grete pereil and drede   4044
To medle thingis deceyvable
Witħ thinges that be delytable.
Sugre and galle acorde nought',
Thogħ they be to-gedre wrought',   4048
Ther is in hem suche variaunce,

"And thingis also of plesaunce,

As be semyng outward glosed,

Witħ fals venym vnder closed, 4052

Is more to drede a thousand folde.

   "And even thus, as I ha tolde,

Is Venus of condicion

In al¹ hir operacion   ¹ alle *in the catchwords.* 4056

Witħ hir dredful double mygħt :

Debonayre vnto the sygħt,

Lusty, fresħ, and amerouse,

But in werkyng venymouse, 4060

Ful of chaunge and variable ;

And in hir erber delytable,

Whicħ I ha to the descryved,

Folkes that ther haue aryved 4064

And al her lyve to hir servyd,

Ful many oon therin hatħ stervyd,

Perysshed witħ-out remedye,

Or they the venym koude espye ; 4068

Swicħe double greyn she hath ther sowe,

Soote and bitter botħ a-rowe,

Delytable in tastyng,

And venymous in werkyng ; 4072

For ay delyt is cast to forn :

Prykyng witħ a lusty thorn,

To ravyssħ a mannys herte,

Or he the treson kan aduerte, 4076

And vnwarly to suppryse,

Or he the venym kan devise,

Til he in the snare falle,

For whicħ take good hede of alle 4080

The myschefes whicħ I ha tolde.

   "And I counsaylle : be not to bolde

To entre in-to that gardyn grene,

Lyst yt turne the to tene, 4084

To sorwe, and gret aduersyte !

For ther may no mene be,

Nor remedye to thy socour,

Yif thow cachche onys sauour, 4088

And lyst nat of wysdam spare

Diana.

So Venus is always double:

[leaf 258]

to sight, fair,

really poisonous and changeable.

In her Garden

many have died.

Pleasure is shown,

but poison lies behind.

Do not enter that Garden!

Diana.

" For to fallen in the Snare,

To stumble vnwar with eyen) blynde,

For which my wordes haue in mynde.   4092

[leaf 258, bk.]
I am to follow
the example
of Ulysses,

'· Take example of vlixes

Touching the drinkes of Circes,

Which, whan) he kn'yw the perilous wrak,

With-drough his foot and went a-bak,   4096

Lyst hys passage wer nat wronge,

Deceyved by Sirenes songe ;   ¶ Hoc fuit sumptum in eppistola
valerij ad Rufum.

who kept
clear of the
Sirens,

For throgh hys noble providence

He ordeyned a dyffence   4100

Pleynly that he kam) no nere.

And as thouching this erbere,

To forn) or thou be put in blame,

My counsayl ys : thow do the same,   4104

Somme other way[e] that thou take,

Myn) ovne frende, for goddys sake,

And entre nat for no folye,

Lyst thou falle in Iupartye   4108

Of flesshly lust throgh fals desire,

and am not
to be reckless
like Empe-
docles,

To be consumyde in the fire,

Yif thou be founde rekkeles ;

As whilom) was empodocles,   4112

Which nat oonly of folye

But also of Malencolye

who was
burnt to
ashes

Was sodeynly to asshes brent.

And even) lyke shaltow be shent,   4116

Yif Venus Marke the with hir bronde,

Which that she holdeth in hir honde ;

The fire of whom), who kan) take hede,

Ys of perel more to drede   4120

Than is the fire, I dar wel seyn),

on Mount
Etna.

Of smoky Ethna, the mounteyn),

Wher empodocles was dede,

Be-cause that he took noon) hede   4124

To do by counsayl of the wise,

Therfore he brent in his emprise.

¶ **Her Diane maketh A maner rehersayl of al**   *Diana*
the pereils to for seyde in the herber of Deduit.

"Kepe the wel and make[1] the strong   [1] make] maketh F. A.   bids me stop my ears

And stoppe thin eres fro the song   4128   against Sirens' song,

Of Sirenes passing soote,   [leaf 259]

Ageyn[e]s which ther is no bote!

And kepe the fro the bestys felle   keep from wild beasts,

Of whiche thou hast herde me telle!   4132

Hunte hem nat whil they be rage,

Lyst yt turne to thy damage!

And yif thou lyst shortly be sped,

Kepe the fro the perilous bed   4136   from Vulcan's bed,

Wher **Mars** and **Venus** lay y-fere,

Wher thou mayst beholde and lere

The trappus, made by Vulcanus,

To cachche **Mars** and eke **Venus**,   4140

Hem to dystourbe in ther solace!

Eschewe of wysdam al suche place,

And kepe the fro the welles clere   from poisonous springs,

That so fresshly do appere,   4144

Which ben with mortal venym meynt,

In which so many men ar dreynt!

And kepe the, lyke as I ha tolde,

From alle the pereils in that holde,   4148   in the Garden of Pleasure,

Eschewe al wayes that be derke!   .

For who wil nat by counsayl werk[e],

Ful ofte sith to his represe

Falleth in sorowe, and meschefe,   4152

And in grete mysauenture,

Which he ne may lyghtly recure.

   "And yif thou lyst to haue in mynde,

Ful many story thou mayst fynde   4156

To preve, that counsayl of the wyse

Dooth profyte in many wyse,

Namely of folkys that be sage,

As the revers dooth gret damage.   4160

Examples preve yt mo than[2] oon: [2] than] that F.   and not do like Icarus and Phaeton.

By ycharus and ph[a]eton;

For first this ylke ycharus,

I

Diana.

[leaf 259, bk.]

" That sone was to Dedalus,   4164

Was desirous to lerne fle

Ouer the gret[e] salt[e] se,

Icarus's father Daedalus made him wings of wax and feathers,

And hys fader dyde his peyne

For to make him wynges tweyne   4168

Of wex and fethres knet y-fere,

And his fader dyd him lere:

Teschewen̉ al aduersyte,

In swich a mene for to fle,   4172

What maner wynd that euer blowe,   ¶ nota

Nowther to highe nor to lowe;

and told him not to fly high, near the sun,

For yif ageyn̉ hys fader lore

That he to high alofte soore   ¶ id est flye 4176

Almost to the shene son̉ne

With hys fethres white and don̉ne,

or the wax would melt;

The wexe with hete wil relente,

Ageyn̉ hys fadres pleyn̉ entente,   4180

Than̉ his fethres wil dissever,

Which he shal recure never,

That sodeynly he shal descende,

The whiche no man̉ may amende;   4184

or too low,

And yif also he fle to lowe

With hys wynges sprad a-lowe,

as the feathers would freeze together.

Sodeyn colde, as he shal fele,

Shal hys fethres so congele   4188

That thay may gedre wynde nor air;

From al hope put in dyspair

He shal ploun̉gen and a-vale.

And by example of thys tale   4192

The middle path is always best.

In̉ alle maner of werkyng

A mene ys good in alle thing;

For, as the philisophe assenteth,

Who dooth by counseyle nat repenteth,   4196

And by recorde of thise clerkys

Counsayl is good in al[le] werkys,

As storyes telle moo than oon̉.

Take warning too by Phaeton.

" Make eke thy merour of Pheton̉,   4200

And by example of him be war,

When̉ he lad his fadres char,

How, throgh vnhappy aventure,

"Be-cause he koude no mesure   4204
Nouther a-twixen[1] hoot nor colde, ¹ a-twixen] A twen A.
But of presumpsioñ was bolde   Phaeton
drove his Fa-
ther's chariot
wrong,
To take oñ him the gouernaunce,
For which, throgh hys vr happy chaunce, 4208
As poetys lyst to descryve,
For he ne koude hys stedys[2] drive, ² stedys] stodys F.
Al a-wronge her cours they went,
For which al the worlde they brent, 4212 and burnt
the world:
Lost him self and eke hys wayñ;
Ther was as thoo nooñ other gayñ,
Al went to dystruccioñ;   4215
Oonly throgh his presumpsion,[3] ³ presumpsion] presupsion) F.
By disposicioñ fatal,
And lak of counseyl caused al.
Poetys make mencioñ
That the heveñ fil adouñ[4] ⁴ adouñ] doune A. 4220 the heaven
fell:
To grete hynderyng and Damage
Amonge the floodys fel and rage.
By which example to hys avayl
Ech mañ werke by counsayl,   4224
And take oñ him noñ empryse
Without[e] consayl of the wyse.

⁋ **Her declareth Diane many meschefs that felle**
  in the gardyn of Deduit by example of many
  sondry stories.

"And yif that thou of necligence   For fear all
this is not
Lyst nat yive no credence   4228 warning
enough for
me,
To that thou hast herd me declare,
Yet for al that I wyl nat spare,
How I ha ryght and thou hast wronge,
And to make my partye stronge,   4232
Touching pereils which I ha tolde,
Ful many story newe and olde
To my purpose I shal applye,
And in ordre specefye   4236
By resemblaunce and figures :
The sorowes and mysaventures,   Diana will
tell me the
sorrows
The meschef, and the violences,

Diana.

[leaf 260, bk.]

"And the Inconvenyences 4240
That loves folkys ha suffred there.

that Love's
folk suffer in
her Garden
of Pleasure.

And first as wysdam) dooth vs lere,
And the same afferme I dar,
He ys wyse that wyl be war 4244
And him self chastise kan)
By trespace of another man),
Prudently to taken) hede
Of another mannys¹ dede,   ¹ mannys] mans A. 4248
The foly wisely to eschewe
To fleen) a-way and nat to sewe,²   ² sewe] shewe A.
Where as he seeth yt be[t] to do.
For which take good hede therto 4252
Thy selfe of foly nat tencombre,
For by examples out of novmbre
I shal reherse to purpose,
Which ha be-falle[n] in that close 4256
With swich as wern) with love atteynt :

1. Narcissus
was drownd
there.

First how Narcisus was ther dreynt,
Rede Ouide and he kan) telle,
Beholdyng at the mortal welle 4260
Hys ovne shadwe and figure,
Wherby of fatal aventure
And of foly he was ther dede ;
And eke also, yif thou take hede, 4264

2. Pygma-
lion,

The crafty man) Pigmalion)
To grave in metal and in ston)
Made and wroght' to his delyte

who made
a statue of
ivory,

An ymage of yvore white, 4268
Most mervelous of entaylle,
To tellen al the apparaylle :
Most excellent in fairenesse,
Bothe of shap and semelynesse, 4272
And amyable of visage,

went madly
in love with
it.

Which him brought' in swich a rage
That he wex verray furious ;
Love him made so amerous, 4276
In Ouide as it ys tolde,
Al be that yt was ded and colde,

[leaf 261]

Which made hym selfe [for] to stryve,

"Lyche as hyt had[de] ben̄ alyve.   4280   *Diana.*
Of whos fooly thou mayst lere
To be war and come no nere.
    "In Naso eke thou maist se,
How, yore agoon̄, that Phasiphe   4284   3. Pasiphae
With Venus brond was made so hoot   was enam-
                                                                                ourd of a
To be enamowred on̄ a goot,   goat.
And how Mirra eke therto   4. Mirra lovd
Hir ovne fader lovede also   4288   her father;
Vn-to hir confusion̄,
And also eke, how Menafron̄,   5. Mena-
In poetis as ye may lere,   phron, his
                                                                                mother;
Lovede his ovne moder dere   4292
Ageyn̄ naturys ordynaunce,
To fulfillen hys plesaunce ;
He was so brent in Venus fire
To a-complysshen̄ his desire,   4296
As in bookys ys expressed,
He wolde hir falsly have oppressyd
And by force dovne y-drawe.
    "Eke Phedra lovede hyr sone yn̄ lawe,   4300   6. Phædra,
Whos love was superstycious ;   her son-in-
                                                                               law;
And, as I fynde, Tereus   7. Tereus, his
Lovede the suster of his wyfe,   wife's sister;
That cause was of ful gret strife,   4304
Hir afforcynge throgh hys myght'
Of fals lust, ageyn̄ all ryght'.
Silla also, to hir represe,   8. Silla, her
Fil for love in grete meschefe ;   4308
She thought', hyt was to hir so swete
To love Minos, kyng of Crete,   father's foe,
Which enmy to hir fader was ;   Minos, who
In swich dysioynt she stood, allas,   4312
Whan̄ he the cyte of Athene   won Athens
Beseged in hys mortal tene,   thrᵤher,
                                                                                   ᴧ
To wyne hyt throgh hys hygh renoun ;
But he hyt gat by hir treson̄,   4316
Love, allas, made hir so bolde   [leaf 261, bk]
To stele a-way the heer of golde   ¹ grewe] growe A.   and for whom
                                                                                she stole her
Which grewe¹ vpon̄ hir faderes² hede.   ² faderes] fader A.   father's Hair
                                                                                of Gold.

Diana.

Minos was turnd into a merlin,

and Silla into a lark.

" Thus was she cause that he was dede,   4320
Thorgh goddys disposicion)
Tourned to A Merlyon),
And she to A larke was transmewed
Ay of hyr fader to be sewed,   4324
For contrary, of condicion),
The larke and the Emerlyon)
I-founde be of ther nature,
Philosophres vs assure.   4328

9. Medea slew her 2 children.

    " Medea also did hir peyn)
For to slen) hir children) tweyn)
In gret dispyte of Duke Iason),
Whan) he was falsly fro hir gon) ;   4332

10. Phyllis hangd her-self.

Eke Phillis, as thou kanst recorde,
Heng hir selven) with a corde ;
And eke thou hast yrad also,

11. Dido kild herself.

How the worthy quene Dido   4336
Slough hir self, as thou maist see,
For the love of Enee,
The ryche quene of Cartage,
Whan) he was goon) on) hys viage,   4340
Virgile writeth[1] pleynly thus ;   [1] writeth] wrythe A.

12. Thisbe and Pyramus committed suicide.

And Thesbe eke and Pyramus
For love bothe two wer lorne,
As thou hast herde me tel afforne.   4344

¶ **Here maketh Diane a co[m]parison) a-twene hir Forest of chastite and the Herber of Deduit.**

Thus I may see the troubles of Love,

" By these exaumples thou maist se
The errour and contrariouste
That ys in love, yif thou take hede,
Which quyteth folke with cruel mede,   4348
Whos merveylous condicion)
Ys contrarye to reson) ;

[leaf 262]

Yt ys so ful of sorwe and tene.
For which I rede the abstene,   4352
Lyst thou repent[e] in the fyn,

and decide to stay with Diana in her Forest of Chastity.

Nat to entre in hys gardyn) ;
But abyde and make arest
Her with me in my forest,   4356

" Which hath plentevous largesse
Of beaute and of fairenesse ;
For, shortly, throgh my providence,
Her ys noon Inconvenience,   4360
No maner fraude, deceyt, nor wrong
Compassyd by Sirenes songe,
Nor be nat no bestes rage,
Dredful for to do damage,   4364
And ther thou shalt no wellys fynde
But that be holsom of her kynde,
The watir of hem ys so perfyte,
Who drinketh most hath most profyte.   4368
Eke in thys forest vertuus
No man taketh hede of Vulcanus
Nor of hys decepcion,
For the tren in ech seson   4372
Geyn al assaut of stormes kene
Of fruyt and lefe ben al-way grene,
Perdurable of nature
In ther beaute to endure,   4376
They ben of¹ kynde so notable
That they be neuer corrumpable,¹
I-lyche fresh and neuer olde,   ¹ corrumpable] corrumptable A.
And somme of hem bere fruyt of¹ golde,   4380
Swich as Alysaundre founde.
Whan he had wonne euery londe.
Ther is no fruyt, to rekne al,
That may therto be peregal,   4384
For thilke fruyt, as thou maist se,
Perseuereth ay in hys beaute,
And thyse tren, in comparison,
Passe of vertu and renoun   4388
The treen both of Mone and sonne,
Which clerkes so wel preyse konne ;
The fruyt ys so confortatyf
To preserve a mannys² lyf   ² mannys] mans A.   4392
Longe from al corrupcion,
By kyndly dysposicion ;
Of whos Applis thou maist se
The noblesse and the dignyte,   4396

Diana.

"Yif thow abyde in thys forest.

Alexander rode into India, but couldn't find golden apples,

For Alysaundre, in his conquest,
In hys story thow mayst fynde,
Rood in-to the ferther ynde,   4400
Of entent[e] to enquere
Swich maner fruyt to fynde there;
But he founde noon, in special,
That to thys fruyt was [per]egal   4404
Nor semblable to hys avayle,

tho' he consulted 2 trees sacred to the Moon and the Sun,

Al be that he took hys counsayle
Of two tren al to sone :   4407
The ton y-sacryd[1] to the mone,   [1] y-sacryd] Isacrifysyd A.
[2]The tother halwed to Phebus,[2]   [2—2] *om.* A.
Philysophres writen thus,

where his fate was told him.

Wher hys fate was nat sparyd
But openly to him declaryd,   4412
In greke and hebrew tonge sovnyd,
And hys fyn clerly expovned,
He myght eschew hyt by non art,

But, had he eaten Diana's apples, he'd have won more victories, and livd longer.

But had he ete and take his part   4416
Of this fruyt which I of telle,
Which al other doth excelle,
He had contunyd in hys glorie,
And bet acheved hys victorie,   4420
And prolongyd eke his lyf :
Hyt hath swych A prerogatyf

[leaf 263]

And of vertu so grete myght.
For the shadwe of kyndly ryght   4424
Ys allone so comfortable
And to profyte most notable.

The Herbs in the Forest of Chastity are ever fair,

The erbys also, of nature,
In ther beaute euer endure,   4428
And kepe alyche her grennesse,
Bothe her beaute and fayrenesse ;
Ther flour[e]s euere fresh and glade,
And for no maner stormys fade,   4432
For they be so vertuous,

and no poisonous beast can get near them.

That no best[e] venymous,
Serpent in kave nor in Roche,
Ne may in no Wyse aproche,   4436

" Nor ther vertu amenuse ;

For al swich venyme they refuse,

For which with al thy ful[le] mygħt

Thou sholdest be ful glad and lygħt   4440

Here to abyden and presever

And neuer hen[ne]s to dissever,

First considre*n* of prudence

In thy self the dyfference   4444

Atwene this habitacio*n*

And the amerous mansyo*n*

Of Deduit and of Cupide,

And set both*e* two asyde ;   4448

And al thys thing consydred wel,

¹Peysed and novmbryd euerydel,¹   ¹—¹ *om.* A.

Thow sholdest chese here tabyde

Perpetuelly, and nat devyde   4452

Of thin ovne volunte,

Syth thou hast swich lyberte.

For more to the kan I nat sey,

It longeth nat me to prey.   4456

For yt may happe so par case :

The more men prey[e]*n* a gret pase

The more som*m*e folkys wil declyne

For tobey[e] my doctryne."   4460

So I ought
to be glad to
stay with
Diana in her
Forest,

seeing its
advantage
over the
Garden of
Pleasure,

for I have
free will.

[leaf 263, bk.]

¶ Thansuer of the auctour vn-to Diane.

The Author.

" Madame," quod I, " with thys that ye

Be nat displesed now with me,

I wil lyke my*n* oppinio*n*

Make a replicacio*n*   4464

To that ye han rehersed here,

Which ys mervelous to here,

That by your wylle I shold[e] tarye

In thys forest solytarye ;   4468

To which, yif I dyde assente,

I sholde sone me repente.

But trusteth pleynly wel ther-to,

My purpose ys nat to do so,   4472

This verray sooth, me lyst nat fey*n*) ;

Therby thogh I mygħt atteyne

I tell Diana

that if I stayd
in her soli-
tary forest,

I should soon
repent ;

and I don't
mean to stay.

" To the prowesse of Ector,
That was so worthy her to for,   4476
Nor to the wisdam, botħ in oon),
Of Dauid and kyng Salamon),
Nor to wynne al the tresor
Of the kyng Nabugodonosor.[1]   4480
Al thys ne mygħt[e] me compelle
In this forest for to duelle,
Thogħ ye reherse al y-fere :
The dyuers trees, the wellys clere,   4484
The herbys, nor the flour[e]s fayre,
Nor al the bestys debonayre :
Al yfere avaylle nogħt',
To do me consent in my thoght'   4488
For to holden here hostage ;
Yt acordetħ no thing witħ myn age
For this habytacion)
To myn) Inclynacion).   4492
For I se here no plesaunce
By no maner resemblaunce :
Ioye, myrthe, nor gladnesse,
But al-to-gedre hevynesse,   4496
For whicħ I preyse[2] yt nat a myte.
Me list as ӡet be noon hermyte
Nor solytarie of lyvynge.
For, fynally, thys duellynge   4500
Ys nat acordyng witħ my lyfe ;
The place ys so contemplatyfe,
I wer a fool, here to soiourne,[3]
Alway to compleyn) and morne,   4504
Ever in oon, [both] day and nygħt'.
I sholde do ageyn) al rygħt',
To contrayre in werkyng
The preceptys and byddyng   4508
Of Nature, my maistresse,
Of alle the world[e] gouerneresse ;
Whicħ bad me, as I kan report :
' Go se the world ' and me disport,   4512
And theryn) oonly me delyte :
Goon) about[e] and vysite

[1] Nabugodonosor] nabugodonyʒer A.

[2] preyse] rayse A.
[This line added in the margin.]

[3] soiourne] soioure A.

" Places which that be Iocounde,

Wher as myght' ys most habounde   4516

In my selfe, to knowe and see

On) hir werkys the beaute,

The merveylles and vnkouth*e* thing*es*

Of hir w*,*onderful werkyngys,   4520

And of hir forge the secrees,

Mysteries, and the prevetees,

Whic*h*, in sot*h*, be nat apert

But wonder cloos and ful covert.   4524

And for I ha so grete plesaunce,

With al my hool[e] attendaunce

Of ful desire to folwe hir lust,

I wil hir siwe of verray trust,   4528

And abyde no lenger here

Myd thys forest, in no manere,

Wher I kan se noon) avauntage

To my profyte but bestys rage,   4532

Ne party that I kan) devyse,

And I wil in no maner wyse

Nouther offende nor trespase,

Lyst I wer put out of grace,   4536

Ageyn) myn) hest, in soth[e]nesse,

Made to Venus, the goddesse,

I wil hir serve and euer shal,   *nota*

What euer fal, loo, here is al !   4540

Thus to doon) ys most myn) case,

Wher so yt greve yow or please,

This[1] myn) entent in eu*er*y cost,   [1] This] Thus A.

And wher as men) me blame most,   4544

Ther shal I be most ententyf

Hyr to se*r*ven al my lyf.

For without comparyson),

Ther ys noon) of swic*h* renou*n*   4548

As my lady, dame Venus,

Humble, and benigne, and g*r*acious,

Faire a-bove al mesure,

Both of shappe and of stature,   4552

And to speke in wordys pleyn),

Fairer than ever was Eleyn),

The Author.

Nature told me to view the beauty of her works;

and I mean to do so. [leaf 264, bk.]

I promist Venus I'd serve her,

and I will,

for she's a most

lovely lady.

The Author. " Ryght' bontevous and ynly fre,
And of lyberalyte   4556
She excelleth, I dar expresse,
Of port also and loulynesse.

No one can estimate Venus's power Ther is no man) this day so wys
That to the fulle kan) yive aprys   4560
Of hir myght' nor hir highnesse,
Of hir pover nor noblesse.
I dar yt wel expresse and telle

and renown. That she of renoun dooth excelle   4564

[leaf 265] Alle tho that ever I koude of rede,
For to speke of frendlyhede.

Diana is to blame for saying that And in oo thing ye wer to blame,
That ye lyst declare hir name   4568
By wrong interpretacion)
In your exposicion),
Which openly seyden thus :

'Venus' meant 'venom': That of venym was seyde Venus.   4572
This was your oppinion)
Contraire to myn) entencion).
For I dar pleynly specefy
That, for she hath the maistry   4576
And al represseth with hir myght',
Therfore of verray due ryght'
She hath hir name, who taketh hede,
To be callyd, yt is no drede.   4580

It means 'vanquishing,' Venus ys sayde of venquisshing,
For she venquyssheth euery thing.
I say yt out, me lyst nat rovne,
Thus ye shuld hir name expovne,   4584

for no one can resist her. For noon) may make resistence
Ageyn[e]s hyr magnificence,
For which I ha set myn) entent
To ben at hir comandement,   4588
Me to agreen) to hir wille
In euery thing, as yt ys skylle ;
For which I shal do my power

I shall hasten to Pleasure's Garden. To hast[e] me to thilke herber   4592
Wher Deduit hath gouernaunce
With Ioy and play and al plesaunce.

"For in my wit I kan) nat se,

That swiche perel sholde be   4596

In that place, lyke as ye seyn),

Ye blame yt ydelly in veyn),

And maken) a comparyson)

Of the dedys of Iason),   4600

Of Pheton), and of Icharus,

That wolde fleen, ye tel[le] thus.

But I me cast[e] nat to fle

With y-charus ouer the se,   4604

Nor with Pheton) al my lyve

The chare of Phebus for to dryve,

Nor for to wynne the flees of golde,

Of which to forn) ye han) me tolde.   4608

Of al her foly wilful dede

I wil take no maner hede;

But I desire the knowleching¹

Of the hevene and his mevyng¹,   4612

And also of the salt[e] see,

And eke what thing yt myght[e] be,

Why the flood, as clerkys telle,

Folweth with hys wawes felle,   4616

And after that the ebbys sone

Folweth the concours of the Mone,

The reson) out I wolde fynde

After the course oonly of kynde;   4620

Thogh I ha this effeccion

Prentyd in myn) oppinion),

Vn-to yow is noon) offence.

For, vtterly, thys my sentence :   4624

I wil go serve my maistresse,

I mene Venus, the goddesse.

I wil ther-of make no delay,

Lo, here is al ! I goo my way."   4628

¶ Here ansuereth Diane vn-to the Auctour.

"Thogh I al day do forth my peyne,

By force I may the nat restreyne,

Nor I wil nat the conterplete

Nouther in colde, nouther in hete,   4632

Marginal notes:

The Author.

Diana has compared Venus's followers

[leaf 265, bk.]

to Phaeton and Icharus.

But I'm not going to fly over the sea,

or drive Phaeton's chariot.

I want to understand the motion of heaven, of sea, and tides.

I'll go and serve Venus at once.

Diana.

Diana
says she'll,
leave me to
[leaf 266]
fall into
Venus's trap,

"Nor the afforcen by the lappe,
Til thou falle in Venus trappe
By somme vnhappy frowarde chaunce,
That thow falle in repentaunce   4636
Of thing wherin) thou doost offende,
And seyst : thow mayst yt nat amende,
Nouther by wyt nor purveyaunce,
Thorgh foly of thy gouernaunce,   4640
That thow lyst the nat provyde
To caste aforn), on) euery syde,

The perel of thyn) auenture,
Which thou art lykly to endure.   4644
Ther may be made noon) avoydaunce ;
Thow hast nat yet swich aqueyntaunce
On) euery part of thy maistresse,
Whom thow callyst thy goddesse,   4648
In euery cost, both fer and nere,
And yivest to hir so gret powere,
As al wer lacyd in hir cheyne,
As thogh she myghte al restreyne ;   4652

But yif thow wistest euerydelle
And knew what she were[1] ryght' welle,   [1] were] war A.
Al hir maner and hir gyse,
In hyr thow sholdest in no wise   4656
Han so grete affeccion)
Nor swyche ymaginacion),
But ageyn) hir lust debate

I should hate
her, and slash
her with my
sword like
Diomed did.

And haten hir of gretter hate   4660
Than) euer dyde dyomede,
Which with his suerde made hir blede.
To hir he gaf so grete a wounde
So mortal and so profounde   4664
That withont[e] more abood
She shoold ha deyed, so yt stood ;
Ther was now) other mene weye,
Yif goddys myght' of kynde deye,   4668
But deth hath, in conclusyon),
In hem no dominacion).

For thingys which that be dyvyne
Vnto deth may nat enclyne.   4672

" And thus consydred eue*r*y thyng

Of hyr wonderful wyrkyng,

Thow sholdest not, and thou wer wys,

Yife to hir so grete a pris,   4676

Yif thou knyw in thy reso*n*

The noble sentence of **Caton**,

Which comaundeth, thus I mene,   ¶ *parce* laudato.

A ma*n* to preysen in A mene,   ¹ *parce*] *per te* F. A.   4680

Both in high and low degre,

And by no super*fl*uyte,

Lyst after be no lak y-founde ;

And wher as² thou lyst the to grounde,   4684

To sustene thy grete errour,   ² as] *om.* A.

To make nature thyn Auctour,

That she³ sholde ha co*m*maundyd thus   ³ she] *om.* A.

The to folwe Dame Venus,   4688

Which was no thing hir entent

Nor fy*n* of hyr comaundement.

For I dar sey*n* and yt expresse

That nature, the goddesse,   4692

By recorde of wysest clerk*es*,

Hath noo*n* errour in hir werk*es*.   ¶ *quia* dirigit*ur* ab intelli-
                                        gencia no*n* erra*n*te.

For god, which goue*r*neth al

By hys pover eternal   4696

And hys dyvyne sapience,

Hath throgh hys myghty providence

Dame nature ordeyned so

That she may noo*n* errour do   4700

Nor forfete to no maner wyght.

Thow v*n*derstood hir nat a-ryght,

To comp*r*ehende in thy felyng

The cler entent of hir menyng ;   4704

She bad the, nouther fer nor nere,

To soiourne in the Erbere,

By no maner feyned weye,

Wher ydelnesse bereth the key,   4708

Nor wher as she ys porteresse

Of the gate and chefe maistresse,

Wher as **Deduit** was first fou*n*dour,

Lord, and sire, and gouernour,   4712

Diana
says I'm not
wise to praise
Venus so
highly.

I should
follow Cato's
advice, and
be moderate.

I've also
mistaken
Nature,

who never
bade me
follow Venus.

Nature is per-
fect in all her
works.

God made
her so.

She never
bade me stay

[leaf 267]

in the Garden
of Pleasure.

Diana

warns me
that Pleas-
ure's Garden

"Oonly ordeyned for delyte
And voluptuouse appetyte.
¹For botħ the host and the hostel¹   ¹⁻¹ *om.* A.
Ben) so peɾilouse and cruel   4716
That, to rekene hem oon) by oon),   ¶ *id est* pericula.
A man) wer bet in sooth to goon),
Who al the peɾeils kan) espye,
In-to the dredful host[e]rye,   4720

is worse than
the house of
Lycaon,

A-forne consydred euery thing,
Wher Lychaon) was, lord and kyng'   ¶ Ille lychaon interficie-
Of Archadie, the myghty londe,   bat hospites suos.

who murderd
all his guests.

Which slough and mordred witħ his honde   4724
Hys gestys soothly euerychon);
Whan) they kam), he spared non).
But thys erber, as I ha tolde,
Is wel wors a thousande folde,   4728
For whicħ consydre in thy thought'
To be war, thou entre nought'."

The Author.

¶ How thauctour ansuerede Diane.

I tell Diana

"Madame," quod I, "witħ your leve,
Wher yt offend[e] yow or greve,   4732
I may nat knowe the meschefe,
Ther-of tyl I ha made a prefe ;
But happe what euer happe may,
I thynk for to make assay,   4736
For the conceyt of my reson)
Contrarieth your oppinion) ;

that she and
I differ in
opinion.

Ye and I ful gretely varye :
Our Iugement[es]² be contrary,   ² Iugementes] Iugement F.,
And stonde also at discordaunce   Iugemente A.
Touching the gardyn) of plesaunce.   4741

[leaf 267, bk.]
She says the
Garden of
Pleasure is
harmful :
I say it's
agreeable.

Ye seyn), yt ys contagious,
And I, how yt ys gracious,   4744
Agreable, and debonayre,
And ye holde the contraire,
This your fantasye at al.
And thogħ yt wer[e] as mortal,   4748
As horryble³ and foule also,   [This line added in the margin.]
As ys the paleys of **Pluto**,   ³ As horryble] [ho]rrible F.
                              ¶ Pluto est deus infernalis.

" And as ful of blak derkenesse,

Of sorwe, and of wrechchidnesse,   7452

Yet fynaly, how euer yt bee,

I shal assayen and go see,

Afforce me and do my myght

Therof in hast to haue a syght¹ ;   7456

For thyng that may nat be eschiwed

But of force mot be sywed.

Yt semeth a maner destane,

The which, in sooth, no man) may fle,   7460

For which ye lese your langage."

The Author.

However bad the Garden of Pleasure is,

I mean to see it.

That's my fate.

¶ Diane.

Diana.

" Thow seyst sooth, I am nat sage

To make so a long sermon)

Ageyn[e]s thyn oppinion) ;   4764

For what so ever I devyse,

Thow wilt folwe thyn) ovne guyse.

Thou gest of me no more langage,

I put al the surplusage   4768

In thyn) ovne eleccion)

After thy discrecion),

To chese or leve, sith thow art free,

At thyn ovne liberte."   4772

And with that worde **Diane** anoon)

Tooke hir leve and ys a-goon)

As fast as she hir tale brake,

And I neuer after with hir spake,   4776

For she without[e] more arest

Took the thykke of the forest.

As I'm determind to go my own way,

¶ Auctour.

Diana leaves me.

¶ How the Auctour took hys wey towarde the herber of Deduit.

Withouten any lenger space

I gan on) my waye trace   4780

And Diane anoon) forsooke,

And forth the ryghte wey I tooke,

Bothe throgh felde and throgh forest,

Forth ryght¹, as me sempte best,   4784

Gan) to crosse dovne and dale²

[leaf 268]

The Author.

I follow the right-hand road.

² dale] talle A.

K

The Author. And ouer-twerteŋ hille and vale,

I press on,   The next[e] wey as was myŋ happe,

Spared nouther busʒ̄ nor gappe,   4788

Felte nowher[1] no greuaunce   [1] nowher] nowgher F., nouther A.

feeling happy,   For [my] ioy and my plesaunce,

Boʒ̄ in countenaunce and chere ;

As I neghed the herbere,   4792

Me thought', I gaŋ encresse more

And to helthe me restore,

Evene lyke as was my fate,

till I reach the gate of   Til I kam vn-to the gate.   4796

¶ Here the auctour maketh a descripcioŋ of þe place.

the garden where Pleasure and Cupid dwell,   This lusty herber delytable,

Above al other most notable,

Wher **Deduit**—the story tolleʒ̄—

With **Cupide**, hys brothir, duelleʒ̄,   4800

The whicʒ̄ entende never a day

But vn-to myrthe and vn-to play ;

as well as Cupid's followers.   And al[le] tho that there abyde

In the seruise of **Cupide**   4804

Ha nooŋ occasioŋ

But lyke to her affeccioŋ

In that fressʒ̄e, lusty place

Hem to disporte and solace.   4808

For this the gardyn and the cloos,

The whiche haʒ̄ so grete a loos,

[leaf 208, bk.]   And, for the excellent fayrenesse,

Is remembred, in soothnesse,   4812

Of many clerkes as be writyng'

For the faire, fresʒ̄ beldyng'.

Among them was Guillaume de Lorris, who wrote the *Romance of the Rose.*   Among[e] whiche ther was oŋ

Most specialy of euerychoŋ,   4816

I mene hym, witʒ̄-out[e] glose,   ¶ Nota quomodo auctor allegat historium de Rosa.

That gaŋ thᵉ romaunce of the rose ;

The whiche drempte in his slepyng',

How erly oŋ A morwnyng'   4820

He was vn-to this gardyŋ broght'

And so longe aboute haʒ̄ soght',

Til he fonde a smale wiket, *The Author.*

The which ageyn[e]s him was shet; 4824

And fonde as thoo noon) other weye, Guillaume de Lorris

Til that he gan[1] knokke and praye; [1] gan] kan A. knockt at the gate.

And, without[e] more delay,

Ther was no wight[t] that sayde nay 4828

Nor made thoo no straungenesse,

For the porter ydelnesse The porter Idleness let him in,

Lete hym in, and that in hast; ¶ Ociositas.

And whan) he was the entre past, 4832

He fonde a place of grete delyte to a delightful place,

Most plesant[t] to his appetyte.

The beaute was so souereyn),

For which he felte ful gret peyn), 4836

He had so gret affeccion) where he longd for a girl's Rosebud,

To han yt in possession)

Oonly for beaute of A roose,

Of which the levys wer ful cloose 4840

In maner of A rounde boton),

That herte and hool affeccion),

He gafe therto in soth[e]nesse,

For thexcellent[e] swet[e]nesse 4844

The which environ) dyde sprede, [leaf 209]

Ful desirous yt to possede.

For love of which, in substaunce, for love of which he wrote the *Romance of the Rose,* an

He compiled the romaunce 4848

Callyd the **Romavnce** of the Rose,

And gan) his processe so dispose

That neuer yet was rad noo songe

Swich a-nother in that tonge, 4852

Nor noon) that in comparysoun) incomparable poem.

Was so worthy of renoun),

To spekyn) of philosophie,

Nor of profounde poetrie; 4856

For, sothly, yet it doth excelle

Al that ever I herd of telle.

And in[2] this book most notable, [2] in] *om.* F. A.

Most lusty and [most] agreable, 4860

The Auctour pleynly doth declare,

Openly, and lyst nat spare,

The Author. How he first in that erber

G. de Lorris
did homage
to Cupid for
his girl's
rosebud, Bekam) a trew[e] homager   4864
Vnto **Cupide,** and dide homage.
He was so rent witħ lovys rage
For the feyre, fressħ boton),
Swettest in comparison),   4868
Most goodly and delycious,
For whicħ he was so amerous
Felt in his hert[e] ful gret peyn)
To forn or he myght atteyn)   4872
At hys lust yt to possede.

and at last
gaind it : But at the last[e] for his mede
Of Aventure thus yt fil :
He had hit at his ovne wil,   4876

and the
*Romance of
the Rose* And al the maner and the guyse
The romaunce dotħ deuyse,
Ful of mystery and secres

[leaf 269, bk.] And many vnkoutħ prevites,   4880

tells you all
the process. As the processe kan yow lere.
So ful of pitħ is the matere
That swicħ a book in Romaunce
Was neuer yet [y-]made in Fraunce   4884
Nor compiled in sentence,
It is so ful of sapience.

¶ Here tourneth the auctour ageyn) to
hys matere.

I'll now try
to describe
this Garden
of Pleasure
to you. And of thys lusty, fresħ herbere,
Most agreable and most entere,   4888
To declare yt and expresse,
A-noon) I wil my style dresse
And ther-of make mension)
To kome to myn) entencion) ;   4892
For ellis myght I in no wyse
Al the maner here deuyse
Touching hooly myn) estate,
To tel, how that I was chek mate,   4896
By and by myn) aventure
Touching my discoṃ-fyture
And hooly the occasion),

As I haue maked mencioṇ,   4900   *The Author.*
For whicħ Venus, the goddesse,
My lady eke and my maystresse,
Sent[e] me vn-to that place,
Callyd the herber of solace.   4904
Now shal ye here, and ye take hede,   I'll tell you how I sped.
Al the processe of my spede,
Botħ the gyṇnyng and the fyṇ,
And how I kaṇ to that gardyṇ,   4908
And the maner of myṇ entre,
Wonder desirous for to se ;
And first gaṇ in my self recorde,   I was anxious to see,
Wher the beaute dyde acorde   4912 whether this Garden of Pleasure was like my
By any maner Resemblaunce,   [leaf 270]
Touching¹ my dreṇ¹ in substaunce,   ¹ dreṇ] dreen F. dream-garden.
Wher yt be lyke in any thing,
I mene as thus, wher my dremyng,   4916
Whicħ in this book I shal disclose,
Be lyke tke Romaunce of the Rose
Oonly, in conclusyoṇ,
Touching our bothe avysioṇ.   4920

¶ **Here declaretħ² the auctou*r* the thing*es***
that he saugħ witħout the herber.

First I wol touchen and declare   ² declaretħ] dyscryvyth A.
Al the maner and nat spare
Of the Ryver environ,   Its River flowd thru
Whicħ that ys descendyd dou*n*,   4924 the green mead,
Euer flowede, as I took hede,
The lusty, freshe, grene mede.
The water was so cristal clene   ¶ Ita aqu*a* no*n* e*st* sine
And as gold the gravel shene,   misterio fluu*ius* d*icitur* qu*ia* fluit / v*nde* Ouid*ius* de ar*te :*
And this Ryuer, in certeyṇ,   ludite eu*nt*³ anni more fluen*tis* aque // Nec que p*ra*teriit &c.
Lasse was somdel than sayne,   ³ eu*nt*] e*ss*ent F. A.
And the cours of thys Ryuer
Raṇ throgħ-out the grene herber   4932
Witħ his stremys fresħ and colde,
That yt was Ioy for to beholde,   and was a joy to behold.
Whicħ refressħed al my chere :
The watir was so pure and clere.   4936

The Author.	And witħ myn) hool[e] ful entent
	By ryght' good avysement
	I saugħ by clere[1] in-speccion) [1] clere] good A.
Outside the Garden-walls I saw Pictures of	Vpon) the wallys environ) 4940
	Many wonderful ymages,
	Ful ougly of ther vysages,
	Purtreyd higħ vpon) the wal, 4943
	And what they wern I tel[le] shal : ¶ Iste decem imagines ex*tra*
	viridarium[2] depicte con-trariantu*r* amori.
1. Hate, 2. Felony, [leaf 270, bk.] 3. Villainy,	I saugħ first hate and[3] Felonye, [2] viridariu*m*] veridariu*m* A.
	And next besyde vylenye, [3] and] *om.* A.
4. Covetousness,	And in ordre **Covetyse**
5. Avarice,	And[4] hir suster **Auarice;** [4] F. and A. insert *in* after *And* 4948
6. Envy,	And after next I sawgħ envye,
	Fulfilled of malencolye,
7. Sadness,	Tristesse [eke], pale of visage,
8. Age,	And next besyde croked age, 4952
	Tremblyng as she wolde dye,
9. Hypocrisy,	And bysyde ypocrisie,
	Dedly of chere lyke a rynde ;
10. Poverty,	And pouerte stood al behynde, 4956
	Foul of face and nothing faire ;
	And al they wer[e]n) ful[5] contrayre [5] ful] *om.* A.
	Vnto love, yt is no dout ;
painted high up.	Ther-fore they wer set witħout 4960
	Higħ vpon) the wal[le] peynted,
	Deduit witħ hem was nat aqueynted
	Nor witħ hem lyst nat abyde,
	And also eke the god **Cupide** 4964
	Hatħ no lust witħ hem to be,
	They wer so frowarde for to se.
Looking at them did me good.	And al the whiles I ther stood,
	Me thought', yt dyde me gret good 4968
	To be-holde the purtreytures
	And the wonderful figures
	Witħ ther ougly countenaunces,
	By al maner accordaunces 4972
	Euerycħ lyke to hys degre
	Arrayed, as they shold[e] be,
	Bothe in shap*pe* and (in) portrayture,
	And eche of hem, y yow ensure, 4976

Pretendede in signifiaunce   *The Author.*
By there chere[1] grete displesaunce   [1] chere] clere A.
Froward of in-speccionᛁ.
And yet as of proporsionᛁ   4980
They[2] wer by craft made ful sotyle,   [2] They] There A.   [leaf 271]
As I behelde aryght grete while ;
Til that I kamᛁ to the wiket,   The wicket of
Whicħ was closed and y-shet,   4984   the Garden of
And first fonde ther ydelnesse,   Pleasure was shut.
Whiche bere the key as porteresse,
The whiche was vn-to me Warde
Nouther straunge nor[3] frowarde,   [3] nor] nother A.   4988
But let[4] me ynᛁ and that in hast ;   [4] let] lat A.   Idleness let
And whanᛁ I was the gate past   me thru it,
With al mynᛁ hool[e] hert entere,
I thanked hir onᛁ my manere   4992
That she wolde nat debate
To suffre me entre at the gate.

¶ Here reherseth the auctour, how he was res-
     seyved and accepted of a lady callyd Curtesy,
     whiche graunted him lyberte to goo wher
     him lyst.

And ryght anoonᛁ, whanᛁ ydelnesse[5]   [5] ydelnesse] I ydelnesse F. A.
Oonly of hir gentilesse   4996
Hatħ me receyved witħ glad chere   and receivd
In-to this lusty, fresħ herber,   me gladly.
As she that was my first[e] gyde,
I saugħ after stond asyde   5000
Vnwarly, as I koude espye,   Then I saw
A lady, called **Curtesye,**   a lady, Courtesy,
The which of hir benignite
Took hir way towardys me,   5004
And seyde thus witħ ryght glade face :
" Ye be welkome to this place,   who welcomd
Ordeyned oonly for comfort,   me, and said the Garden
For solace, and for disport ;   was meant
In the whicħ, shortly to telle,   5008   only for amusement.
Nonᛁ[6] other manere folkes duelle   [6] Nonᛁ] Neon F.
But swycħ as lyketħ to obey,   [leaf 271, bk.]

Courtesy. " To disporte hem and to pley,   5012
And ha noon) other attendaunce
But in Ioy and in plesaunce,
For they nat ellys have ado ;
And for your self ben) oon) of tho,   5016

I may walk
about as I
like.
Ye shal ha fully lyberte
To walke a-bout[e], and to se
Euery thing that may yow plese,
Or tourne yow to hertys ese   5020
With swiche folkys as ye sen),
Yif yt lyke yow to ben)
As oon) of hem, her tabyde.

Courtesy will
make me
joyous.
I shal my self for yow provyde   5024
That ye shal han al suffisaunce
Of¹ Ioye without displesaunce.
For nature and love also
Han so ordeyned bothe two.   5028

Mirth and
play always
go on.
For in thys place eve and morwe
Is merthe and play with-out[e] sorwe,
Devoyde of heuynesse and thoght',

Every one
does as he
likes,
For here no man) doth ryght' noght'   5032
But what so euere him best lyketh.
Here no wight¹ sorweth nor siketh   ¹ wight] wyte A.
But to be besy and espye,
Euerych lyke hys fantasye   5036
To fynden out somme pleyes newe
Ther corages to renewe,
Ther obseruances² to observe,   ² obseruances] obseruantes F. A.

and serves
Pleasure.
Of oon) entent[e] for to serve,   5040
As for her chefe and best refuit,
To ther lorde, callyd Deduit,

[leaf 272]
That shortly, as I tolde rathe,
The folkys here hem selwen) bathe   5044
In Ioy and play and in noght' ellys,
Al[e] tho that here in duellys,

Nowhere else
are such nice
folk.
That no man), I dar wel seye,³   ³ seye] seyn F. sayne A.
Such a-nother peple seye⁴   ⁴ seye] seyn F. seyne A. 5048
Met to gedre in oo place.
And to conclude in lytill space,
Of entent they euerychon),

"Withouteɳ variaunce of onɖ,   5052   *Courtesy.*
The lawes folwe nygĥ and fer
Which that whilom **Iubiter**   Jupiter made
Establysshede of entencioɳ   laws to
In hys myghty regioɳ,   5056
To enclyne folke in dede   lead folk to
To lust oonly and flessĥlyhede   fleshly
                                       pleasures.
And to woluptuous delyte ;
And this[1] hooly[2] the appetyte   [1] this] thus F. A.   5060
                            [2] hooly] the holy A.
Of al the folke that duelletĥ here,
By processe as thou shalt lere,
Yif thou lyst thy wyt applye."
  And in thys wyse **Curtesye**,   5064
Lusty, fresĥ, benignie and fre,
Ful goodly hatĥ receyved me
And made me ful noble chere,
And al about[e] the herbere   5068   I was free,of
                                        the Garden of
Witĥ-outen any straungenesse   Pleasure.
Oonly of hir gentillesse
She graunted me, and that anooɳ,
Wher that me lyst[e] [for] to gooɳ,   5072
Oonly witĥ this condicioɳ :   The only con-
                                       dition was,
That by no collusyoɳ
She myghte fynde nor espye   that I
That I dide vilenye,   5076   shouldn't do
                                       damage to
Throgĥ my defaute nor trespace,   any growing
                                       thing.
To no thing growyng in the place,   [leaf 272, bk.]
Sitĥ al the gardyɳ environ
Was frely put in my bandoɳ   5080
And al hooly in my garde,
For which, as I koude awarde
And deme in myɳ oppynioɳ,
Here requeste kaɳ of resoɳ.   5084

¶ How the auctour commendetĥ the Herberɔ.

Whaɳ I behelde this lusty place,
So ful of beaute and of grace,
And had ecĥ thinge apparceyved,
Me sempte, I was nat[3] deceyved   [3] nat] *om.* A.   5088   I thought I
                                         should like to
In sucĥ a place to abyde,   stay there.

For, truly, vpon eue*r*y syde,

As I behelde to my plesaunce,

I think the
Garden of
Pleasure   Me thogħ[t], I fonde al suffisaunce,   5092

As of delyte ther lakkyd nogħt'

That was ravisshed in my thogħt',

And held my self verrayly

Passyng ewrous and happy   5096

That ever I had[de] swicħ a grace

For to entre*n* in that place.

Yt was so glad, and so Iocunde,

joyful   And of al Ioye most habounde,   5100

So excellent and so notable,

Surmou*n*tyng and delytable,

That shortly, as I kan dyffyne,

and divine,   It sempte werrayly dyvyne,   5104

As me thogħt' in my demyng'

Pleynly, And noo*n* ertħly thing';

For of beaute and of renou*n*,

To make iust comparison),   5108

Yif I shal the trouthe telle,

excelling all
places,   Placys al yt dyde excelle,

To whos beaute was noo*n* lyche :

[leaf 273]   Soothly nat the paleys ryche,   5112

even that in
which the
Gods live,   I mene the house celestial

Wher the goddys immortal

Witħ Iubiter, gretest of mygħt',—

The sterry place ful of lygħt'—   5116

Abydetħ in the higħe hevene,

Brighter than) the firy leuene ;

and the
palace of
Apollo.   Nor the paleys of Phebus,

Whicħ is so ryche and curious,   ¶ *Regia solis erat.*   5120

To rekne al, yt wil not be

To be resembled of beaute

To this place, higħ nor low.

For as fer as I coude know,   5124

Eue*r*y where in my walkyng'

No glad or
sweet thing
is lacking.   Ther lakked[e] no maner thing'

Of Ioye, merthe, nor gladnesse,

Of holsom) ayr, nor of swetnesse ;   5128

And ay the more I ga*n*) to presse

The more my Ioy[e] gaɳ tencresse ;[1] [1] tencresse] toencrese A.
And yif I sholde aryght' descryve
The beaute during al my lyve,   5132   The beauty of
The tyme wold[e] not suffise   the Garden of
                                              Pleasure
To tel the maner and the guyse
Of the excellent fairenesse.
And eke also the noblesse   5136
Of this herber most renomed,
Who so lyst aryght' take hede,
Ful many day or I was borɳ
Hath be descryved her to forɳ,   5140   was described
Both in metre and in prose.   of old by G.
                                               de Lorris
I take recorde of the rose   and other
And of many mo Auctours.   authors.
The which of blosmys and of flours   5144
And of herbys vertuous
Is euery wher so plentevous
That to euery maladye   [leaf 273, bk.]
A maɳ may fynde remedye   5148   Its herbs will
                                               cure every
To preserve a mannys[2] lyf.   [2] mannys] mans A.   disease.
Ther nature is so sanatyf
That the leche most famous,
Callyd Esculapius,   5152   Æsculapius
                                               could find
Yif' he wold[e] ther be kynde   there all
Àny maner herbe fynde :   grains and
                                               gums for sick
Outher bitter outher soote,   folk,
Greyɳ or gomme, rynde and roote,   5156
Pertinent vnto physike
To helpe folkys that be syke,
Of frutys holsomme vpoɳ tres,[3]   [3] tres] tre F.
Of many sondry [divers] gres,   5160
Yt nedede[4] him no more enquere,   [4] nedede] nede A.
For he sholde fynde hem there
As fresh in wynter and as grene   as fresh in
                                              winter as in
As in the lusty somer shene ;   5164 summer.
For ther may no corrupcioɳ
Haue there domynacioɳ.
And of the herbys thise the chefe,
Who so lyst to make a prefe,   5168
Ther ys no venym, nor poysoɳ,

The Author. Nor noon) intoxigacion)

Of adder, serpent, nor dragon),

Made nor contreved by treson)   5172

But that the herbes of Nature

Vertu han yt to recure,

The Garden of Pleasure And with al this yit ouer more

A man) to helthe to restore   5176

Of kyndly sekenessys and foreyn).

And here and ther vpon) the pleyñ

Amongys al thise glade thingis

containd fresh Springs to water Ther be ful freshe wel[le] springis,   5180

That with her holsom lycour clere

Ouerspredden the herbere,

[leaf 274] The Rotys, greyn[e]s, and the sedes,

the meads, And the smothe softe medes,   5184

Fletyng with bawme sanatyf[1]

Of kynde most restoratyf[1],

That yf ther wer in any[1] londe   [1 any] ony A.

where a love-struck man A man) ybrent with lovys bronde,   5188

Or with his dredful arwe woundyd,

Yif he wer ewrous to be soundyd,

could get heald. This place wer most convenient

Vn-to his amendement :   5192

To duel among the freshe flours

As folk that love paramours.

For ther they myghte fynde and se

Wher-with they shal recuryd be.   5196

And myddys of the soote herbage

Wild beasts were there, Ther be bestys eke savage,

Grey and falwe, white and blake,

Euerych pleyng with hys make,   5200

Bothe on) hillys and on) vales

and Night-ingales on cedars. Ther herde I also nyghtyngales

Syngyng on) the Cedres trene,

Tavoyde away al sorwe and tene   5204

With her hevenly nootys clere,

Euerych of hem with his fere,

With so melodious acorde

That ther was founde no discorde ;   5208

For y suppose, ther[2] is no man)   [2 ther] the A.

That aryght[?] reporte kan)

The wherbles, nor the vnkouth touns,

Nor the ravysshinge sowns,   5212

Nor the sugryd melodye

Of ther soot[e] armonye,

So aungelyke vn-to the Ere

Throgh the gardyn) her and there   5216

That ther is no man) in hys wyt

The whiche koude ha[1] levyd yt   [1] ha] he A.

Nor demyd yt in his entent,

But yif he had[de] be present.   5220

The Author.

No one can describe the angelic harmony of the Nightingale's song.

[leaf 274, bk.]

¶ How the auctour espied first the god of love.

And among al thys plesaunce

Yt fil in-to my remembraunce

And gan) to wonder ful gretely

That **Diane** was hardy   5224

Touching this gardyn) of delyt,

How she durst haue yt in despyt,

Which to me she hath so blamyd ;

She oughte for to be ashamyd   5228

Yt to lake in any wyse.

And while that I gan me avyse

And my looke[2] to[3] cast a-syde,   [2] looke] book F. [3] to] om. A.

Y saugh **Deduit** and Cupide   5232

With her folkys a gret Route,

Al the herber rounde aboute,[4]   [4] aboute] a bounte F.

By hem self[e] tweyn) and tweyn),

Ful besely to don) her peyn)   5236

Hem to play and to solace

In that lusty, mery place,

Euerych glad and fresh of chere.

And tho I gan) aproche nere   5240

To seen the vnkouth countenaunces[5]   [5] countenaunces] countenaunce A.

And ther gracious ordinaunces,[6]   [6] ordinaunces] ordynaunce A.

Goodly fresh and debonayre,

As an Angel fethred faire.   5244

In karol wise I saugh hem goon),

And formhest of hem euerychoon)

Diana ought to be ashamed of herself for abusing the Garden of Pleasure.

In it I see Pleasure and Cupid, and their folk

as glad as

Angels, dancing.

I saugħ **Deduit**, and oɲ his honde,

Confedred by a maner bonde,   5248
Ther went a lady in sothnesse,
And hir name was gladnesse,
Lotħ a-sonder to dissever',
For they wer to gedyr ever'   5252
Fresħ of hewe and no thing pale ;

And as any nyghtyngale

She sange that Ioye was to here,
That the lusty nootys clere   5256
Of **Sirenes** in the see
Ne wer nat lyke, in no degre,
To the soot[e], sugryd song'
Whiche they songeɲ euer a mong'   5260
Of Ioye, myrthe, and lustyhede.
      And in my walke, as I took hede,
I saugħ **Deduit** amongys other

Witħ Cupide, his ovne brother,   5264
By kyndly generacioɲ
Bothe of oo condicioɲ,
Moder to whoɲ was **Venus**.
But of name most famous   5268
Was **Cupide**, for oonly he
Had allone the dignite,
The honour, and the chefe renouɲ,

And the domynacioɲ,   5272
And hooly al the gouernaunce
Of this herber of plesaunce.
And for his higħe worthynesse,
For his power and noblesse   5276
Al to him they dide enclyne ;
For ther [is] nooɲ that may declyne,
For to rekene al the **Route**,
But that he kaɲ make hem to lowte   5280
Vn-to his subieccioɲ,
For his Iurysdiccioɲ

May constrey[e]ɲ higħ and lowe ;
And who that lyst his power knowe, 5284
The proudest he kaɲ make tame ;
For ther is nouther halt nor lame,

So hawteyꝛ) nor so surquedous,　　　　　　*The Author.*
So lusty nor so coraious,　　　　　　5288
Nor the goddys eternal,　　　　　　　　[leaf 275, bk.]
Ertħly nor celestial,　　　　　　　　　Even the
　　　　　　　　　　　　　　　　　　　Gods obey
But they must of diwe rygħt,　　　　　Cupid.
Maugre al her grete myght,　　　　　5292
Stonde vnder his obeyssaunce
To a-byde his gouernaunce.

¶ **Here**[1] **declareth the auctour the maner**
　　　　of hys corowne.　　1 Here] He F.

The same tyme stille y stood
　　And consydred and a-bood　　　　5296
With a sobre countenaunce,
Seyng the gret[e] suffisaunce
Of this god most dredeful,
Most myghty, and most wonderful.　　5300
And sodeynly, as I took hede,　　　　On his head.
I sauġh a corowne vpoꝛ) his hede,　　is a crown set
　　　　　　　　　　　　　　　　　　with stones,
Passing riche and curiouse
And ful of stonys preciouse,　　　　5304
Fet out of the ferther ynde,
Which by vertu of ther kynde
Made euery maꝛ) in his estat　　　　which make
Ryght ewrous and ryght fortunat.　5308 folk fortun-
　　　　　　　　　　　　　　　　　　ate,
For somme were so graciouse,
So myghty, and so vertuouse
To make folkes amyable,　　　　　　amiable,
And other to be honourable,　　　　5312
And other, as I caꝛ) reporte,
With good hoope to confort,　　¶ Spes.
To kepe a maꝛ) in al gladnesse　　　merry,
And avoyde of hevynesse;　　　　　5316
Somme had vertu and renoun
To kepe a maꝛ) from) al poysoꝛ),
And somme hadde suffisaunce
To kepe a maꝛ) from) al grevaunce,　5320 and free from
　　　　　　　　　　　　　　　　　　harm.
And somme in Ioye to conserue
And fro sorwe to preserue
And with myrthe to releve　　　　　[leaf 276]

The Author.
That noon) hevynesse greve;   5324

Some stones
in Cupid's
Crown keep
folk free from
disease.

And somme gaf perseueraunce

Ageyn) al maner perturbaunce,   ¶ perseuerancia.

Manly of force to sustene

Al disese, peyne, and tene,   5328

And euery maner aventure

Good and evel for tendure,

That, to rekne oon) by oon),

Ther ne was no maner stoon)   5332

Set in his corovne but of value

And but yt were of gret vertue,

Euerych of hem in his degre

Of grete power and dignite.   5336

¶ Here declareth the auctour the maner of clothyng⟩ of Cupido.

Cupid's
clothing

Hys clothyng eke, yif ye lyst here,

Was wonder dyvers of Manere,

The vnkouth werke y-made of ohle

Nouther of silke nouther of golde   5340

was of ever
changing
colour

But of a mater wonder straunge,

Ever redy for a[1] chaunge   [1] a] to A.

In-to as many folde colours

As in erthe growe flours,   5344

Outher on) hilles, vale, or playn);

And euer yt was in non) certayn),

Of what colour yt myghte be,

For ther was of noo degre   5348

not to be
described.

Nor in this worlde no man) a-lyve

That konnyng hadde to descryve,

Of what colour was his clothing,

It was so dyuers of chaungyng.   5352

He had two
wings on
his shoulders,

And this god hadde eke also

On his shuldres wynges two,

[leaf 276, bk.]

Al vnwarly and vnwist

For to fle wher euer hym lyst   5356

As any swalwe swifte of flyght⟩;

of feathers
like Angels'.

And of fethres he was as bryght⟩

As an Aungel of paradys,

That I hadde in my devys   5360

And in myn̄ hert[e] grete plesaunce   *The Author.*
To beholde his gouernaunce ;
And eke this god, in special,
As he that ouercometh̄ al   5364
And daunte kan̄ [bothe] yong and olde,
Was wonder fair for to beholde :   *Cupid was fair, fresh,*
Yong, lusty, fresh̄, and also eke
Symple and as dovwe meke,   5368   *meek,*
Debonaire and amyable,
Curteys, large, and honourable,   *and courteous,*
And fulfilled of gladnesse,
Of myrthe, play, and lustynesse,   5372   *full of mirth,*
And¹ wel y-cheryd of lokyng,   ¹ And] a A.
And his eyen̄ ay laughyng,   *with laughing eyes,*
Clere, and gray, and eke drawyng,
And plesaunt eke of beholdyng   5376
To lure folkys and to drawe
And to constreyn̄ hem to his lawe ;
Thogh̄ somme seyn̄, in special,   *not blind, as some folk*
That he seeth̄ ryght' nogh̄t' at al,   5380   *say,*
But is² as blynde as stok or ston̄,   ² is] it is A.
But what they Ianglen̄ euerychon̄,
I espyed by hys chere
That his sight' was ryghte clere.   5384
And his eyen in lokyng'
Weren, me thoughte,³ ryght' persyng'   ³ thoughte] though A.   *but piercing.*
And ryght' faire in apparence,
And, short[e]ly, thus, in sentence,   5388
I sawgh̄ this myghty god certeyn̄
In his estate ful wel be-seyn̄.

  ¶ **Here telleth the auctour, how the god of love**   [leaf 277]
    lad on hys one⁴ hand gladnesse and Doultz
    regarde.   ⁴ one] om. F.

And this dredeful god Cupide,   *Cupid can give his servants weal or woe.*
That kan̄ departen̄ and devyde   5392
To hys servauntes wele or wo,
Ryght' as him lyst, for bothe two
Ben̄ in his honde fully committed,
Tabyde sure or to be flytted,   5396

The Author. Al stant in his gouernaunce :

Ioye, myrthe, or displesaunce,

Al ys knet vnder hys bonde ;

Cupid leads with him Beauty, And he lad vpoɯ his honde   5400

A lady, passing fair¹ to se,   ¹ fair] for A.

And hir name was **Beaute**,

A lady of ful gret plesaunce,

For, fynally, hir aqueyntaunce²   5404

Was to him most acceptable ;   ² aqueyntaunce] aqueytaunce F.

Of port she was so agreable,

So debonayre in eu*er*y part.

Sweet-Looks, and Gladness. And witħ him eke was doulz reguart   5408

And a lady, in sothnesse,

Of whom the name was gladnesse.

And this god most³ debonayre   ³ most] *om.* A.

He has two bows, Bare twoo bowes ful contrayre   5412

And arwes eke of sondry guyse,

Mervelouse for to devyse,

Witħ whicħ, wher they be square or rou*n*de,

He kaɯ hurte, Mayme, or wounde,   5416

And what tyme kaɯ no maɯ knowe.

And touching hys first[e] bowe,

one smooth, Whiche that is so pleyɯ and smothe,

Is wroghtᵗ and made, this verray sothe,   5420

of ivory, and white ; Al to gedre of yvory,

Y-piked out ful craftyly,

As any snowe passing white,

And to be-hold of grete delyte.   5424

[leaf 277, bk.] The tother, hydouse and ryghtᵗ blak,

the other black, and full of knots, Wroughtᵗ al oonly for the wrak,

Ful of knottys and of skarrys,

The tymber is so ful of warrys.   5428

to shoot his arrows as he likes. And of his arwes to devyse,

This is of hem pleynly themprise :

To shete hem, whaɯ he is purposyd,

Lycħ as hertys be dysposyd   5432

And enclyned of nature,

Ryghtᵗ so love dootħ his cure

To markeɯ hem, in conclusioɯ,

Most covenally in ther sesoɯ   5436

After dyuersyte of men̅); *The Author.*
And they wer in novmbre ten ; Cupid has
ten Arrows,
Thise arwes whicħ that I reherse
Sharpe fyled for to perse, 5440
And there namys[1] by and by [1] namys] nannys F. A. whose names
are given in
Be rehersed ceriously the *Romance*
of the Rose.
In the Rose, who taketħ hede,
In ordre ther ye may hem rede, 5444
Her names and condicion),
Her force, her power, and renoun ;
Ther he may her kyndes knowe.
And fyve vnto the first[e] bowe 5448 Five belong
to his first
Ben) of nature pertynent, bow ;
Rygħt' faire and rygħt' convenient ;
And to reherse hem oon) by oon),
The first and hiest of echon), 5452
Most to be drad, as thought[e] me,
Of ryghte callyd was beaute, and are
1. Beauty,
The lady whicħ that **Cupide**
Lad in the erber by his syde. 5456
The secounde callyd was symplesse, 2. Simplicity,
And the thrid, in sothfastnesse, 3. Truth (cald
Freedom in
As the Rose lyst to devyse, the *Rose*),
Was ynamed ek fraunchise, 5460
Of whicħ the fethres and the hede
Wer verrayly, who kan take hede, [leaf 278]
Fulfilled with al curtesye.
The fourthe was callyd companye, 5464 4. Company,
The whiche by fervence and desire
Kyndletħ ever lovys fire,
Comfortable and rygħt plesaunt.
The fythe was callyd beausemblaunt, 5468 5. Good-
Looks.
The whiche at the sharpe poynt
Witħ soot[e] bawme was enoynt, [2] sharpnesse] shapnesse F.
The sharpnesse[2] to asswage ¶ Iste *predicte* sagitte mouent
pruritus[3] et alliciunt amatores.[4]
And to allayen) the Damage [3] *pruritus*] priuitus F. A.
In hertys, bothe yong and olde. [4] amatores] amarores A.
And al the hedes wern of golde, All have
heads of gold.
Passyng sharp and rygħt' kervyng
And to hurte eke percynge, 5476

The Author.	Of temper̃rure they wer so fyne
	Thorg̃ an hert[e] for to Myne,
	That where so as they dyde assaylle
	Diffence noon myght̃e avaylle. 5480
The Five Arrows of Cupid's 2nd bow are black and foul :	The tother fyve wer nat faire,
	Ful hydous foule and ryg̃ht̃ contrayre,
	Mortal of condicioꝰ ¶ *quia ille affligunt amatores.*
	And of colour blak and brouꞥ, 5484
	And so foule that yt was wonder,
	More dredful than stroke of thonder,
	And hateful vpoꝰ euery syde.
1. Pride,	The first of hem was callyd pride, 5488
2. Felony,	And the seconde Felonye,
	The fetheres fret with̃ villenye,
3. Shame,	And the thryd[e] callyd shame,
	Al envenymyd with̃ dyffame, 5492
4. Despair,	And the fourth̃e disesperaunce,
	Which̃ with̃ vnhap and meschaunce
	Wondeth̃ hertys to the dethe
	And many hundred folkys slethe, 5496
5. Change of mind;	The fyfte chaunge of thoughtys newe :
	Echooñ ful hidouse of her hewe,
[leaf 278, bk.] all pointed with lead,	And the poyntes of eche hede
	Nat of Ireꝰ but of lede, 5500
	Whiche tokne was of sorwe and woo ;
	Cupide had hem forgyd soo
	Perilouse and hevy at the poynt,
and tipt with poison,	For with̃ venym they wer enoynt, 5504
	To make menꝰ, who vnderstood,
	To wexe furiouse and wood.
	And thise arwes most hateful
	With̃ sorwe make menꝰ so dul 5508
	Throg̃h̃ her mortel Auenture
so that their wounds are almost deadly.	That yt ys harde a maꝰ recure
	With-out[e] deth̃, this douteles,
	That the arwe of hercules 5512
	Was nat of pereyl lych̃ therto,
	Ther venym was ytempred so.
	And al thise arwes euerychoꝰ
	That I ha tolde of ooꝰ by ooꝰ, 5516

Bothe of Ioy and eke of peyne,   *The Author.*
And also eke the bowes tweyne
Doulz regarde bare by hir syde,   Sweet-Looks
As hir lyst hem to devyde,   5520   bare Cupid's 2 bows and
And many other arwes kene,   his arrows.
Wonder dredful to sustene.

   And thus **Cupide** and **Dame beaute**   In his train
And **doulz** regarde, thise ylke thre   5524   were
Wente y-fere, this no doute,
And folwyng hem a ful grete route.
And first of al[le] kam rychesse,   1. Riches,
And next fraunchise and largesse,   5528   2. Freedom, 3. Largess,
And also, as I koude espye,
After hem kam **Curtesye**,   4. Courtesy,
Than ydelnesse and with hir youthe,   5. Idleness,
And thise six, as yt ys kouthe,   5532   6. Youth,
Confedred by a maner bonde,
Euerych vpon others honde,   hand in hand,
Looth a-sonder to devyde,
Suede ay the god **Cupide**,   5536
Ay to gedre tweyn and tweyn,   [leaf 279]
And dyd also her[1] besy peyn   [1] her] hys A.
To serve love and nat repent
With al her hool[e] trewe entent.   5540
And euerych for the more socour   each with his
With him had his paramour ;   paramour.
And al this folke most lusty
Deduit hadde in his company,   5544
[2]Comytted hooly to hys garde :
Ten wythout[e] dowse regarde,[2]   [2] [These two lines added in the margin.]
Yonge, fresh, and lusty of visag[es[3]],   [3] es *cut off.*
As with-out wer ten ymages   5548
Portreyde in a nother guyse,
As ye to forn han herd devyse.

    ¶ **Here reherseth the auctour the Mynstralcyes**
       that Weren in the gardyn of Deduit.

O[f] fortune yt is thus falle
     Among thise lusty folkys alle   5552
That they nentende nyght nor day

The Author. But vn-to merthe and vn-to play ;

And folke of al condicion)

In Pleasure's
Garden stayd
also Gods, Duellede in that mansion),   5556

Of eche cost that men) kan) nevene.

And goddys also of the hevene,

For merthe oonly and solace,

Soiournede in that lusty place,   5560

And hadde Ioy ther to abyde

in honour of
Cupid. In hononr of the god **Cupide**,

Havynge al thingis at ther wille.

And yt syt nat me to be stille   5564

But tel[le], how they were devyded,

They had
musical in-
struments: And also how they wer provyded

Of Instrumentys of Musyke,

For they koude the practyke   5568

Of al maner Mynstralcye

That any man) kan) specifye ;

psalteries of
Germany and
Spain, For ther wer rotys of **Almanye**

And eke of Arragon) and spayne,   5572

[leaf 279, bk.] Songes, stampes, and eke daunces,

Dyue*r*s plente of plesaunces,

And many vnkouth notys newe

Of swich*e* folkys as lovde[1] trewe,   [1] lovde] love A. 5576

And Instrumentys that dyde excelle,

Many moo than) I kan) telle :

harps, fiddles, Harpys, fythels, and eke rotys,

Wel accordyng with her notys,   5580

Lutys, Rubibis, and geterns,

More for estatys than taverns,

organs,
monachords, Orgnys, cytolys, monacordys.

And ther wer founde noo discordys,   5584

Nor variaunce in ther sovns,

Nor lak of noo proporsiou*n*s,

Ther was so noble accordaunce ;

And for folkys[2] that lyst daunce   [2] folkys] folke A. 5588

trumpets,
shalms,
and flutes. Ther wer[3] trumpes and tru*m*petes,   [3] wer] *om.* A.

Lowde shallys and doucetes,

Passyng of gret[e] melodye,

And floutys ful of armonye,   5592

Eke Instrumentys high and lowe

Wel mo than I koude knowe,

That I suppose, ther is no man)

That aryght⁴ reherse kan) 5596

The melodye that they made :

They wer so lusty and so glade.

They do no thing but pley and syng⁴

And rounde about[e] goo dauncyng, 5600

That the verray heuenly son)

Passed in comparison)

The harpis most melodious

Of Dauid and of Orpheous. 5604

Ther melodye was in all

So heuenly and celestiall

That ther nys hert, I dar expresse,

Oppressed so with hevynesse, 5608

Nor in sorwe so y-bounde,

That he sholde ther ha founde

Comfort hys sorowe to apese

To a-sette his hert at ese. 5612

The Author.

The folk in
Pleasure's
Garden sung
and danced,

making
heavenly
melody.

[leaf 280]

¶ Here declareth the auctour, how he sawgh the Rosys and the Rosier, and the place wher Ialousye set bialacoil¹ in prison, and the welle of Narcisus. ¹ bialacoil] bralacorl F.

Whan) y had beholde and seyn)

    Myd of the gardyn) in a pleyn)

Thise folkys al of oon) entent,

So bysy and so dylygent 5616

To folowe and sywe² ther delytes, ² sywe] serve A.

With al maner appetytes

That may the god of love queme,

As ferforth as I koude deme, 5620

With euery maner circumstaunce,

That was ther hool attendaunce

Al-way there to lyve in Ioye,

And I a-noon) vpon) my weye³ ³ weye] woye F. 5624

Gan passe forthe and let hem be,

And went[e] ferther for to se

Al the estrys envyron),

And as I walked vp and doun, 5628

After seeing
all these folk
enjoying
themselves,

I went on.

The Author. I saugh the flour[e]s delytable

And herbes ful medycynable

And eke ful many holsom̅ roote ;

In Pleasure's Garden I saw the famous Rosary once kept by Danger   And ther I saugh the **Rosys** soote   5632

And the famous fressh **Roser**

Whilom̅ y-kept by **Daunger**,

Whan̅ the lover was I-blamed,

Oonly for he wolde ha tamyd   5636

Tan touched yonge **Rosis** new,

Wonder soot and fressh of hew,

from the lover who would have toucht one Rosebud ;   And specialy for oon̅ boton̅

He had Indignacion̅,   5640

That he was hardy outher bolde

To touche hem in that ryche holde.

[leaf 280, bk.]   Reson̅ myght' him nat restreyne,

Al be that she dyde her peyne,   5644

What she sayde, yt stood for noght',

In oon̅ poynt to with-drawe his thoght'.

also the Dungeon in which Jealousy put Balaceuil ;   And also there I dyde espye

The place, wher that **Ialousye**   5648

In a myghty strong **Dongon**ᵎ

Pute byalacoyl in prison̅,

Whan̅ Malebouche by treison̅

Made hys accusasion̅,   5652

But yet this castell large and longe

Myght*e* neuer be made so stronge

but Cupid could break thru it.   But that **Cupide** anoone ryght'

Gat hyt by force throgh hys myght' ;   5656

.For ther was no resistence

Ageyn̅ hys myghty violence.

And as I went[e] to sen aH,

Further, I saw   I saugh a place in specyaH   5660

Which surmou*n*tede in beaute

The remenant al, as thoght*e* me,

And was most excelent of pris,

I sey as vn-to myn̅ devys,   5664

Seuered by ther self asyde,

Ful desyrous ther to abyde,

In which, shortly for to telle,

I sawgh the noble, ryche welle,   5668

Callyd the welle amerous, *The Author.*
And eke the welle dangerous the Danger-
ous Well
Whicħ **Diane** of enemyte
Had[de] lakked so to me, 5672
At the whiche **Narcisus** at which
Narcissus fell
Loved his shadwe, she tolde thus; in love with
his shadow.
But, in sootħ, for al hir speche,
And who so that she kan me teche, 5676
I wiħ aproche to haue a syght,
What ever fal anoone ryght'. [leaf 281]
Who so ever do his peyne,
Ther shal no maɲ me constreyne; 5680 This I re-
solved to
But, fynaly, I wol goo see look at.
To beholde the beaute,
Aħ the maner, and the guyse.
    And first I saugħ in what wyse— 5684 So I saw the
graven le-
By *lett*res graveɲ in the stooɲ, gend which
tells how
Whicħ declarede me anooɲ Narci*s*us
was slaiɲ,
The maner hooly and the cas—
How **Narcisus** slay[e]ɲ was 5688
And his woful Auenture,
Whicħ no wyght' koude tho recure.
And whaɲ I had the *lett*res rad,
Whicħ in the stonys hard and sad 5692
Wer profoundely and depe y-grave,
The scripture for to save
Wryte of olde antyquyte,
To conserve[1] the beaute, [1] conserve] coserve F. 5696
I wexe astonyed in partye and I was
shockt
And abasshed sodenly,
Touchyng the pereyl of the welle at the danger
of the well,
Of which ye han herd me telle; 5700
But I,[2] in sootħ, no pereil caste [2] I] *om.* A.
But gan assure me as faste,
And thoughte first in my corage
That he deyed of out-rage 5704
This Narcisus and of folye, or rather, of
Narcissus's
In sooth, this was my fantasye: folly.
The welle no maɲ blame myght',
Thogħ he deyecl' wytħ a syght' 5708

The Author. Restynge him self on the stronde.

For I do yow vnderstonde

[leaf 281, bk.] That thys welle most Ioyouse

This well lookt so fresh and fair to me Sempte vn-to me ryght' graciouse,   5712

Fressħ and faire a-bove mesure,

That me thoughte, Dame Nature

Koude in no maner wyse

A more goodly oon devyse.   5716

The watir was so clere and fyne

Of colour verray cristalyne,

Boylyng vp ay of that hewe

Witħ his quyk[e] stremys newe   5720

Vpon the preciouse gravel.

Me lykede euery thing so wel

That to departe, in verray sootħ,

I was in herte wonder lootħ.   5724

And yif that I disseuer sholde,

that I wanted to wash my hands and face, A forne I thoughte that I wolde

Wassħ myn handes and visage

For myn grete Avauntage,   5728

Yif so were that I myght',

Yt was so plesaunt' to my syght'

That, yif I hadde had lyberte,

and bathe in it, Ful fayn I wolde ha bathyd me,   5732

Yif reson wolde ha consentyd

That I sholde ha nat repentyd.

For of swetnesse and of odour',   [1] flauour] fauour F., fauoure A.

Of tast also and of flauour,[1]   ¶ *quantum* ad iudicium 5736
                                                                        sensitiuum.

for it was sweeter than rose-water, It was swetter than watir rose

A man in helthe to dyspose.

Ay[2] at a poynt, as yt was prevyd,   [2] Ay] At F.

Dyane oughte be repreved   5740

This welle for to blame so ;

and its gravel was full of rich stones. Of whiche the grauel eke therto

Was so ful of ryche stonys,

Preciouse ryghte for the nonys,   5744

So orient[e] and so shene,

Bothe perse, rede, and grene,

[leaf 282] And[3] other' colours many oon,   [3] A inserts *many* after *And*

That I trowe, ther was no stoon   5748

Throgh-out the worlde, nor in ynde,
But men) shulde ther y-fynde.

¶ Here declareth the Auctour how he loked in-to tLe welle.

As I behelde, by gret avys,   This Well of
                                                         Narcissus
Among thys stonys of gret pris,   5752
Doun by the bothme wonder lowe,
I sawgh, so I koude knowe,
That this wel[le] most royaH
Was y-pavyd with cristaH,   5756   was paved
                                                    with crystal,
Shewyng¹ by refleccion)
Al the estris environ)
By Apparence vnto the syght¹,
Who that koude looke aryght¹,   5760
With-out[e] trouble, so clere yt was,   which re-
                                                    flected all
As in A merour or A glas,   the sights
                                                    of Pleasure's
And al the syghte¹ of the herbere.   ¹ syghte] syyt F.   Garden,
The watir was so pure and clere,   5764
So fresh of syghte and so shene,
The cristal pulshede was so clene
That ageyn) the sonne bright¹
It gaf so merveylous a lyght¹   5768
That men) myghten), out of doute,
Beholden al that stood aboute.
And in this merour² merveylous
Behelde the proude Narcisus   5772
Hys ovne beaute and lyknesse,
As ye to forn) have herd expresse,
Ground and roote of al hys woo.
    And I beheld therin alsoo   5776
With many dyuers circumstaunces
Ryght¹ wonder vnkouth resemblaunces,
In the cristal stoonys clere,
And many figure eke appere: 5780
Of Cupide the lyknesse,   [leaf 282, bk.]
Of Deduit and of gladnesse,   as well as
                                                    the figures
Of youthe also and of beaute,   of Cupid,
                                                    Pleasure,
Arrayed lyche to hir degre,   5784 Youth, and
With al that other companye   Beauty.

The Author.
Whiche ye haue herde me specifye.

All the folk
in Pleasure's
Garden drew
into a corner
of it.
And I sawgħ al the maner, how

In-to Angle how they[1] drow   ¹ they] ther A.   5788

Of al the gardyn) oon) and aħ

For somme thyng' of newe faħ ;

And I gan) neghen), of entente

For to wete what they mente,   5792

And shortly, yif ye lyst to lere,

I fonde gadryd al y-fere

The god of love and his menye.

And I wol tel anoon), yif ye   5796

Lyst heren) of entencion)

What was her occupacion).

¶ How the Auctour founde Deduit pleying'
at the ches.

Pleasure
Deduit first, y yow ensure,

Whicħ hatħ of no thing no cure   5800

But of Ioye and of gladnesse

And to avoyde al hevynesse

And to exclude al sorowe and tene,

sat on the
grass,
Sat vpon) the smothe grene,   5804

The whicħ eke, as I kan) reporte,

Lovis folkys to disporte

Even) amydᵗ of the herber',

and cald for a
Chessboard.
Bad bring[e] fortħ a chekker' ;   5808

For to that play[e] most Royal

He had a love in special,

Ther at to pley[e]n) oft[e] sythe,

And I wil tel[le] yow as swythe,   5812

[leaf 283]
In that place, so as I kan),

How to pley[e] they began)

Ceriously and that anoon).

The game
was for the
love of a
beauteous
maiden.
And for the love, in sootħ, of oon)   5816

That was A mayde ful entere

The pley began, as ye shal here ;

And yif ye lyste to leve me,

She excelled of beaute   5820

Botħ of shap and eke of face.

And for disport and for solace

This goodly yong[e], fresh of hewe,

The Author.

Y-entred was and kome of newe　　　5824

This pretty
young girl
had come
into the
Garden to get
acquainted
with Pleasure
and Cupid.

In-to this herber of counfort,

Oonly for play and for disport

And also for the more pl.saunce :

For to kachchen aqueyntaunce　　　5828

Of Deduit and of Cupide

She caste awhile ther tabyde.

And this mayde of whiche I telle

Had a name and dyde excelle　　　5832

She was a
splendid
chess-player,

To pleyen at this noble play,

She passede alle, yt ys no nay,

And was expert and knyw ful well

Al the maner euerydell.　　　5836

Ther was nat fonde, to rekne all,

without an
equal,

That was in craft to hir egall,

For she surmountede euerychoon.

But for al that, Deduit anoon,　　　5840

but Pleasure
undertook to
play her.

Ryght lusty and fresh of port and chere,

Caste him for to pley y-fere

With this goodly yonge mayde,

Most excellent, lych as I sayde,　　　5844

And folke gan drawe to anoon,

All the folk
crowded
round them.

Of the garlyn euerychoon,

Croude¹ aboute hem environ　　　¹ croude] koude F. A.　　　[leaf 283, bk.]

To seen a ful conclusyon,　　　5848

Which of hem shal lese or wynne.

And ful demurely they begynne

As by maner of batayle

To diffenden and assayle ;　　　5852

But yt was don of noon hatrede

But of love and frendelyhede

They playd
for love, to
ease their
hearts,

And her hertis to releve ;

For noon lyst other for to greve　　　5856

But, lyke as I haue memoyre,

Oonly for to han victoire

With-oute surplus² of wynnyng　　　² surplus] surplus F. A.

Of any other foreyn thing ;　　　5860

For they play for no profyte

But for Ioy and for delyte.

just for joy.

The Author.
That was ther entencion),

And yet men) knowen) of reson),   5864

But every
one wants
to win,
How that euery creature

Desireth kyndly of nature

To han victoyre and maistrie

in whatever
he does.
In euery maner Iu-partye   5868

And in euerych high emprise.

And tho I gan) me to devise

To fynde a place covenable

To sen ther play[e] most notable.   5872

I got into a
place where
I could see
all the game,
And fortune shoop so for me

That I myght' beholde and se,

Without[e] let, ech maner thing'

Fro poynt to poynt of ther pleyng,   5876

And as I took good hede therto,

Anoon) I was supprised so,

Of verray lust and high plesaunce,

For to sen her contenaunce,   5880

Al her port, and goodly chere,

and the
players'
moves.
The sotilte, and the maner

Of her Draughtes most crafty,

[leaf 284]
And I was
so enthrald
by it that I
forgot Juno
and Minerva,
That I was ravysshed outerly,[1]   _{1 outerly] enterely A.} 5884

So ferforth that al other thing

I forgat throgh her pleying :

Of Iuno pleynly the rychesse,

And of Pallas the goddesse,   5888

Al the wit, and the prudence.

and wanted
just to stop in
this joyous
place,
For hooly al myn) aduertence

Was to abyden) in that place,

So ful of myrthe and of solace.   5892

I wolde haue had no more rychesse,

Wysdam, force, nor prowesse,

Nor noght'[2] ellys in myn) entent,   _{2 noght] ought A.}

But ay to be ther present   5896

with love's
folk.
With tho folkys amerous,

I was therto so desyrous,

I thoght' on) no thing ellis-where

But euer in on) to abyden) there.   5900

¶ **Here declareth the auctour, aftir play was** *The Author.*
ended, how the god of love made hym **playen**
at the ches with the Damesele,

Wha\u0274 the play I-ended was
   Atwex hem two, thus stood the cas :
Without a maat o\u0274 outher syde.

Pleasure
and the
Maiden's
game is
drawn.

Anoo\u0274 the myghty god Cupide   5904   Cupid praises
Ga\u0274 to preyse the partye
And gretly to Magnefye,
I mene the *partye* of this mayde,   the Lady's
And swich a pris vpo\u0274 hir layde,   5908   play,
Touching this play o\u0274 eu*er*y part,
As she that koude al the art
Ful parfytly, who lyst take hede,
And for hit was gretly to[1] drede, [This line added in the margin.]   and, that she
                                may not get
Lyst for disuse, throgh ydelnesse,   ¹ to] or A. 5913   out of prac-
                                   tice,
She fil in-to for-yetylnesse,
For which this myghty god Cupide
Seyde he wolde so provide   5916
That she sholde nyght' and day
Haue exercise of thys play   [leaf 284, bk.]
                                   says she shall
With the folke of his covent :   play day and
                                   night with all
This, he seyde, was his entent.   5920   his folk,
For by hir crafte he knyw anoo\u0274
She sholde maat[e] many oo\u0274,
Therof he was ryght' wel certey\u0274,
Or eny sholde hir maat agey\u0274 :   5924
Of play he gaf hir swich a name.
Deduit recorded eke the same,
That yonge and olde bothe two   to improve
                                   them ;
Myght' lerne of' hir[e], and also   5928
In the crafte gretly amende,
Bothe to assaylle and to deffende,
And take of hir examplarye
To Afforcen hem to her contrarye.   5932
" For which my wil ys this," q*uod* he,   and she shall
                                   start with
" Thys yong[e] ma\u0274, which that ye se,   me.
Whiche shapeth him her to abyde
With my brother, the god Cupide,   5936 .

The Author. " Of hys retenyw to be oon),
And for hys¹ skyl, nat yore agoon),   ¹ hys] this F. A.

Venus has sent me to the Garden of Pleasure to learn Love-Chess. My moder **Venus** of entente
Specialy him hyder sente,   5940
For he sholde haue exercise
Of this play in al[le] wyse,
That his tyme he nat lese,
Syth he ys her wher he may chese."   5944
  Thise wordys eke and many other
Deduit spake vnto hys brother,
And **Cupide** yaf ful assent.
And so they bothe, of oon) entent,   5948
And specyaly the god of love,
Which hath lordshippe al above
And souereynte more than) alle,

So Sweet-Looks brings me Cupid's order
[leaf 285] Bad **doulz regarde** me to calle   5952
With that goodly debonayre
And fairest eke of al[le] faire
And of beaute sovereyn),
That I sholde me ordeyn)   5956

to play Chess with the fair Maid. In al hast with hir to pley ;
And I ne durste disobey
Vn-to his comaundement,
Lyst afterwarde that I wer shent   5960
Or in any wise blamed,
But I was first sore ashamed ;
And yet for al that, in certeyn),
I ne durste nat with-seyn)   5964
Hys biddyng in no maner wyse.
  But what so that I kan) devyse,
Without[e] respite or awarde
. I sayde ageyn) to **Doulz regarde**   5968

I agree to take my chance for weal or woe. Pleynly that yt sholde be do,
Outher for wele outher for wo,
Or what may turne to plesaunce
With euery maner circumstaunce   5972
Vn-to **Deduit** or to **Cupide**,
I shal fully ther on) abyde,
Til I haue of ful entent
Fulfilled her comaundement.   5976

For I was I-bode thus

The Author.

Of my lady, **Dame Venus.**

  Anoon) with humble reue*r*ence

I kam) forth to presence,   5980

Lyke as I comaundyd was,

And sat dou*n* on) the smothe gras   I sit on the grass oppo-site the pretty Maid,

Thilke part that was contrayre

To the goodly freshe faire,   5984

That was fairer, as thought[e] me,

Tha*n*) is hir self, **Dame** beaute :

Of porte as any dowve meke,

Symple of maner, and also eke   5988

She was, shortly for to telle,   [leaf 285, bk.]

Of womanhed[e] Sours and welle,

Trew exaumple of Curtesye.

And of hir ovne gent[e]rye   5992   by her bid-di*n*g.

She made me to sytte a-dou*n*

To for*n*) hir, of entencyo*n*)

That I sholde with hir pley.

And I lowly dyde obey,   5996

With-out[e] more, to hir biddyng'.

And ther ne was no more tarying',

But in al hast[e] a chekker,   A chessboard is brought,

Passing ryche and ful enter,   6000

Was brought' forth, and that anoo*n*),

And the meyny eue*r*ychoo*n*) ;   and the men.

And pleynly [for] to specyfye,

She chese first for hir p*a*rtye   6004   She took such pieces as she liked;

Suche as hir lyst of the meyne,

As she sholde of duete,

And I the tother ful lowly   I had the rest;

Tooke, to diffende my p*a*rty.   6008

And tho we set our o*r*dynau*n*cys

With al maner circu*m*stau*n*cys,

That longe v*n*-to the pley of ryght',

And our bataylles anoo*n*) ryght'   6012   and we ar-ranged our battalions.

We set hem, as the play requereth,

In ordre so as crafte vs lereth.

  But yif ye lyst to taken hede,

To for*n*), or I ferther procede,   6016

M

The Author.

I wil descryve the maner

Both of the chesse and the chekker,

Our chess-
board and
men were

By and by clerely expresse

The beaute bothe and rychesse.   6020

For in this worlde, I dar wel seyn),

Wer neuer noon) so ryche seyn)

Of oo Meyne a-rowe sette,

finer than
Lancelot's
and Guine-
vere's,

Nat thilke chesse that launcelet   6024

Pleyed on) with quene[1] Guenore   [1] quene] queme F.

Ne wer nat lyke for neuer a fore ;

[leaf 286]

Ther wer no chesse to a-covnten al

Of swich matere, in specyal,   6028

Nor half so worthy of renoun ;

For in her composicioun

and were
made of gold
and jewels.

Ther was ryght' noght' but golde and stonys

Chose and piked for the nonys.   6032

In al my lyf I saugh noon) lych,

For the preciouse gemmes rych

Were of vertu so entere,

So oriental, and eke so clere,   6036

That I kan) nat to ther value

Fully descrive the vertue

But parcel, yif ye lyst to here,

As I kan), I wil yow lere   6040

The maner hool of the Meyne,

And alderfirst, as ye shal se,

The vnkouth craft of the tabler[2]   [2] tabler] taller F.

And the poyntes of the cheker.   6044

¶ Here descriveth the auctour[3] the cheker *and* the meyne.

The chess-
board was
four-square,
of adamant.

The crafty cheker by mesure

Was foure square of figure,

[3] descriveth the auctonr]
the auctur discrivyth A.

Lusty to syght' and avenant   6047

Wroght' out of an adamant,

¶ Iste lapis attrahit ferrum
durum et semper respicit
polum septentrionalem
que est pars inferior cell /
Polus enim meridionalis
est sursum et polus sep-
tentrionalis deorsum.
¶ Philosophus 2° celi et
mundi.

The whiche ston), who loke wel,

Hath in magyk naturel

Ful gret vertu and gret renoun

By kyndly disposicion).

And hys aspect be kynde most   6053

Draweth towarde the north cost,

And Maryners euerychon͐,

By nelde and vertu of that ston͐,   6056

Know her cours and her passage

And also eke her loodmanage.

It draweth yren and eke stel,

By which ye may noten ful wel   6060

That love throghe[1] myght' of his werkyng'[1 throghe] throght F.

Draweth to him euery thing,

Be yt never so strong nor harde,

Contrarious or frowa[r]de,   6064

And folke constreynyth to his lawe,

To seylle in many perylouse wawe

Amonge the Rokkys ful of stryf

During' al a mannys[3] lyf

Her in this worlde, which ys a see

Medled with gret aduersyte.

And of this ston͐ I speke of here

Was y-makyd the cheker,   6072

By crafte ywroght' ful smothe and pleyn͐

Eche other poynt in certeyn͐.

  And of this chekker amerous,

So dyuers and so mervelous,   6076

Of poyntes al the remenaunt

Y-Ioyned to the adamaunt

Wern͐ of awmber ryche and fyn,

Pulshed ful clene out of the Myn͐,   6080

Wonder soot[e] in smellyng',

And ryght' myghty in werkyng',

By concours of naturys[4] lawys,

For to drawe to him strawys,

To holde hem that they parte noght':   4 naturys] *om.* A.

So fareth love, yif yt be soght',

Who that ys kaught' in his seruise

And y-bounde to his emprise,   6088

It is ful harde for woo or peyne

To go fre out of his cheyne,

Yif' that he[5] be onys bounde ;   5 he] *om.* F.

At assay the preffe ys founde.   6092

And thus of Awmbir half the poyntes

Marginal notes:

The Author,

By this Adamant or Loadstone, sailors guide their course.

¶ *id est per* magnetem diriguntur naves et veniunt ad portum.

It attracts iron,

1 throghe] throght F.

¶ *Nota quod* in campo amoris attrahuntur homines non solum fragiles[2] et iuuenes imo eciam homines prudentes et durissimi.

2 fragiles] fratiles F, 3 mannys] mans A.

and by it Love makes folk sail among rocks in this worldsea of adversity.

[leaf 286, bk.]

¶ *id est* de minera.

The squares of the Chessboard were rich Amber,

¶ *per quod* denotatur *quod* amor attrahit debiles et fortes.

which attracts and retains straws,

like love does its votaries.

The Author. Wer ful cloos made in the Ioyntes

The jointings of the amber and adamant [leaf 287] And adamauntys knet y-fere,

Wroght' in so sotile manere   6096

That the operacion)

Passed my wyt and my reson);

For noght' devysed was in veyn),

The poyntes squared eke so pleyn)   6100

were not perceptible. That the Ioynyng was nat sene,

The werkmanshippe was so clene.

And to considren) euery thing',

The devys and the makyng',   6104

When) I considred euery del,

Yt lyked me ryght' wonder wel :

The Mistery and the privete.

The Fair Maid's Chessmen   And touching also the Meyne   6108

Whiche she had on) hir partye,

I shal declare and specefye,

As I remembre in my thoght' :

were of rich stones, Of ryche stonys they wer wroght'   6112

And I-made ful sotily ;

But I merveled ful gretly

That al hir meyne, oon) by oon),

and all had shields on their shoulders, Wern) y-armed euerychoon)   6116

With sheldys on) her shuldres square,

And also eke, as I was ware,

carven and painted. Ymages thervpon) depeynt

With freshe colours no thing' feynt ;   6120

Somme in the mater depe grave,

And many stonys that they have,

Which of figures ofte varie,

Be called in the lapidarie,   6124

Some were stones found in Israel, Stonys in ysrael y-founde,

Somme square and somme rounde,

Enprinted of ther owne kynde,

For crafte was ther set behinde,   6128

For I trowe that no man)

Swiche seelys grave kan).

[leaf 287, bk.] graven by Nature. For nature, who taketh kepe,

Passeth soothly werke-man)-shepe ;   6132

For crafte ys subget vn-to kynde,

And mannys wyt kaꝺ nat fynde, *The Author.*

By resemblaunce of no figure,

To be egal vn-to Nature. 6136

   And swich ymages as I ha tolde,

Newe echoꝺ and no thing olde,

Ech of hir menꝺ had in his shelde The Maiden's

Mid enprinted of the felde, 6140 chessmen all had figures on their

Ordeyned al[le] for batayle shields.

Lych menꝺ of Armes to assayle.

Arrayed thus menꝺ myght' hem senꝺ,

Except al oonly that the quenꝺ 6144 But the Queen had a

Had in soth, as I took hede, crown of gold on her head.

A crowne of golde vponꝺ hir hede,

And al the tother, in swich wise

As ye[1] to fornꝺ hanꝺ herd devyse, [1] ye] *om.* F. 6148

With many [a] wonderful figure

Ordeyned wernꝺ, y yow ensure.

And I me cast[e] nat to spare

Al the maner to declare 6152

Her in ordre, verreyly,

Of al hir Meyne by and by.

¶ Here maketh the auctour a descripcioꝺ of al hir Meyne and first' of hir povnys.

Her povnys all, y yow ensure, The Maiden's

I-forged wernꝺ[2] of oo mesure, ¶ Primus pedinus. pawns were made of emeralds.

Wrogbt' and made by crafte ful clene [2] wern] was A. 6157

Al of Emeraudys grene,

And lych as I vnderstood

The first[e] povne, which that stood 6160 Thé 1st

Onꝺ hir ryght' hand, was callyd youthe, pawn was Youth,

Which in his sheeld, as yt ys kouthe, with a cres-

Bare a cressaunt Mone shene, 6163 cent moon on his shield.

To declare, thus I mene, ¶ primus pedinus in bello mu-

lieris ponitur Iuuentus et por- [leaf 288]

That youthe in his grene age tat in suo scuto lunam nouam que in suo lumine multiplici-

Varieth ofte of corage, ter variatur. et sicut luna in modico tempore multa signa

Redy for to chaunge soñe peragrat[3] / Ita Iuuentus per- transit multa pericula ante-

After the nature of the mone ; quam perfecerit cursum suum. [3] peragrat] pargrat A.

But of chaunge the properte 6169

Longeth nat, in no degre,

The Author. Vn-to woman) of Nature,

They be so stable and so sure

In ther trouthe to persever',

Women's hearts never change: For ther hertys chaunge never,

Wher they be set, they wil abyde,

They voide chaunge to ben) her gyde, •   6176

they are not moonlike Ther sect ys no thing lunatyke,

Nor of kynde they be nat lyke

To no monys that be wane,

or vanelike. They turne nat as dotħ a phane   6180

With vnwar wynde, god forbede

That ther sholde in womanhede

Ben) any monyssħ tache at al,

But stedfaster than) ys a wal   6184

In what thing that they ha to don).

They be nat lyche the hornyd moon)

That kan) encrese and wanse ageyn),

Swiche a faute was neuer seyn)   6188

In woman) yet afore thys tyme ;

They hate that any newe prime

Wer founden in her kalender,

They are perfect and stable, They be so perfyt and enter   6192

And stable in her sykernesse,

That cloude noon) of doubilnesse

Eclypse may the clere lyght',

ever shining Nor difface the bemys bryght'   6196

Of her trouthe, whicħ wansetħ never

[leaf 288, bk.] But in hys fulle lastetħ ever,

like the sun. Nat lyke the mone but the sonne,

That fadetħ witħ no skyes donne,   6200

Ryght' so the bryghte bemys glade

Of her trouthe dootħ never fade.   *¶ per contrarium.*

¶ Sed absit quod aliqua variacio foret reperta in sexu muliebri qui non habet aliquam influencium variacionis a luna / per Antifrasim.

¶ The seconde povne on hir partye.

The Maiden's 2nd pawn was Beauty, The secounde povne next arowe

Was callyd, as I koude knowe,

Beaute by name or fayrenesse,

A povne of grete worthynesse ;

with a Rosebud on his shield. And he bare in his sheelde a Rose,

Budded as hyt wolde vnclose,   6208

¶ Secundus pedinus fuit pulcritudo que significatur per Rosam que cito marcessit et nascitur inter spinas.

Oonly for to signifie

That beaute, who that kan) espye,

By naturel Inclinacion)

Lasteth fresh but a seson),   6212

No mor' than) doth a Rose newe

Which with a storme chaungeth his hewe,

For al his soote levys glade

Ful vnwarly yt wil fade;   6216

And so, in sooth, doth al fairenesse

With sodeyn) storme of somme sekenesse,

Both in man) and woman) bothe,

Wherso they be glad or lothe,   6220

Lat no woman) ther-of han pride,

For yt wil no while a-byde

But passe, as dooth a Rose flour,

Al vnwarly with a shour,   6224

For age, or they taken) kepe,

Lyche a thefe wil vnderkrepe

And appallen) the beaute,

From) whos stroke they may nat fle;   6228

For ther may no crafte avayle,

Whan) that age dooth assayle,

And youthe last but a seson)

And hath eke this condicion):   6232

Whan) he ys goon), be wel certeyn),

He wil never resorte ageyn),

Of kynde yt may be noon) other;

And beaute, which is youthes brother,   6236

Whan) youthe ys goon), wil nat appere,

For comounly they goon) y-fere,

And after **Age** doth defye

Al[le] merours in to prye.   6240

For pleynly youthis herytage,

Who look aryght', ys crokyd age;

And of beaute this is the fyne:

Whan) he draweth to declyne   6244

With age for to be allyede,

It may of no wyght' be denyede

In noon) estate, who taketh hede;

For age taryeth for no mede,   6248

The Author.

Wher so he be nygħ or ferre,
Hys tyme sette for to differre,
For no request of kyng nor queŋ,
Hys manacyng they may nat fleŋ.

6252

¶ The thridde povne.

The Maiden's 3rd pawn was Simplicity,

The thridde povne callyd symplesse,
 Which be kynde dootħ expresse
Innocence and loulyhede
That sholde be in womanhede,
And humblesse that they sholden have.

with a lamb in his shield,

Therfore in his sheelde was grave
A lambe ful meke and debonayre,
Whiche is a best[e] nat contrayre
No more, in sootħ, than woman be,
For oonly of humilyte

6260

as women suffer humbly [leaf 289, bk.] and silently men's bad words.

They suffreŋ al that men wil seyŋ,
And kaŋ nat speke a worde ageyŋ ;
Meknes hath so her tonge nayled,
Thogħ they witħ anger be assayled,
They be as Muet as a stoŋ.

6264

A mouthe they haŋ, her tonge ys goŋ,
For of kyndly providence
They be professed to silence.
Ther ys no maŋ that wyl sey nay
That hatħ hem preved at assay.

6268

6272

¶ The fourthe povne.

Her 4th pawn was Sweet-Looks,

The fourthe povne ful plesaunt
 I-callyd was doulz semblant,
Which had grave, as I behelde,

with a rain-bow in his shield.

A reyne bowe amyd hys sheelde,
Of colour rede and watry grene
Shewyng ageyŋ the sone shene ;
And as the philisophre seythe,
To whom men muste yiveŋ feythe,

6280

Yt causetħ trees, crope and Rote,
For to smelle wonder soote,

He leads folk to love.

And folke enclynetħ by desyre
For to be brent witħ lovys fire,

6284

¶ *Tercius* pedi[n]us vocabatur *simplicitas que significatur per agnum / et conuenienter per agnum intellegitur illa simplicitas siue* ma[n]suetudo[1] *que pro maiori parte in mulieribus reperitur.*

[1] ma[n]suetudo] masuetudħ A.

¶ *Quartus* pedinus vocabatur *dulcis aspectus qui portauit* Iridem[2] *in scuto / Nam secundum philosophum /* Iris est grata aspectu *et reddit arbores super quas cadit odorabiles et mouet desiderium in amatoribus / Item significat pluuiam pietatis que omnia possunt applicari ad mulieres / que cito mouentur ad lacrimas pietatis. //*

[2] Iridem] Iride A.

And yt betokeneth also reyn).

The Author.

And even) lych, I dar wel seyn),
And afferme in soth[e]nesse,
Women) be cause of al swetnesse ;

6288 Women are
the cause of
all sweetness.

For who hem serveth eve and morwe,
Hath neuer cause for to sorwe.
This knoweth ech man) that ys wis,
How that yt is a paradys

6292 It is Paradise
to be with
them.

For to abyde in her presence.
They kan) make no resistence
In no thing which that is honest ;
For ther ys noon) so meke a best,

6296

So humble, in soth, no more suffrable,
And eke they be nat variable
But of Nature hool and pleyn).

[leaf 290]

And as a Reyn bowe tookneth reyn),

6300

Ryght so the dewe of goodnesse
Descendeth doun from)[1] her mekenesse,

[1] from] for A.

They give out
the dew of
goodness

That, wher yt falle on) crope or roote,
The bawmy dropys be so soote,

6304

They fade never in no gardyn),
And eke her stremys cristallyn)

and the
streams of
devotion.

That fro her chekys stylle doun
Kam) al of deuocioun.

6308

They kan) nat wepe of no Rancour,
For holsom) as the Aprile shour
Fallyng on) the erbes newe,
Ryght so I holde her wepyng trewe,

6312

Devoyde of al Malencolye,
What so men) Ianglen of envye.

¶ The Fyfthe povne.

The Fyfthe povne, yif ye lyst here,
Y-called was **Port** and **Manere**,

6316

The Maiden's
5th pawn was
Deportment
and Manner.

Which ys a maner condescence
For to ha gret excellence
In contrevyng, how that oon) may
Excelle another in array,
So that array and port y-fere
Accorde lyke and that Manere,

¶ Quintus pedinus vocabatur[2]
in gallico fetitesse que in-
ducit aptitudinem et con-
descenciam corporis et ha-
bitus exterioris[3] que optime
per anulum designantur /
quia si striccior vel largior
quam deceat digito non
congruit. /
[2] vocabatur] vocabitur A.
[3] exterioris] exteritores A.

The Author. Botħ of chere and cou*n*tenaunce,

Haue a maner Resemblaunce, 6324

Lad and conveyed by prudence,

Speech should agree with its substance. Witħ this that specħ and elloquence

Procede lyke to the matere

Witħ ful acordaunce of the chere, 6328

Be yt of Ioye, or of gladnesse,

Outher of sorwe, or hevynesse,

As for the tyme ys most sittyng'.

The Maiden's 5th pawn had a Ring on his shield, And this povne bereth eke a ryng' 6332

Myd of hys sheelde, to signifye

That, yif yt sholde aryght' aplye

[leaf 290, bk.] Vpo*n* A fynger,[1] Iust to sytte,   [1] fynger] synger F. singer A.

Nouther to nor fro to flytte, 6336

Yt may nat be to streyt nor large.

Ryght' so of Maner this the charge :

to show that every one should keep within bounds, In eu*er*y thing to kepe a Mene,

To refuse and voyde clene 6340

Of excesse aħ surplusage

Aftir doctrine of the sage.

And who considereth eu*er*ydeħ,

Ther is no wyght' ka*n* do so weħ 6344

To holde A Mene in eu*er*y thing,

as women always do, As wome*n* ka*n* in ther werkyng.

They be so prudent and so wyse,

What eu*er*e thing they shal devyse, 6348

And in what thing they shal procede,

A Mene dootħ her brydel lede ;

as well in mirth For in Ioye and in solace

Òf wit they ha so grete grace. 6352

They be gou*er*nyd by mesure,

And yif hyt falle of Auenture

as grief. That hevynesse a ma*n* assaylle,

Her' counsaylle may so moche avaylle, 6356

Yif hem lyst her witte applye,

They have a remedy for every ill. They ka*n* fynde a remedye

Al sodenly, without[e] more,

Vnto eu*er*y maner sore. 6360

Her counsayl ys of swycħ noblesse,

And touchinge also secrenesse

Ther is no wight' more prive,

The Author.

And what ye lyst to ha secre,   6364

If you want a secret kept, tell it to a woman.

Tel yt a woman) boldely,

And thow maist truste feythfully

Thow shalt never here yt more,

Thogh at hir herte yt sitte sore,   ¶ Cui*us* contr*arium* *est* verum.

Lever she had, for any peyne,

Ewene for to breste a-tweyne

Than) a counsayll to discure ;   [leaf 291]

Of her mouthe they be so sure,   6372

She'll be as close as a ring.

First and last in euery thing,

And as cloos as ys a rynge.

¶ The Sixte povne.

The syxte povne of grete renoun)

I-callyd was by good reson)

Substancyally, as in sentence,

Purveyaunce or providence,

To sen aforn) what shal falle,

Nat oonly sugre but the galle   6380

Of worldly mutabylyte,

In Ioye and eke aduersyte,

Consydre by discresion)

The sodeyn) transmutacion)   6384

Of al erthely felycite,

Whiche selde a-byt in o degre,

That wel ys him that kan) beforn)

The chaffe dessever fro the corn).   6388

And for this skylle, of entent,

This povne hath graven) A serpent

Myd of his sheelde ful craftyly,

To signefye fynally   6392

That of Nature the serpent,

To eschewen) al enchauntement,

Dooth to forn) hys besy peyne

For to stoppe hys erys tweyne,   6396

By defnesse to make him stronge,

That the soote sugryd songe

Of thenchauntour by hys wyle

For lak of prudence him begyle,   6400

¶ Sext*us* pedin*us* *est* bona sens*uum* disposicio *et* bona providencia *que per* ser-pentem* designat*ur* qui obturat au*r*es suas ne de-cipiatur ab incantatore / v*n*am scilicet ex t*er*ra, al-t*er*am ex caud*a* / Ita Mulier prude*n*s obturat au*r*es suas ne audiat deceptore*s* /.

The Maiden's 6th pawn was Provid-ence,

or Foresight of worldly change,

and on his shield was a Serpent,

which stops its ears against en-chanters' song.

<table>
<tr><td>*The Author.*</td><td>Whan) yt ys late for to stryve.</td><td></td></tr>
</table>

The Author. Whan) yt ys late for to stryve.
But ther ys serpent noon) alyve,
Wher he wake or ellys slepe,
Provided bet him self to kepe   6404

[leaf 201, bk.] Than) ys a woman) provident
A foreseeing woman is To kepe hir from) enchauntement
Of al deceyt of flaterye.
  They kan) crafte so wel espye,   6408
And hem preserve by prudence
For to yive noon) Audience,
as deaf as a stone But ben as deffe as stok or ston,
What they here, they let yt gon,   6412
For they lyst nat to aduerte
Nor to enprynten in her herte
to sugard words. The sugryd wordys that they here;
Of newe they be nat for to lere,   6416
For to a-voyde and to Refuse,
And with delayes hem excuse,
And longe for to holde on) honde
Folkys bothe free and bonde.   6420
Women are wise as serpents, strong as lions. They ben) of wisdam) Serpentyne
And of force leonyne
To kepe hem fre fro the panter,
And pleynly vn-to her daunger   6424
They al constreyn), ther skapeth noon).
They be so prudent euerychon),
Myghty to assaylle, strong at dyffence;
And al ys this but providence,   6428
They win, and are not won. For to wynne and nat be wonne
Of nature the crafte they konne;
And for they be to forne so wis,
Of providence yif hem the pris.   6432

¶ The seveneth povne.

The 7th pawn was Bounty, The seveneth povne, as ye may se,
  Was by name callyd bounte,
A povne of grete worthynesse,
Of grete renoun and grete noblesse,
with a Panther on his shield. And in his sheelde, yif ye lyst here,
Hath enprented a pantere,

¶ Septimus pedinus [in] gallico vocabatur bounte que per panteram significatur cuius cutis est multis coloribus distincta et odor suauissimus et ideo omnia animalia ipsam libenter insecuntur / et est eciam animal mansuetum et ita mulier bona et virtuosa odorem suauissi-

Myd of the felde to his socours,

²A beste of many folde colours,

Hys brethe swettest of sauour²

And most holsom) of Odour

And passingly restoratyf ;

And he hath a prerogatyf   6444

That al[le] bestys specialy

Desire of kynde hys companye

And to be in hys presence.

  And semblably, in sentence,   6448

Bounte, which ys of fredam welle,

Al[le]³ vertues dooth excelle,

And ys preferred of renoun

In euery maner Region) :   6452

Gretly in erthe magnefied,

And in the hevene stellefyed

Amongys goddys celestial

As the vertu most Royal.   6456

And thys vertu specialy   [This line added in the margin.]

Ys apropred naturely

Of Iuste reson) to womanhede

Oonly for ther goodlyhede.   6460

For fredam, bounte, and largesse,

Worship, honour, and kyndenesse,

Norture, and al curtesye

Ben so nygh of hir allye   6464

That fro the welle of her goodnesse

Springeth out all⁴ gentylesse.

They be Merours of al bounte,

So large of giftes and so fre ;   6468

Who⁵ axeth hem, they sey nat nay,

Her fredam maketh no delay,

They yive, but they wil nat take,

Her kynde ys pleynly to forsake,   6472

Al[le] giftes to Refuse ;

Al be somme folkys hem accuse

And apeche and seyn) exprese:

They be wolfes⁶ of gredynese,   6476

And ther with al more capcyus

Than) is the Mawe of Tycyus,

Marginal notes (left column):

mum emittit per bonam famam¹ et sic de alijs proprietatibus //

¹ famam] fomam F. A.

²—² om. A.

³ Al[le] of A.

⁴ all] of F.

⁵ who] whom F. A.

⁶ wolfes] swolfe F. A.

Marginal notes (right column):

The Author.

The Panther's breuth is so sweet [leaf 292]

that it attracts all beasts.

So Bounty

is held by the Gods as the most heavenly virtue,

and is given to women,

from whom all gentleness springs, and all generosity ;

they give, and will not take ;

tho' some folk say they're wolves, in greediness.

More Rauenous in takyng

And of desire more fretyng   6480

Than) Tantalus, whicħ ys in helle

And may never ete his felle,

The hunger fret on) him so sore.

Yet somme folke seyn) that wel more   6484

Ys the hunger more vnstaunchable,

More gredy, and in-saturable

Of wommen, for to Acroche and take,

Ther leveth noght' byhynde her rake;   6488

Their Etike abydeth no respyte,

So fretyng ys her appetyte

That watir noon) stauncheth the fire

Which that brenneth in her[1] desire.   [1] her] hys A. 6492

Thus somme folkis of malys,

I mene folys that be nat wys,

Delyten hem wommen to blame;

To seyn) hem harme *and* to diffame: 6496

This al her lust, bothe eve and morwe.

I prey god yive hem evel sorwe

And short her tongys witħ myschaunce,

Which ys y-whet witħ fals plesaunce   6500

For to a-peche her Innocence,

Which kan) nat stonden) at diffence

But kepe hem Muet and sey ryght' noght',

Devoyde of malys in her thoght'.   6504

Who so ever that hem dere

They ne kan) no malys bere.

They be so good euery-choon)

That I dar seye ther is neuere oon)   6508

But she ys good or ellys wolde

At the lest[e] so be-holde,

That the panter in hys kynde,

Which that is yfounde in ynde,   6512

Hatħ on) hys bak nat mo colours

Than) Women) han) of *ver*tu flours,

For of prudence and wyt also,

What euer thing that hem lyst do,   6516

With-out[e] any long soiour

They kan) fynde a colour

By short avys hem self to excuse,

For the whicħ lat no man) Muse   6520

Of Malys nor of cursydnesse

Hem to apeche of doublenesse.

¶ The viij. povne.

The viij povne for prowesse

     Was I-callyd higħ noblesse,

Passyng of grete Auctorite,

Vpon) whos shelde men) myght[e] se

The myghty figure Imperial,

I mene the foule most Royal

Whicħ hath fethres grey and donne

And perceth eke the shene sonne,

Golde tressyd witħ his bemys bryght',

Whan) he is most fervent of lyght',   ¹ omnia] omnia omnia F. A.

Soring higħ vp in the ayre,   6533

Whan) the wynde is smothe and faire.

    This Royal foule, most of renoun,

Whicħ hath in swicħ subieccion)   6536

Foulys al and ys her kyng,

And evene lyke, in many a thing,

Who hath such noblesse and renoun

By kyndely inclinacion)   6540

In vertu for to floure and shyne

As nature femynyne,

Or who is of so grete value

To flen) so higħ in al vertue,   6544

As is a woman), who lyst se !

For the grete humilyte

Of a woman), this no drede,

The seconde persone of the godhede   6548

Took flessħ and blood and be-kam man).

Now as me semeth truly than)   ² worshepe] worsheped F.

Men sholde worshepe² hem and preyse,

Her honour eke exalt and reyse,   6552

Oonly for the sake of oon),

By whos exaumple they echoon)

Han the wynges of al pride

In ther flight' y-leyde asyde.   6556

Marginal Latin note:

¶ Octauus pedinus in bello mulieris vocabatur nobilitas que tria / includit / primo anime excellencia / que est vera nobilitas / 2o / generis potencia 3o / quedam excellencia apparatus / hec omnia ¹ optime designantur per Aquilam que aspicit solem . id est racionem et abicit pullos // qui hoc nequiunt facere / Item in arduis nidificat . id est in magnis et honestis actibus.

Marginal English glosses:

The Maiden's 8th pawn was Nobleness,

with an Eagle on his shield,

gilt with the sun's rays,

soaring high.

And as this bird is King,

so woman

is highest in all virtues.

For, in her, Christ became man ;

[leaf 293, bk.]

and men should praise and honour her.

The Author.
They be nat pompous nor elate,

They hate women are meek, and simple in dress;
But humble and meke in eche estate,
They love noon) excesse of array,
Al swyche cost they[1] caste away.   [1] they] the F.   6560
For they kan), as in substaunce,
In lytel thing ha suffisaunce,
They ben) atyred with humblesse,
Ther Porte ys founded on meekenesse,   6564

they hate high horns.
They dedely haten highe crestys
And to be hornyd lych as bestys,
With lytel they kan holde hem payed,
And which of hem gooth best arrayed,   6568

They never envy better-drest women;
Another haueth noon) envye ;
For al pompe and surquedye
Wommen naturely eschewe,
And from) her hert[e] they remewe   6572
To bern hem high : for of Nature
Ther is no meker creature
Nor loulyer of countenaunce,
And also of her dalyaunce   6576

they never use double meanings,
They be so verray innocent
That doublenesse in ther entent
Ther groveth .noon) : for mouth and hert
Ben) al oon), who kan) aduerte.   6580

or change.
They varie neuer for word and thoght',
At a prefe discorde noght' ;
This her vse in al[le] londys,

I appeal to their hus-bands.
Recorde I take of her husbondys,   6584
[leaf 294] . That knowe best experience
Of her mekenesse and pacience.

¶ The quene or the fers.

Now I've de-scribed all the Maiden's pawns.
Touchyng hir povnes, by and by
     Ye ha conceyved, how that y   6588
Haue declared in substaunce
The maner and the ordynaunce
Of ther stondyng, and ther with all
Rehersed eke in special   6592
Her power gret and ther renouns
And hooly ther condicions.

And now I cast[e] to procede,

How hir fers, as I took hede, 6596

Stood arrayed in the place,

By hir name callyd grace,

Wroght out of a ryche stoon),

Most in value of echoon). 6600

In this worlde, I dar exp*r*esse,

Ther was noon) of swich rychesse,

For this Royal stoon) famous

Was a Ruby vertuous, 6604

Which hath by kynde the dignite

Of stonys and the souereynte,

Most of vertu and most of pris,

As clerk*es* knowe that be wys. 6608

 And this quene, as I was ware,

I saugh vpon) hir breste she bare

Of golde y-wrought' a ballaunce,

To signefyen) in substaunce 6612

That she oghte by mesure

In *euery* maner auenture

Voyde al fauour outterly

And wey[e] thingys ryghtfully. 6616

 And me semeth, out of drede,

That Iustely vn-to womanhede

Grace ys apropryd kyndely ;

For ne wer grace fynally,

Seruise in love wer but in weyn)

And oppressed by fals disdeyn).

And sith the tyme that Genivs,

That hooly prest of Dame Venus, 6624

Was doun fro the hevene sent

For to cursen) of entent

And hys pover to pronovnce

And Rygorously to denovnce 6628

Hys curse vpon) the folkys all

Which that in the sentence fall

From)[2] his lawes for to varie,

I mene folke that be cont*r*arie 6632

To serve love with al her cure,

Lych as hem techeth nature,

Sidenotes:

The Author.

The Maiden's Queen was Grace.

She was made of a Ruby,

and had, on her breast, a Balance

to show that

she'd weigh all things fairly.

And surely Grace belongs [leaf 294, bk.] naturally to women.

For, since Genius came from heaven

to cure all folk

who won't serve Love,

Latin sidenote:

¶ Nota quod gracia habet magnam efficaciam in amore et importat quandam condescenciam in gestu et loquela et in motibus et ideo—satis conuenienter—per[1] equilibram designatur eo quod omnia faciat cum modo et mensura. //

[1] per] om. A.

[2] From] fron F.

N

The Author. He cursed hem with book and belle,

And after, as ye haue herd telle,   6636

and then made the air smoky with his torch, Anoon) as he his torche hath queynt,

The smoky air' with curse ymeynt

Ran) so fer in lengthe and brede

That sodenly, or they took hede,   6640

so that women had to sneeze, Women) kaught [it] in her nose,

The whiche broght' hem in a pose,

That, for drede of infeccion),

They had abhomynacion)   6644

Of the curse and the sentence,

Lyst yt engendred pestilence ;

they vowd They made avowe with al her hert

That it sholde hem nat astert,[1]   [1] *hem nat astert] nat them starte A.*   6648

Bothe in high and lowe degre,

they'd give up disdain, But daunger sholde exiled be,

Vnmercy[2] also and dysdeyn) ;   [2] *Vnmercy] yn mercy A.*

and not re- fuse men who askt them. And how they wil no more with-seyn)   6652

Folkys that goodly hem requere,

So Grace is theirs. By whiche exaumple ye may lere

[leaf 295] That grace, mercy, and pyte

Longen to femynyte,   6656

They can't hate a man for loving them. For yt is not reson) nor skylle

To hate a man) for his good wille.

And grace eke, for his worthynesse,

Resembleth by lykelynesse   6660

Vnto the Rubye Vertuous,

Which is a stoon) Most plenteuous

Of vertu, yif I shal nat tarye,

Preferred in the lapydarye,   6664

With grace and hap a man) to avaunce.

The Queen's balance and scales show And touching also the balaunce

Set in the quenys brest to forn)

With the skalys evene born),   6668

Declareth clerely to our syght'

that women weigh mercy against cruelty. That wommen) sholde of verray ryght'

Peysen) mercy and pyte

Ageyn) Daunger and cruelte,   6672

Nat execute ther Rygour

But of grace don) fauour

To cherysh folke that hem *serve*,

Nat of daunger dow hem sterve,   6676

Lest **Genivs** efte ageyw

Curse hem newe for her dysdeyne.

But I hope they wyl provyde

Teschewe curse on eue*r*y syde,   6680

And, lyst they fall[en] in sentence,

Make no more no resistence.

¶ The two knyghtys on hir pa*r*tye.

Next I saugh hir knyghtys tweyne,
     By craft y-wrogh*t* ful souereyne,   6684

Made of Saphirs oriental,

Of chere and look ful Marcial,

And bothe to myw inspecciow

Ful knyghtly of proporsiow,

Of cher and port ful of pride.

And the knyght' ow hir ryghte syde

Bare in his shelde an vnycourne,

Which in his forhed had an[1] horne

Passing sharp and pe*r*ilouse,   [1] an] a A.

Whech is a beste Surquedous,

Spook of in many straunge londe.

And the knyght' ow hir lefte[2] honde   6696

Bare an hare vpow his shelde,   [2] lefte] ryght F. A.

A beste swyfte in pleyw and felde,

Of hys Nature fugytyfe,

With-out a reste or any stryfe,   6700

By whiche bestys, who taketh hede,

Is vnderstond[e] shame[3] and drede   [3] vnderstond[e] shame] vnderstood I hame A.

Which to wo*mm*en apartene,

In honeste to kepe hem clene.   6704

For but shame were her guyde,

Chastite wer sette a-syde,

They wer won*n*e without stryfe,

But drede hem made fugytife,   6708

Lyghter to take than an hare,

But shame and drede doth hem spare

That they lyghtly wil nat be won*n*e;

But her cours ys ofte ro*n*ne   6712

The Author. To be pursuyd in her flyght':
Thus some folkys ageyn) ryght'
Iangle of hem of yre and mood,
Which kan) neuer speke hem good.   6716

¶ The two Rokys on) hir partye.

The Maiden's 2 Rooks or Castles were of citrine topaz,

Hyr Rokys, at eche corner oon),
Wer makyd of a ryche stoon),
Of a Thopas wonder fyne,
Which of colour ys citryne,
A stoon) of grete worthynesse,
Lyke as clerkys bere wytnesse
And expressen in her bokys.

¶ Duo Roci in bello amoris ex parte mulieris fuerunt Doulz Regarde and Bialacoil / primus per Caladrium designatur quia totus albus / certificat de morte et vitam egrotantis / Secundus Bialacoil multum proprie designatur per sirenam quia suo cantu dulcissimo suoque aspectu grato nautas allicit et attrahit inexpertes ita vt ob dulcedinem dormiant et finaliter deuorentur / Applica ad propositum.

and were named Welcome and Sweet-Looks.

[leaf 296]

And the namys of thise Rokys:
Bialocoil and **Doulz Regarde,**
As I loked thiderwarde,
They wer callyd so of ryght',
Whos names ben) of ful gret myght'   6728
To maat a man), or he be war.
And they vpon) her sheldes bare:

One had a Mermaid on his shield;

The toon, lyke as I koude se,
A Meremayden) of the se,   6732
Whos songe ys most souereyne
To bryng[e] folkys in-to a treyne,
It is so ful of armonye,
For the soote melodye   6736
Bryngeth folkys in gret sklaunder;

the other a Lark,

The tother roke had a calaundre
Vpon) his shelde him self to assure,
A bridde of merveylous nature,   6740

which can foretell a man's death

The whiche kan), as clerkys seye,
Shewe a man) yif he shal deye;

by flying away from him.

Yif he withdrawe and tourne away,
Of deth ther ys no more delay,   6744
And yif he look vpon) hys face,
Of lyf he shal haue lenger space.
Ryght' so, in sooth, doth Doulz Regarde:
Whan) a womman) hath no rewarde   6748
With her eyen of pite
Vpon) hir servant for to se,

Ther ys vnto hys maladye   ¶ *Nota.*   *The Author.*

But detħ witħ-out[e] remedye.   6752

And as syrenes witħ her song   As Syrens

Make a man) to saylle a-wrong,

Tyl he be drovnyd and y-slawe   drown men,

Witħ ouer-tournyng of som*me* wawe :   6756

So bialacoil or fair semblavnt   so Welcome and Sweet-Looks

For a seson) ful plesavnt

In womanhede falsely feyned

Hath ful many man) constreyned   6760   delude men

In the se of doublenesse,

Y-plonged in ful gret distresse,   [leaf 296, bk.]

That he neuer was socouryd,   and ruin them.

Karibdys hatħ him so devourid   6764

That ther myght' helpe him no lecħ.

     Thus lyst som*me* folke wom*men*) apecħ,   Some men

I mene swicħ as hem delyte

To put on) wom*men*) al the wite[1]   [1] wite] white F.   6768   blame women wrongly.

Hem to diffame wrongfully.

In sootħ, they syn*n*e ful gretly

That wom*men*) put in suche trespace.

I prey, god yive hem sory grace,   6772   May God requite them!

Al tho that be bolde to seyn)

That women) ar nat hool nor pleyn).

¶ The two Awfyns on hir syde.

And of Awfyns eke also   The Maiden's two Bishops

On) hir syde she had two,   6776   were made of the gem Heliotrope,

Wroght' of a ston) of grete fame,

Eliotropia was the name,

A ston) of passing grete rychesse,

The lapydary bereth witnesse,   6780

Whicħ yiveth a man) hap and grace

To be welkome in eue*ry* place,

And also, yif yt be credible,   which renders a man

Maketh a man) Invisible.   6784   invisible.

And on) her sheldys thyse awfynes

Bare emprynted for her sygnes :   [2] dowve] dowbe A.

The toon) a dowve[2] humble and meke,   ¶ Duo alfini fueru*nt* Frau*n*chise and pite *pri-ma signi*ficatur *per* co-*lumbam* q*uia* felle caret   One had a dove on his shield.

And the tother grave had eke,

The Author.	Lych as I report[e] kan),
The other Bishop had a Pelican on his shield.	In her shelde a pellican),
	By the dowve[1] first to exp*r*esse
The Dove typifies the meekness of women,	The loulyhede and the meknesse
	That women) han) of her nature,
	The whiche, for noon) auenture,
	Kan) nat gruchche, for noon) offence.
[leaf 297]	They be so ful of pacience,
	And as a dowve[2] they ha no galle,
	Whos mekenes dooth neuer apalle,
	Thogh men) wolde day be day
	Her humblesse put at assay.
	For yif that[3] men) hem preue wel,
who are true as steel,	They be as trewe as any stel
	Her worshipe to kepe and save,
	Whos herte harder ys to grave,
	Touching her honour, than) ys glas.
	They be so pleyn) in eu*er*y cas,
	Al be that clerkys bere witnesse
and not like glass—	That glas ys ful of brotelnesse,
	And also, as they specefye,
ready to break, not bend—	Redy[4] to breke but nat to plye
	Nor to bowe on) nouther syde,
	Yt wil the hamer not abyde.
	Men) kan) nat maken yt plicable
	Nor forge yt to be Malliable.
	But surely wom*m*en) fare nat so,
	For they be redy to and to
but obedient, yielding like wax.	Tobeye as wex, and[5] kan) nat let
	To eu*er*y prynt that men) lyst set,
	And to receyve al figures,
	Thise sely tendre creatures,
	For stryfe of kynde they ne kan),
And like the Pelican, they'll shed their blood sooner than offend their husbands.	And also, lyche a pellican),
	Her herte blood they wolde spende
	Rather than) they sholde offende
	Her husbondes wrathe or greve.
	Who that lyst may thys beleve,
	For I dar sweren) yt on) a booke.
	Ye woot wel, how Alceste tooke

Side notes (right margin):

et nullum ledit / pari forma mulieres no*n* ha-bent fel scil*icet* amari-tudinem *etc.* Secu*n*da designat*ur* per pelli-canum / *quia* pullos quos ¶ occidunt ex indignacione reviuificat ex pietate illis natura-liter attributa.

1 dowve] dowbe A.

2 dowve] dowbe A.

3 that] than A.

4 Redy] Rede F. A.

5 and] an A.

Line numbers (right margin):

6796
6800
6804
6808
6812
6816
6820
6824
6828

Mekely her deth hir lorde to save,

And ches to goon) vn-to hir grave

Wilfully, without[e] stryve,

For to save hir lordys lyfe, 6832

Which ys Merour and pat.onesse,

To yive example of stedfastenesse

To women) throgh hir noble fame,

That wyfes al[le] do the same; 6836

And so they wolde, yt ys no nay,

Yif they were put at assay.

The Author.

[leaf 297, bk.]

As Alcestis gave her life to save her lord,

so would all women do.

¶ Of the kyng¹ on hir partye.

Hir kyng which in myddes stood

In value was worthe mychel good, 6840

Y-forgyd by ful gret avys

Of A diamaunt of grete prys,

For never in book I herde expresse

Of noon) that was of swych gretnesse, 6844

Nor by kynde of swych entaylle;

And ordeyned for batayle

He sate vpon) a large stede,

Which was wroght¹, as I took hede,

Out of a wondir dyuers stoon),

That was called albeston),

Ryght¹ mervelous, as I behelde.

And thys kyng had in hys shelde

A turtyl grave craftyly,

To signefye that fynaly,

With-out[e] Mutabilyte,

That in Femynynyte

Trouthe sholde lasten) euere

In her hert and nat dysseuere,

Wherso that they slepe or wake.

And as a turtil from) hir make 6860

Departeth by no maner weye

In-to the tyme that he deye,

And after pleynly he be dede,

Far wel al Ioy and lustyhede, 6864

Fare wel myrthe and al solace,²

For solytary in euery place

¶ Rex *vero* in bello amoris ex *parte* mulieris *per* turture*m* intelligi-*tur que* si semel¹ com-*parem* amiserit sem*per* alio carebit [et] in de-*serto* / habitat solivaga. Sic Mulieres post mor-te*m* viri sem*per* depost solitarie viuu*nt* pro dolore / *sed* voluntas illaru*m* *pro* tunc est libera / Idem Rex pro-prie *vocabatur* volun-tas / et inde vbi vult se / co*n*uertit / sicut Rex in isto ludo tr*a*hit ad omn*em* parte*m* / Pari forma volu*n*tas mulie-ris *est* q*u*asi girovaga ad om*n*em parte*m* hinc inde se tr*a*usferendo *et* nu*n*quam in eode*m* statu permanendo.

¹ semel] fel F. A.

² al solace] also lace A.

The Maiden's King was made of a diamond.

He rode a big steed of Asbestos,

and had on his shield a Turtle,

showing that women's love is everlast-ing.

The Author.

[leaf 298]

The turtul playneth euer in woo

That hir make ys thus agoo,   6868

And lyst nat for his peynes kene

To resten in weyes grene,

Nor on trees but bareyn

For the constreynt of hir peyn: 6872

When women are

Thus women¹ for verrey dool,   ¹ Thus women] Thus for women F.

Whan they allone be left sool,

They kan nat do but wepe and pleyn,

Swich sorwe dooth her hertys streyn.   6876

left by their husbands,

Whan her husbondes be departed,

With wo they be throgh-out y-darted,

That for to stynte her mone

Ther is no thing but deth allone,   6880

For they wil deye and nat abyde.

they sorrow,

Ther grete sorwe they kan nat hyde,

Her ioy, her myrthe goth to wrake ;

and dress in black.

They kan nat clothe hem but in blak,   6884

Al other colours, in certeyn,

They han hem in so gret dysdeyn :

Rede and white, blyw and grene ;

Of entent they be so clene,   6888

They hate al chaungys that be nywe.

   Ther ys no turtul halfe so trewe

As they may iustely make avaunt,

They are as stedfast as a diamond, which goat's blood alone can break.

For stydfast as a dyamaunt,   6892

That breketh nat but with gootys blood,

Ryght¹ so be they bothe trewe and good

And stedfast founde in ther estate,

And kan abyde desolate   6896

Solytarye in gret distresse,

In morenyng, and in heuynesse,

They wail till men court them again.

Ful many day [they] wepe and wayle,

Tyl that men of newe assayle   6900

Her tendernesse, and begynne

By somme engyne hem to wynne,

By grete avys and purveaunce

And by longe contynywaunce   6904

Of seruise for hir trouthe.

This causeth women to ha routhe,

And to take a man) to grace,
Rather than) deth hys herte arrace, 6908
Of pite and of tendernesse
For to rewe on) hys dystresse ;
Of prudence they take hede
That no man) be for hem dede. 6912
   Thogh [t]he[y] harde as dyamaunt,
Mercy maketh hem plyaunt
For pyte, who that kan) aduerte,
Renneth[1] sone in gentyl herte :   [1] Renneth] ronneth A. 6916
Water that droppeth euer in oon)
Myneth ful depe in-to A stoon),
And castel ys ther non) so stronge,
The sege ther-at may be so longe 6920
That at the last yt wil be wonne ;
Ne ther ys noon) so large a tonne
That men) may wyth a Fauset smal
Devoyden) out his lycour al ; 6924
Nor woman) noon) so sted[e]fast
That, whan) mowrenyng tyme is[2] past,   [2] is] y F.
She may of mercy aud pite
Save and kepe hir honeste, 6928
And forsake hir clothes blake,
And chesen) hir a nyw[e] make.

[leaf 298, bk.]
The Author.
Rather than see men die, widows marry them.
(As Chaucer says), 'Pity runs soon in gentle heart.'
A little tap will drain a tun.
And the stedfastest widow will choose a fresh husband.

¶ Her aftir the auctour hath descryved the Meny on hir syde, he declareth and maketh a descripcion) of hys ovne Meyny.

The first[e] povne to specefye,
Whiche that stood on) my partye
To make my game stronge and good,
In ordre on) the lefte hond stood,
The name of whom) to expresse,
Was y-callyd ydelnesse ;
In whos shelde men) myghte se
Ful depe y-grave a drye tre
Without[e] lefe, fruyt, or flours,
Lych as yt hadde be wyth shours 6940
Be made naked and bareyn),
To signyfien in certeyn)

¶ Primus pedinus in bello amoris ex parte viri fuit ociositas que preparat iter ad vitam voluptuosam / super omnia / vnde Ouidius / Ocia si tollas periere / cupidinis[3] arcus / Ociositas ergo per arborem siccam[4] carentem floribus et frondibus significatur et sibi proprissime adaptatur[5] //
[3] cupidinis] cupidis A.
[4] siccam] siccum F. A.
[5] adaptatur] adoptatur F. A.

My first pawn,
on my left,
was Idlenesse.
On his shelde was a barren tree.
[leaf 299]

The Author. That ydelnesse, to declare,

This barren
tree showd
that Idleness
bares a man, | In vertu maketh a man) ful bare, | 6944

And bryngeth in al maner spices

Of' vnthryfte and [of] al[le] vyces

And of voluptuous desires,

and kindles
the fires of
lust in him. | And yt kyndeleth eke the fyres | 6948

Of Venus bronde by fals delyte,

A man) to folowe hys appetyte

Thorgħ the arwes of Cupide,

To set al reson) fer asyde. | 6952

¶ The secounde povne.

My 2nd
pawn was
Sight. | The secounde povne of gret[e] mygħt'

In ordre next was callyd sygħt',

On his shield
was a big
Key, | Whicħ in his shelde, shortely to y-sey,

Bare y-grave a large key,

To specefy erly and late :

That, as a key vndooth a yate,

showing that
Sight opens
the gate to
all vices. | Rygħt' so the sygħt', who kan) se,

To vices al[le] yiveth entre | 6960

Throgħ hys wyket as porter,

And ys the hertys messager ;

And of tresour and Rychesse,

Of golde and siluer, in sothenesse, | 6964

Of semelynesse, and of beaute,

And of al wordly vanyte :

The eye, by fals collusion),

Ys Rote and chefe occasion). | 6968

¶ *Secundus* pedin*us* in bello amoris ex *parte* viri vocat*ur* in gallico Regars / *qui pro* claue intelligit*ur* . et merito q*uia* sicut *per* clauem aperit*ur* introitus do-m*us* ita *per* visum in-troit*us et* porta amoris aperit*ur* / visus enim *primo presentat* cordi ꝺⸯectabilia que sunt in muliere //

¶ The thridde povne.

My 3rd pawn
was Sweet-
Thoughts. | The thrid[e] povne made and wrogħt'

I-called was suetnesse of thogħt'

And in the Frensħ Doulz penser,

Whicħ at the hert[e] sytte ful ner,

[leaf 299, bk.] | Makyng many fair beheste ;

On his shield
was a big
Tiger. | And in hys shelde he bare a beste,

A Tigre, whicħ that ys so rage

And a best[e] most savage,

Swyftes[t] to renne for his pray.

Whan) his fovnes be lad away,

¶ *Tercius* pedin*us* in bel-lo amŏris ex *parte* viri vocabat*ur* in gallico / Doulz penser *qui per* Tigridem signi*fi*catur q*uod est* animal diuer-s*is* colorib*us et* maculis maculatum / Item velo-cissime mouet*ur*.
¶ Et ita mens et cogi-tat*us* hominis speciali-t*er* amatoris / iux*ta* illud / Ouidij velocis-sime mouet*ur* /
¶ O deus in qu*antis* ani-m*us* vexat*ur* am*antis* / Item[1] speculo decipi-tur / sic mens reuolu*ens* pulc*ri*tudinem[2] q*uasi* in speculo decipitur.

[1] Item] Ita A.   [2] pulc*ri*tudinem] pulcritudine A.

He ys deceyved by merours   *The Author.*
Whicħ the hountys for socours   6980
Caste in the way[e] for a treyne ;
And lyke, yif I shal nat feyne,
Ther ys in this worlde rygnt' nogħt'   Nothing is
Half so swyfte as ys a thogħt',   6984   so swift as
                                       Thought,
Whicħ selde in oon) abydeth stable
But folweth thing*es*[1] delytable,   1 thinges] thynge A.
Swifter also of passage
More than any Tigre rage ;   6988
Now thought ys here, and in A while
It ys hens a thousande Myle ;
Ther may on) thogħt' be noon) areste :
Now in the West, now in the Este,   6992
And where so euer him lyst to be ;
Ther ys no maner thyng so fre,   or so free.
Nor no thing doth so gret disport
To lovers, nor so grete cou*n*fort.   6996
For thought'[2] a thousande tyme a day   2 thought] though A.
Ys where he loveth, who seyth nay?
And ne wer thogħt', lovers echon)   Without it,
Sholde sterue and that anon).   7000   lovers would
                                     die.
Thogħt' ys her shelde and her dyffence,
And thogħt' hatħ most excellence,
Bothe at eve and eke at morwe,
To save lovers from) al sorwe,   7004   It saves them
                                     from sorrow,
For the Eye of thynkyng
Fleetħ with-out[e] more lettyng
Witħ swyfter wynges and more rygħt'
Than) dootħ any foule of flygħt'.   7008
For eue*r*y hour, wher so she be,   [leaf 300]
He wyl his lady oonys se,   and enables a
                                     man to see
Be she fer or be she nere ;   his Lady
                                     hourly,
Of look and Eye he is so clere   7012
Ther may be made noon) obstacle,
But, lyke [a] thyng wrogħt' by Myracle,
Thogħt' fleetħ throgħ wallys *and* throgħ tours,   thru walls
He spareth nouther wynde nor shours,   7016   and towers.
That [ever] wil goon) and vysyte
Wher as he dotħ most delyte.

The Author.	Thought' wol be holde[1] in no prisonɔ,	[1] be holde] beholde F.
		behelde A.
	Nouther in castel nor doungonɔ ;	7020
Thought pictures the face and look	Thought' kanɔ report[e] the figure,	
	The shappe eke, and the purtreyture,	
	The maner, and the countenaunce,	
	The goodly chere, the dalyaunce	7024
of a man's lady-love.	Of his ovne lady dere,	
	Be she fer or be she nere ;	
	Thought' hath so moche suffysavnce.	
But mirrors of false pleasure	But merours of fals plesavnce	7028
	Make him stynten ofte sythe,	
	Let him that he go nat swythe	
	Throgh deceyt of apparence,	
	Which doth to love gret offence,	7032
deceive him.	Deceyved oonly by wenynge	
	And by fraude of supposynge.	
	Whanɔ myshap guyeth so his Rother	
	To take oo thing for another,	7036
	Thanɔ as a Tigre he ys repeyred	
	And of his pray eke disespeyred.	

¶ The fourthe povne.

My 4th pawn	Next by the povne of thinkyng,	
	So counfortable in al[le] thing,	7040
	Ther stood a povne of gret renoun	
was Delecta-tion.	Callyd delectacionɔ.	

[*From leaf* 300, *back, to leaf* 305, *back, are blank pages, pro-*
bably for the remainder of this poem. Leaf 306 *begins thus:—*
How a Louer prayseth Hys Lady.]

[*Title in the Table on leaf* 2, *back:—*
"The booke of' þe Autoure how he plaid at
þe Chesse and was mated of' a Feerse."]

GLOSSARIAL INDEX.

a

abasshen, v. be abashed, 3968 ; p.p. abashed, 5698.
abhomynacion, s. abhorrence, 6644.
abood, s. delay, hesitation, 3303.
abrayde, v. awake, start up, 489.
absent, v. withdraw, 2574.
abyt, 3 ps. sing. remains, 6386; abydeth, 6489.
abyte, s. dress, 1403.
accordable, adj. going together, 2305.
accorde, s. agreement, 2259, 2368.
accordyng, p. ps. agreeing, 2368.
acorde, s. agreement, 2156.
acorded, p.p. granted, 2336.
acovnten, v. count, 6027.
acroche, v. encroach, 6487.
adamant, s. loadstone, adamant, 6048.
aduerte, v. pay attention to, 1257, 6413, 6580, 6915.
aduertence, s. attention, thought, 5890.
advys, s. opinion, 1855.
aferris, adv. from far, 419.
affeccioun, s. wish, inclination, 600, 4837.
affray, s. dread, 3012.
ageynwarde, adv. in opposite direction, backwards, 650 ; on the other hand, 1266, 1517.
algate, adv. under all circumstances, 3995.
allay, s. admixture, 1331.
allye, s. family, relation, 2280, 2525, 3163.
a-lowe, adv. in a lower part, 4186.
alygiavnce, s. allegiance, 3288.
amende, v. help, 2911 ; improve, 3172 ; p.p. 328.
amendement, s. cure, recovery, 5192.
amenuse, v. diminish, 4437.
among, adv. euer amonge: always, 797, 1172, 2241, 3319 ; somwhile amonge : sometimes, 1125.

angle, s. angle, 5788.
angwissh, s. angry disposition, 2583.
angwysshous, adj. distressed, 901.
annoy, s. trouble, 2370.
apalle, v. fade, 6798.
apayed, p.p. satisfied, 513.
apayre, v. grow worse, 2745.
apeche, v. impeach, 6475, 6501, 6522.
apert, adj. manifest, 4523.
apparayle, s. ornament, 156, 349, 1411.
appetit, *appetyt*, *appetyte*, s. desire, 779, 802, 1236 ; taste, liking, 4834, 5060 ; pl. fancies, 5618.
apropred, *apropryd*, pp. attributed, 6458, 6619.
arest, s. delay, 2111, 4777 ; abode, 4355 ; deliberation, 3746.
armoure, *armure*, s. armour, 1180, 1186, 1192.
a-rowe, *arowe*, adv. in a row, 4070, 6023, 6203.
arrace, v. pluck out, 6908.
aspect, s. —— of the adamant : aspect, direction, 6053.
assaut, s. attack, 4373.
assay, s. trial, attempt, 4736, 6092, 6800.
assaye, v. try, 1337, 4754.
astert, v. escape, 6648.
a-swovne, adv. in a swoon, 3849.
atemperaunce, s. mildness, 184 ; temperance, 1188.
atempere, *attempre*, adj. mild, 130, 932.
attamen, v. to make tame, 2460.
attendaunce, s. attendance, 5013.
attones, adv. at once, 3114.
atwene, prep. between, 783.
auctorised, p.p. recognized, renowned, 2386.
aureate, adj. golden, 1312.
avaler, v. come down, fall, 4191.
avaunte, v. boast, 3156.
avayl, s. profit, 4223, 4405.

avenant, adj. graceful, comely, 1719, 6047.

aventure, s. story, 46; chance, 2492; fortune, luck, 2227; peril, 5509.

a-voutrie, s. adultery, 1611.

avoyde, v. remove, 2863.

avys, s. consideration, opinion, 205, 2078.

avysed, p.p. advised, deliberate, 1864.

awarde, v. make out, decide, 5082.

a-wayte, v. wait, 2495.

awfyns, s. pl. bishops in the game at chess, 6775.

awmonere, s. female almoner, 1364.

b

bandon, s. disposal, 5080.

bareyn, adj. barren, 6871, 6941.

barge, s. small ship, 944.

bay, s. stonding at a ——: standing at bay, 3702.

behestys, s. pl. promises, 2077.

bekome, v. suit, 1401.

beldyng, s. building, residence, 4814.

bere, v. have, show, 728.

be-seyn, p.p. *wel be-seyn:* well provided, 5390.

bet, 3 pt. sing. fluttered, flapped, 2104.

bet, adv. better, 829.

blyve, adv. quickly, soon, 409, 1281.

bokel, s. clasp, 3123.

bonde, adj. unfree, 6420.

bonde, s. obligation, promise, 2355.

bontevous, adj. bounteous, 4555.

boolys, s. pl. bulls, 3551, 3573.

borde, s. table, 1899, 1915.

bote, s. remedy, 3441, 4130.

brotelnesse, s. fragility, brittleness, 6808.

budded, p.p. in the form of a bud, 6208.

byddyng, s. order, 2266, 2350, 2601.

bysye, v. refl. take pains, 33.

by-thynke, v. refl. imagine, 3515.

c

calaundre, s. [O.F. calandre] calandra, a species of lark, 6738.

capryne, adj. resembling a goat, 3376.

case, s. par case: by chance, 4457.

cast, v. hold fast, be determined, 628; cast, 666; conjecture, 1209.

ceriously, adv. minutely, one by one, 1604, 5442.

certes, certys, adv. certainly, 579, 603.

chamburere, s. maidservant, 2268.

chapelet, s. circlet for the head, chaplet, 1573.

charge, s. money, 1497; meaning, nature, 6338.

chastise, v. correct, 4245.

chaunce, s. luck, 2226; chance, 2231.

chesen, v. choose, 165, 645.

clerkes, s. pl. writers, authors, 551, 1342.

cleppyd, p.p. called, 3360.

clode, s. cloud, 3262.

cloos, adj. secret, 4524.

cloos, close, s. cell, 89; enclosure, 2614, 3009, 4256.

collateral, adj. adventitious, 31.

collusion, s. deceit, fraud, 6967.

comfortable, adj. wholesome, 4425.

commonly, adv. generally, 104.

compas, s. circle, 1574, 2732; contrivance, 3773.

compassed, p.p. contrived, 362; brought about, 4362.

concerne, v. interest, 2342.

conceyved, p.p. heard, 2249.

concourse, s. course, orbit, 280, 4618.

condescence, s. aptitudo et condescencia corporis, 6317.

confeccioun, s. mixture of drugs, 3401.

confedred, p.p. conjoined, 5248, 5533.

confortatyf, adj. wholesome, strengthening, 4391.

confounde, v. destroy, 472.

congele, v. congeal, 4188.

constreynyth, 3 pr. sing. compels, binds, 6065; *constreyned,* p.p. led, misled, 6760.

contagious, adj. infectious, harmful, 1943, 3922, 4743.

contek, s. contest, 2580.

contemplatyfe, adj. inviting to contemplation, 4502.

conterplete, v. oppose, 4631.

contrarie, contrayre, v. oppose, 261; contradict, 4507.

contrariouste, s. adversity, 4346.

contrarye, contrayre, adj. obstinate, 6260; different, 5412; contrary, 5482, 5932; opposite, 5983.

corage, s. heart, spirit, mind, 985, 6166; courage, 907.

corbed, p.p. bent, crooked, 1347.

corumpable, adj. corruptible, 1085, 1151.

cost, s. manner, way, condition, 4543, 4649; region, 5557, 6054.

cote, s. gown, 1556.

couched, p.p. placed, laid, 52.

covenable, adj. proper, suitable, 809.

covenably, adv. suitably, 5432.

covent, s. convent, conventual body, 3450, 3683; assembly, 2542.

covert, adj. secret, 4032, 4524.

covertly, adv. secretly, 4023.

craft, s. occupation, 2999; skill, art, 1661, 1668, 5838, 6043.

crafty, adj. skilful, 2296, 2854, 5883; skilfully worked, 6045.

crawmped, unnaturally compressed, 3653.

cressaunt, adj. increasing, 6163.

crestyd, p.p. having a crest, 3621.

cristalyne, adj. like crystal, 5718.

crope and rote : the whole plant, 136, 6281; *nouther crop nor rote :* nothing at all, 2743; *on crope or roote :* anywhere, 6303.

croppis, s. pl. summits, tops, 2732.

cure, s. diligence, care, 33, 549.

curious, adj. wonderfully made, 5120, 5303.

cursydnesse, s. wickedness, shrewishness, 6521.

curteys, adj. courteous, 2114, 3465.

cynetys, s. pl. [O.F. chienettes], swans, 1241.

cytolys, s. pl. [O.F. citoles], small dulcimer, 5583.

cytryne, adj. citron-coloured, 3853.

d

dalyaunce, s. conversation, 2232, 6576, 7024.

daunger, s. disposal, bondage, 6424.

davnce, v. —— *on hir ryng :* follow her command, 3255.

daunte, v. tame, subdue, 5365.

debat, s. war, strife, 1083.

debate, v. quarrel, 4993.

decert, s. reward, 2199.

deceyvable, adj. deceitful, 4045.

dees, s. pl. dice, 2404.

delys, s. delight, 2547.

demeyne, s. possession, 2017.

demonstracion, s. outside appearance, 3927.

demurely, adv. cautiously, 5850.

departen, v. divide, 5392; p.p. divided, 1774, 3874.

despite, s. spite, hatred, 2868.

destane, s. destiny, 4759.

dever, s. duty, 1431.

devis, s. judgment, opinion, 977, 1095, 1959, 2090.

devoyde, short for *devoyded*, p.p. devoid, not possessing, 5031, 6313, 6504.

devoyden out, v. draw out, empty out, 6924.

devyde, v. describe, explain, 2723; divide, 5392.

deynous, adj. fierce, scornful, 1502, 1919.

discomfyture, s. grief, 1066.

disconfyture, s. defeat, 4898.

discordaunce, s. discord, 4741.

disespeyred, p.p. put out of hope, 7038.

disgesely, adv. strangely, in a quaint manner, 3645.

dispense, s. (distribution of) money, 3339.

dispeyred, p.p. bereaved, without hope, 1318.

disposen, dyspose, v. make disposed, 1509; restore, 5738.

disposicion, s. general disposition of character, 3508.

dispreyse, v. blame, disapprove, 819.

distemprid, p.p. furious, 3404.

disuse, s. cessation of practice, 5913.

dolerouse, adj., O.F. douloureux, 3612.

donne, adj. dark, 6200, 6529.

doo, s. doe, 3727.

dool, s., O.F. doel, 3997, 4040.

doom, s. judgment, 1963, 1988.

double, adj. double-sexed, 3888.

doublenesse, s. duplicity, 3477; state of being double-sexed, 3880.

doucetes, s. pl. sweet-sounding pipes, 5590.

doute, s. fear, 2763.

drawen, v. go, move, 3050; turn, 3337; come, 5845; *drow*, 3 pl. pt. moved, 5788.

drede, s. doubt, 695, 1203.

dredful, adj. timid, 3728; dangerous, 4041.

dresse, v. direct, 694.
dyvers, adj. extraordinary, singular, 5338, 5574, 6850; *dyuers of chaungyng:* changeable, 5352.

e

ease, s. delight, 4541.
eban tre, s. ebon tree, 2789.
ebbys, s. pl. low tides, 4617.
effeccion, s. realisation of an intention, 4621.
embrowde, p.p. adorned, 3756.
empeyred, p.p. made worse, 1317.
emprise, empryse, s. enterprise, 3586, 4126, 4225; determination, 5430.
emprynte, enprynten, v. fix, imprint, 1183, 6414.
enbataylled, p.p. embattled, 2655.
enbrace, v. behold, 3630, 3838.
enchace, v. chase away, 1304.
enclyne, v. obey, 259; give way, 1526; bow, 2875.
encombre, v. encumber, 1784, 2415, 3614.
encrese, s. profit, advantage, 470, 500.
endure, v. last, remain, 168, 1190, 1484.
endyte, v. write, relate, 1038, 1757.
enforcen, v. endeavour, 146.
engendrure, s. *membres of .——:* organs of generation, 1300, 1446.
engyn, s. contrivance, 2341, 3169.
engynovs, adj. cunning, artful, 3429.
enlacyd, p.p. entangled, ensnared, 3123.
enprented, enprinted, p.p. imprinted, 6127, 6140, 6438.
entaylle, s. shape, 350, 1801, 4269.
entaylled, p.p. carved, 2656.
entencion, s. intent, 843.
entendement, s. reason, 757.
entent, s. mind, 5, 365, 679, 1789; opinion, 2069, 2094, 2149; intention, 18, 442, 502; intent, 617, 830; will, 2149, 2192; of entent: of intention, 1812; general meaning, 651, 1598.
ententive, ententyf, adj. attentive, 199; anxious, 577.
erecte, adj. uplifted, raised, 394.
ermyn, s. ermine, 2836.
escape, v. get out of, escape, 3517.

eschewe, eschiwe, v. avoid, 504, 714, 856, 883.
estate, s. rank, class, profession, 1907, 1929, 2149; state, 2942; pl. condition, 1692; estates, 1890.
estrys, s. pl. interior, locality, 5627, 5758.
etike, s. [O.F. etique], impatience, 6489.
ewre, s. fatal ewre: misfortune, 1445; good ewre: good luck, 2880.
ewrous, adj. successful, 1084, 5190, 5308.
exaumple, s. model, 324.
except, adj. expert, 1659; prep. except, 6144.
exemplarie, s. example, 360.
expert, adj. expert, 5835.
exprese, adv. expressly, plainly, 6475.

f

prime face: the first glance, 27, 3905, 3950. 3366
facounde, adj. eloquent, 1657.
fadeth, 3 ps. sing. becomes dark, 6200.
fage, s. bragging, swindle, 2801, 3811.
faile, s. *withoute faile:* sans faille, 95, 155.
falle, p.p. advanced, 343.
fals, adj. unlawful, 4306.
falsly, adv. unjustly, wrongfully, 4298.
falwe, adj. fallow, yellowish, 5199.
fantasye, s. opinion, 2068, 2126, 5706; fancy, imagination, 4747, 5036.
farsed, p.p. crammed, filled, 3359.
fatal, adj. bringing death, fatal, 1248, 1270.
fauset, s. faucet, 6923.
faute, s. fault, 6188.
fawchon, s. O.F. falchon, 1802.
faylle, s. doubt, 1022. 2830
fees, s. pl. estates, cities, 3038.
felle, adj. very dangerous, 3435, 3717, 4131.
felle, s. fill, 6482.
fere, s. mate, 5206.
ferforth, adv. far, 837; so ——: to such a degree, 5885.
fers, s. queen at chess, 9, 6596.
fers, adj. fierce, 2761.

fersly, adv. fiercely, 3579.

fet, p.p. brought, 5305.

feyne, v. pretend, 178.

fille, s. fil, enough to satisfy want or desire, 63.

fix, p.p. used as an adv., steadily, 2900.

flees, s. fleece, 3528, 3544, 4607.

flesshlyhede, s. sensual pleasure, 5058.

floure, v. flourish, 6541.

floutys, s. pl. [O.F. fleutez], flutes, 5592.

flytte, v. move, flit, 6336 ; p.p. *flytted*, removed, 2988, 5396.

fon, s. pl. enemies, 1195.

foreyn, adj. [O.F. forain] unessential, 703; superficial, 734; illegitimate, 1650; *sekenessys foreyn:* diseases acquired from without, 5177 ; sometimes used in opposition to ideal, abstract, 5860.

forderked, p.p. darkened, 736.

forfete, s. wrong, 4701.

forour, s. fur, 2835.

fors, s. *they gaf no* ——: they did not care, it was nothing to them, 3218.

fortune, s. *of* —— : by chance, 5551.

for-yetylnesse, s. forgetfulness, 5914.

fosterynge, s. nourishment, 1639.

fonned, p.p. infatuated, enchanted, 3658.

fovnes, s. pl. fawns, 6978.

fraunchyse, s. privilege, 2984.

fray, v. terrify, frighten, 3716.

fre, adj. generous, liberal, 2675, 4555.

freel, adj. frail, 3253.

frendelyhede, s. kindness, 2884.

fressh, adj. fresh, fine-looking, 432, 621, 812.

fret, p.p. set, adorned, 141, 1400, 3756 ; 3 pt. sing. gnawed, 6483.

fretyng, p. ps. devouring, greedy, 6480, 6490.

frosty, adj. hoary, 1438.

frowarde, adj. disagreeable, 4966 ; ungracious, 4988.

fugytyfe, adj. fugitive, timid, 6699, 6708.

fulle, s. fulness, 6198.

fulsomnesse, s. copiousness, excess, 128.

fynally, adv. in conclusion, 663, 776, 894, 1099.

fythels, s. pl. fiddles, 5579.

g

gentilesse, s. noble kindness, 482.

genterye, s. kindness, magnanimity, 5992.

gery, adj. changeable, 1519, 3512.

geterns, s. pl. [O.F. ghisternes], kind of guitar, 5581.

geyn, s. chance, advantage, 3518.

geyn path: convenient path, direct path, 2725.

gomme, s. gum, 5156.

goodly, adj. kind, 486 ; adv. kindly, 501.

goodlyhede, s. kindness, 6460.

goodyest, adj. sup. most excellent, 2358.

gouernaunce, s. providence, 1187 ; demeanour, manner of action, 1602, 3150, 5362.

gouernaylle, s. steering, 3661.

grace, s. pleasure, 2594 ; favour, 6781 ; *of* —— : may it please you, 470.

graciouse, adj. agreeable, 94, 154, 176, 975.

grene, adj. young, 6165.

greuaunce, s. complaint, 2923.

grounde, v. refl. to base one's opinion upon, 4684.

gryffon, s. griffin, 3653.

guerdon, s. reward, 506, 593.

gyle, s. guile, treachery, 3895, 3976.

gyn, gynne, s. contrivance, 49, 1917.

gynnyng, s. beginning, 651, 675, 3353.

h

haboundaunt, adj. abundant, 1315.

habounde, v. abound, 1324 ; adj. abundant, 367, 5100.

hap, s. chance, luck, 2231, 2960, 6781.

hardy, adj. bold, 1518, 3543.

haunteth, 3 pr. sing. dwells, 2579.

haunte, s. abode, 3891.

hawteyn, adj. proud, 5287.

hest, s. promise, 4537.

hewe, s. colour, 98, 138, 150, 234.

hewed, p.p. coloured, 115.

hidouse, adj. turbulent, dreadful, 957.

highte, pt. sing. was named, 1881.

o

holde, s. enclosed place, 4148, 5642.

homager, s. one who renders homage, 4864.

honeste, s. *of honeste*, for honour's sake, 1175.

honourable, adj. meritorious, 591.

hore, adj. hoar, hoary, 950, 1307.

.*host*, s. host, 4715.

hostage, s. residence, abode, 4489.

hostel, s. inn, 4715.

hosterye, s. hostel, 4720.

hyndryng, s. blame, harm, 23; damage, trouble, 4221.

i

ilke, adj. same, 73, 931, 1229, 1709; *thilke:* that, 855.

importable, adj. insufferable, 3356.

j

janglen, v. chatter, 5382.

joynt, s. out of —— : wrong, out of joint, 1107, 2939, 3016.

joyntes, s. pl. jointings, 6094.

joynyng, s. joining, 6101.

k

kachchen, v. get, have, 5828.

karf, 3 pt. sing. cut, 3994.

karol, s. a dance accompanied with singing, 5245.

kepe, s. heed, notice, 6225.

kerchef, s. [O.F. couvrechef], a head-dress, 1575.

knet, p.p., see *knyt*.

knowlychynge, s. intellectual power, 689.

knowyng, s. understanding, 1157.

knyt, p.p. joined, knit together, 2035, 2289, 4169.

konnyng, *kunnynge*, s. knowledge, skill, 318, 355, 410, 981.

konyngly, adv. skilfully, 2398.

kore, s. core, 3929.

kynde, s. nature, 254, 462, 860; natural bent or disposition, 103, 144, 165, 712, 1251, 2306; kind, species, 302, 390; quality, 86, 5447; *of* —— : naturally, 304.

kynde, adj. kind, 1648.

kyndely, adj. natural, 121, 1465, 6052; constitutional, 5177; natural, 5265.

kyndenesse, s. kindness, 1654.

kynrede, s. kindred, family, 1033, 1352.

kyrtel, s. kirtle, 2826.

l

lace, s. snare, entanglement, 3517.

lake, s. a kind of white linen, 3941.

lake, v. blame, dispraise, 5229; p.p. blamed, 5672.

lappe, s. edge of a garment, 4633.

large, adj. liberal, bounteous, 1498, 2675; large, 2721; *large conscience:* wide conscience, 3496.

largesse, s. abundance, 4357.

lasse, adj. comp. smaller, less, 4930.

laxatyf, s. laxative, 3439.

lefte, p.p. left, 2703; 3 pt. sing. remained, 899.

lesse, adj. minor, 552.

lesson, s. description, account, 1535.

let, v. oppose, 6817.

let, s. let, hindrance, delay, 5875.

lettyng, s. hindrance, 7006.

leve, adj. pleased, 1063.

leve, v. rely, 2219.

leve, s. permission, 4731; leave, 4774.

levyng, v. s. opinion, belief, 2216.

lignes, s. pl. offspring, young, 169.

lokkys, s. pl. locks of hair, 1307.

longeth, 3 pr. sing. belongs, 6170.

loodmanage, s. pilotage, 6058.

loos, s. praise, 4810.

lothe, adj. loath, 1063, 2254.

lothe, v. loathe, detest, 85.

loulyhede, s. Lat. mansuetudo, mildness, 6255.

loulynesse, s. gentleness, gentle breeding, 4558.

lownesse, s. lowliness, 1501.

lowte, v. bow, 5280.

lucre, s. lucre, gain, 1335.

lunatyke, adj. affected by the moon, lunatic, 6177.

lure, v. allure, 5377.

lust, s. desire, 67, 4965; delight, satisfaction, 2603; lust, 3189, 3351.

lustes, s. pl. wishes, 2275; lusts, pleasures, 3357.

lustely, adv. pleasantly, 275, 2397.

lusty, adj. pleasant, 101, 126, 159, 180, 433, 920; joyous, happy, 93; adv. pleasantly, 115.

lustynesse, s. sensual pleasure, 3203.

lych, adv. alike, 100.
lyge, adj. *lyge man:* vassal, 2352.
lyppart, s. leopard, 3494.

m

maat, adj. checkmate, 10.
maate, v. checkmate, 5922, 5924.
maistresse, s. mistress, 255.
make, s. wife, 165.
malliable, adj. capable of being shaped by beating, 6814.
man, s. servant, 3291.
manace, v. threaten, 371, 3365.
maner, s. kind, 173.
marchandyse, s. the trade of merchants', 1690.
massife, adj. thick, 2730.
matynge, s. becoming checkmate, 46.
maugre, prep. in spite of, 375, 1484.
mawe, s. maw, stomach, 6478.
mayde, mayden, s. maid, 151, 2357, 2597.
mede, s. reward, gift, 4348, 4874; payment, 6248.
medil, s. waist, 1566.
mene, s. means, 4086; middle way, 4172, 4194, 4680, 6339, 6345; tendency to keep the middle way, 6350.
mene, adj. middle, 4667.
menye, s. company, 5795.
menyver, s. miniver, 2836.
mereles, s. a game, nine men's morris, 2404.
merlyon, s. merlin, 4322.
mervelous, adj. strange, marvellous, 3372, 3380, 4466.
messagere, s. messenger, 1672.
mesure, s. plan, 58; moderation, 134.
mete, adj. able, fit, 2197.
metre, s. metrical work in opposition to prose, 25.
meyne, s. company, 2663; *meyny, meny, meyne,* set of chess-men, 6002, 6005, 6023.
mone, s. complaint, 900.
mood, s. anger, 6715.
mortal, adj. fatal, death-bringing, destructible, 3134, 3406, 3418.
morwenynge, s. morning, 458.
motles, s. plur. coloured spots, 117.
muse, v. wonder at, 1373, 2893.

myddys, adv. in the midst of, 5197.
myn, s. mine, 6080.
myneth, 3 pr. sing. makes a hole, 6918.
mynstralcye, s. music, 5569.
mys, adj. wrong, amiss, 40.
mysaventure, s. misadventure, mishap, 4153, 4238.
myswrought, p.p. done wrong, 2930.

n

name, s. reputation, 5832.
natyvite, s. birth, 1454, 1609.
nonys, for the —— [O.E. for ꝺ̆ām ânes]: for the nonce, for the occasion, 3113, 6032.
norture, s. recreation, 988; nourishment, 1630; good manners, 6463.
notys, s. pl. tunes, 3672, 5575; notes of a song, 5205.
noyous, adj. troublesome, 3959.

o

obeysaunce, s. *vnder hir obeysaunce:* under obedience to her, 1485.
observaunces, s. pl. observations, attention, 197; ceremonies, 5039.
odible, adj. noxious, 715.
of, prep. on account of, for, 4113, 4114.
operation, s. effect, 4013.
or, conj. ere, 28, 361.
ordayned, p.p. prepared, 6141; supplied, 6150.
ordeyn, v. provide, 2295; v. refl. prepare one's self, 5956; *ordeyned,* p.p. arranged, ordered,. 5028; provided, 3509 ?.
ordynaunce, s. arrangement, 6590.
orient, adj. eastern, of a superior kind, 5745. *oriental* 6036
outerly, adv. entirely, 2885.
ouersprad, p.p. covered, 109.
ovmbre, s. the umber bird [Scopus umbrella], 1242.

p

pappes, s. pl. breast, teats, 1643.
papphe, v. paint, 1368.
parage, s. rank, kindred, 3130.
parcel, s. part, 562, 6039.
pardurable, adj. everlasting, 570, 730.
passage, s. way, 616.

passyng, adv. extremely, 1097, 1216, 1411, 1538.

passynge, adj. passing, 681; great, 1687; excellent, 6525.

passyngly, adv. extremely, greatly, 264, 1302, 1352.

pensyfhede, s. melancholy, 2584.

percynge, persyng, adj. piercing, 216, 221, 5386.

pere, s. peer, equal, 2592.

peregalle, adj. fully, equal, 16, 1738.

pereles, s. pearls, 2848.

pereles, adj. peerless, 3686.

perfyt, perfyte, adj. perfect, 578, 750, 754, 2808; exceedingly good, 4367.

perse, adj. of Persian dye, light blue, 1730, 4019, 5746.

persing, adj. piercing, 5386; v. pierce, 5440.

perturbaunce, s. trouble, 5326.

pertynent, adj. that which is necessary, belonging, 2292, 5157, 5449.

pervers, adj. bad, 642.

pes, s. peace, 786, 1492, 1884.

peyse, s. pondus, 1666.

phane, s. vane, 6180.

physike, s. physic, 5157.

pite, s., O.F. pité, 836, 6749.

pithe, s. pith, 740; value, excellence, 4882.

platly, adv. plainly, simply, 1480, 1862.

play, s. music, 1762.

play, v. refl. divert or amuse oneself, 5237.

plente, s. fulness, 5574.

plesaunce, s. pleasure, 189; pleasure, profit, 713; pleasing behaviour, 2809.

pley, v. play, 5012; p. pres. 5200.

plicable, adj. bending, pliant, 6813.

plyaunt, adj. pliant, 6914.

plye, v. bend, 6810.

plyte, s. condition, 3668.

pokokes, s. peacocks, 1427.

pompose, adj. pompous, 3070.

port, s. bearing, mien, 5406.

porter, s. female porter, 2671.

porteresse, s. female porter, 2615.

portreyture, s. set of drawings, 357.

pose, s. [O.E. geposu], cold in the head, 6642.

powne, s. pawn, 6160, 6203, 6206; plur. 6155, 6587.

povste, s. power, 1685.

poynt, s. house of a chess-board, 6074; plur. 6044, 6093, 6100.

practyke, s. practice, 5568.

prerogatyf, s. prerogative, advantage, 6444.

presever, v. remain, 4441.

presse, v. step forward, 5129.

prevites, s. pl. secrecy, 4880.

prevy, adj. covered, 740.

prikken, v. incite, 92.

pris, s. prize, 5908.

privete, s. secret art, 6107.

professed, p.p. used as an adj., bound by oath or vows, having publicly joined a profession, a religious order, etc., 2694, 3450, 3683, 6270.

profoundly, adv. deeply, earnestly, 628.

profre, s. offer, 2308, 2311.

properte, s. quality, inclination, 6169.

proude, adj., O.F. fier et orgueilleux, 3679, 3714.

provyde, v. refl. protect oneself, 3556.

prowe, s. profit, 2945, 3734.

prowesse, s. prowess, valour, 1516, 3566, 4475.

pulshed, p.p. polished, 2851, 5766, 6080.

pyment, s. wine with a mixture of spice or honey, 3398.

pyn, s. pin, 2952.

q

queynt, p.p. put out, 6637.

quiete, s., O.F. qviete, 2198.

quyt, p.p. acquitted, rewarded, 2354.

r

rage, s. passion, 2364, 2460, 3289, 4274; adj. furious, 3662, 4133, 4222, 4363, 6975, 6988.

rake, s. throat, 6488.

ramage, adj. wild, 2858.

rammysh, adj. like a ram, 3378.

rancour, s. malice, 1955.

rape, s. haste, 1664.

raskayl, s. vulgar herd, 2590.

rathe, adv. before, 5043.

rauenous, adj. greedy, 6479.

ravisshed, p.p. enjoyed, 5094.
raylle, v. provide, adorn, 2561.
rebukyng, s. disgrace, 580.
rede, s. advice, 869, 2055, 2627.
refuit, s. help, hope of safety, 2381.
regalye, s. authority, 3068.
reioysshe, v. make rejoice, 103;
   enjoy, 1939; v. refl. feel glad,
   189.
rekkeles, adj. careless, reckless, 1953,
   3732, 4111.
relente, v. melt, 4179.
religion, s. religious order, 2844,
   3248; laws of a religious order,
   2696.
remenaunt, s. rest, 6077.
repair, s. walk, journey, 952.
repente, v. refl. repent, 4470.
repeyred, p.p. kept back, 7037.
reserved, p.p. observed, kept, 1100.
resorte, v. return, 6234.
respite, v. delay, 517; s. delay, 5967,
   6489.
restoratyf, adj. restorative, 6443.
restreyn, v. hold, embrace, 3846;
   restrain, 5643.
retentyf, s. memory, 3735.
revel, v. be active as a minstrel,
   2396.
rewe, v. have pity, 6910.
reyne, s. rein, 2263.
reyne-bowe, reyn-bowe, s. rainbow,
   6276, 6300.
roke, s. rook or castle at chess,
   6738; plur. 6717, 6724.
roo, s. roe, 3728.
roof, 3 pt. sing. stabbed, 3980.
rote, s. *by rote:* by heart, 2393.
rother, s. rudder, oar, 7035.
route, s. rout, company, number,
   1426, 3226, 5233, 5279, 5526.
routhe, s. a pity, a sad thing, 3107,
   3987; compassion, mercy, 6905.
rovne, v. whisper, 4583.
rowe, s. *a-rowe:* in a row, 6023.
ruff, adj. plain, openly known, 1287,
   1879.
ryghtful, adj. righteous, 851.
ryhtwisnesse, s. justice, 836, 1198.
rywle, s. rule, 3136.

s

salt, adj. salt, 1458.
sanatyf, adj. healing, wholesome,
   5150, 5185.

sapience, s. wisdom, 1044.
savage, adj. savage, 2857, 3680,
   3694.
sawtre, s. psaltery, a kind of harp,
   3635.
scarsete, s. scarcity, 1314.
sclaunder, s. disgrace, scandal, 6737.
scole, s. school, discipline, 3208.
scripture, s. literary work, 34, 45;
   inscription, 5694.
se, s. seat, 1297.
secre, adj. covered, secret, 732, 1675.
seelys, s. pl. seals, 6130.
sely, adj. good, kind, 6820.
semelynesse, s. gracefulness, comeli-
   ness, 321.
sene, adj. visible, 332, 4017.
sengle, adj. without company, for-
   saken, 3225.
sensityf, s. [O.F. li sens], perception
   through the senses, 733. *a. 767, 698*
sentence, s. meaning, 35, 473; judgment, 1962; sentence, decree,
   6645; general meaning, 79, 403,
   515, etc.
sere, v. to become dry, wither,
   2736.
serpentyne, adj. resembling a serpent, 4038.
servage, s. servitude, 1795.
set, p.p. determined, 2251; fallen,
   placed, 3201, 6175.
shap, shappe, s. figure, 4975, 5821.
shapen, v.; *shapeth him,* 3 ps. sing.
   intends; *shoop,* 3 pt. sing. provided, worked, 5873.
shene, adj. bright, 107.
shent, p.p. scolded, punished, 807,
   5960.
shewyng, p. ps. appearing, 6278.
shroude, v. clothe, cover, 353.
skorneth, 3 ps. sing. deludes, 3394.
skye, s. cloud, 1007; pl. 6200.
skylle, s. a reasonable thing, 765;
   reason, 2994.
sleyght, s. contrivance, sleight, 1917,
   2758; plur. devices, 3277.
slough, 3 pt. sing. destroyed, 148.
slouthe, s. sloth, 461, 472.
slyper, adj. light, unscrupulous,
   3295.
smotry, adj., O.F. laide, dirty, 3791.
socour, s. relief, help, 3851.
solace, s. amusement, diversion, 2386,
   2516, 2859.

solace, v. indulge in diversion or pleasure, 3537.

soleyn, adj. solitary, uncouth, 1504.

sondry, adj. various, 98, 109, 116, 534, 707.

sool, adj. alone, 2703.

sore, adv. sorely, 6483.

sothfastnesse, s. truth, 69, 181.

sotil, sotyle, adj., O.F. soubtible, 710; cunning, 1917; very fine, 1150; excellent, 1393.

sotyltee, s. cunning, 3567; plur. subtilty, skill, 1700; difficult questions, 2429.

space, s. space of time, 291, 5050.

spede, v. make prosperous, 1154; *sped*, p.p. sped, 4135.

spere, s. sphere, 270, 276.

spere, s. spear, 1196.

spices, s. pl. species, 6945.

spoote, s. defect, 332.

spouse, s. husband, 153.

stampes, s. pl. [O.F. estampiez], a kind of dance, 5573.

stellefyed, p.p. received into heaven and there glorified, 6454.

sterre, s. star, 118.

sterred, p.p. covered with stars, 114.

sterry, adj. starry, 5116.

sterve, v. die, 6676.

stille, v. drop, 6307.

stoor, s. store, possession, 3199, 3259.

streyn, v. press, vex extremely, 6876.

streyt, adj. tight, 6337.

stryf, stryve, s. strife, doubt, 697; struggle, 768; hesitation, 6831.

stynte, v. shut, stop, 1954, 6879, 7029.

subjet, adj. subordinate, 6133.

substaunce, s. *in substaunce:* an expletive phrase with no distinct meaning, 645, 688, 894.

suasion, s. persuasion, 1994.

subieccioun, s. governance, 5281.

subtil, adj. skilful, ingenious, 49.

suffysaunce, s. contentment, 190.

surcote, s. upper coat, 1392.

surplusage, s. the rest, 4768; surplus, 6341.

surquedous, adj. proud, over-confident, 5287, 6694.

surquedye, s. arrogance, presumption, 2581, 6570.

surquidrie, s. over-confidence, 2452.

sustene, v. endure, 3570.

swarte, adj., O.F. obscure, 3791.

sweren, v. affirm by oath, 6827.

swin, s. pl. pigs, 3428.

swythe, adv. quickly, 5812.

syght, s. expression, condition, 396.

sykernesse, s. steadfastness, confidence, 6193.

sythe, s. *ofte sythe:* oftentimes, 768, 2314, 3320; *many sythe:* oftentimes, 772, 3211.

sywe, v. follow, 503, 660, 1426; attain, 586; step forward, 1387; *suede*, 3 pl. pt. followed, 5536.

t

tabler, s. chess-board, 6043.

tables, s. pl. the game of "tables," 2404.

tache, s. defect, 6183; *tachchis*, pl. manners, 3798.

taketh, 3 ps. sing. puts on, 155.

talent, s. inclination.

tamyd, p.p. ventured, undertaken, 5636.

tapite, v. cover, 2766.

tarage, s. flavour, 3812, 3931; natural disposition, 3943.

taraged, p.p. disposed, 3378.

tarye, v. delay, 4467.

tempred, p.p. tempered, 1808.

temprure, temperrure, s. quality of a tempered metal, 1191, 5477.

tene, s. grief, trouble, 4084, 4351, 5204, 5328, 5803; hate, 4314.

throwe, s. short space of time, 2455, 2673.

thrust, s. thirst, 68.

to, prep. before, in presence of, 220.

tonne, s. cask, 50.

touche, v. *touchinge:* quant à, 251, 315, 347, 407, 1464, 1539, 2091, 2278, 2974, 2982, 3301.

touns, s. pl. musical notes, 5211.

trace, s. trace, steps, 2107, 2206.

travayle, s. labour, 610.

treble, adv. threefold, 3648.

tresourere, s. a female treasurer, 1363.

trespace, s. *put in trespace:* accuse, 6771.

treyne, s. trap, 6734; pl. 3599; delay, 6981.

trewe, s. compliance, 639; fidelity, 5576.
triacle, s. remedy, especially against poison, 3414.
trouble, adj. troubly, not clear, 3887.
trumpes, s. pl. [O.F. trompez], trumpets, 5589.
trumpetes, s. pl. small trumpets, 5589.
tusshes, s. pl. tusks, 3699.
twynne, v. depart, 3492.

V

variaunt, adj. varying, 1551.
varie, v. deviate, 6631.
vayllable, adj. valuable, 948.
vegetatyve, adj. quickening; *vertu vegetatyve :* virtus vegetativa, 2747.
venemyth, 3 ps. sing. poisons, 3391.
venym, s. poison, 3651.
venymous, adj. poisonous, 3405.
ver, s. spring, 187.
verray, adj. very, real, 80, 112, 182.
vertu, s. gift, faculty, 687, 692, 698, 716, 721, 767, etc.; quickening power, 920; magic influence, property, 1741, 1769, 6035, 6038.
vesture, s. clothing, 347, 1144.
vileyn, adj. rude, base, 1508.
vileyns, adj. villainous, 3800.
vncouth, adj. strange, 1987, 2391, 2751, 4880; uncommon, striking, 4519, 5339.
vnhap, s. misfortune, 5494.
vnknet, p.p. untied, 3202.
vnleful, adj. unlawful, 3189.
vnnethe, adv. scarcely, 1327; almost, 1334, 3132; *vnnethis*, adv. scarcely, 2148.
vnthryfte, s. folly, 6946.
vntweyne, adv. in twain, 1774.
vntwynen, v. unwind, 1252.
vnwar, adj. unexpectedly changing, 6181.
vnwarly, adv. unexpectedly, 4077, 5355.
unwist, adj. without being known, 5355.
vnwrie, v. unveil, 18.
voyde, v. avoid, 6340, 6615; p.p. removed, 1208.
vpcast, p.p. uplifted, 399.

W

walkne, s. sky, 1007.
walyve, s. value, 2812.
wanse, v. decrease, 6187; 3 ps. sing., 6197.
war, adj. aware, 804, 2241.
wardeyn, s. guardian, 2604.
warrys, s. pl. knots, 5428.
wavering, p. ps. to be undetermined, irresolute, 2901.
wede, s. garment, 1934.
wende, pt. plur. supposed, 3777.
wene, s. doubt, 1319.
wer, *were*, s. doubt, 51, 326, 1263, etc.
were, v. defend, 1195.
werkyng, *werching*, s. working, acting, 1640, 1705, 3169; pl. modes of working, operations, 620; deeds, works, 1467.
werre, *wer*, s. war, 1083, 1492, 1936.
wete, v. know, 5792.
wexe, v. become, 5506; 1 sg. pt. became, 5697.
wherbles, s. pl. warbles, 200, 1249, 5211.
whilom, adv. once, 3685.
whily, adj. wily, artful, 2758.
white, s. blame, reproach, 6768.
wilde, adj. *wilde fire :* violent fire, 3802.
wilful, adj. unreasonable, obstinate, 463, 3254.
wilfully, adv. voluntarily, 6831.
willed, p.p. willing, 3158.
wonder, adv. extremely, 813.
wont, adj. accustomed, 3023; usual, 3140.
worshippe, s. reputation, 3333, 3342.
wrak, s. wreck, destruction, 5426.
wrake, s. vengeance, persecution, 1451.
wrechchidnesse, s. misery, 4752.
wreke, v. avenge, 369.
wrynkled, p.p., O.F. tissu, mazy, 3607.
wylfulnesse, s. wilfulness, 2244; thoughtlessness, 3316.
wympled, p.p. wearing a wimple, 2837.
wynne, v. get, gain, 739.

Y

y-blent, p.p. made blind, 3659.
y-darted, p.p. pierced, 6878.

LIST OF PROPER NAMES.

Absalon, 3689.
Achilles, 1883.
Adonydes, 3685, 3731.
Adriane, 432.
Agenor, 3260.
Alceste, 6828.
Almanye, 5571.
Alysaundre, 4381, 4398.
Antropos, 369, 1254, 1261.
Archadie, 4723.
Argus, 422, 1781, 1810.
Aristotiles, Aristotle, 314, 340.
Arragon, 5572.
Arthour, 3141, 3178.
Athene, 4313.
Atlas, Athlas, 1618, 2754.

Babel, 3436.
Breteyne, 3176.

Caribdes, Karibdys, 3664, 6764.
Cartage, 4339.
Caton, 4678.
Cerberus, 377, 1382, 1746.
Chymere, 3370.
Cibeles, 1349.
Circes, 3421, 4094.
Cloto, 375.
Colchos, 3525.
Crete, 1346, 4310.
Cupyde, 2438, 2486, 2488, 2496,
 2532, 2569, 2609, 2629, 2641,
 3536, 3863, 3891, 4004, 4446,
 4800, 4804, 4865, 4964, 5232,
 5264, 5269, 5391, 5455, 5502,
 5523, 5536, 5562, 5655, 5781,
 5829, 5915, 5936, 5947, 5973,
 6951.
Cytheron, 3690.

Danne, 3263.
Daphne, 2467, 3267.
Dauid, 4478, 5604.
Dedalus, 3604, 4164.

Deduit, 2382, 2488, 2496, 2508, 2518,
 2524, 2529, 2539, 2559, 2570,
 2595, 2601, 2609, 2629, 2641,
 2646, 3534, 3866, 3897, 4447,
 4593, 4799, 4962, 5232, 5247,
 5263, 5544, 5782, 5799, 5829,
 5840, 5946, 5973.
Denmarke, 2712.
Dido, 4336.
Dyane, Diane, 2970, 4773, 4781,
 5224, 5671, 5740.
Dyomede, 4661.

Empodocles, 4112, 4123.
Enee, 4338.
Esculapius, 5152.
Ethna, 4122.
Europe, 3259.

Flora, 921.
Fortune, 47, 1358, 1364.
Fraunce, 4884.

Grece, 1891; Grekys londe, 2036.
Genivs, 863, 6623, 6677.
Guenore, 6025.

Hector, Ector, 1804, 4475.
Heleyne, Eleyne, Eleyn, 1876, 2037,
 2168, 4554.
Hercules, 1803, 2755, 5512.

Ida, 1971.
Iason, 3524, 3542, 3565, 4331, 4600.
Iubiter, 1035, 1037, 1317, 1345, 1447,
 1527, 1852, 1967, 3104, 3256, 5054,
 5115; Gen. Iubiteris(es), 1288,
 1625, 1984; Iovis, 2975.
Iuno, 1282, 1284, 1341, 1350, 1363,
 1605, 1625, 1641, 1653, 1826,
 1861, 1944, 1995, 2059, 2109,
 2133, 2201, 3334, 5887.

Lachesis, 375.   *

APPENDIX.

SPECIMEN PASSAGES FROM THE TEXT OF THE *ÉCHECS AMOUREUX.*

(From the MS. O. 66 in the Royal Library at Dresden.)

THE following specimen passages from the hitherto unedited original of Lydgate's poem are already given in my book on *Les Échecs Amoureux*. But nevertheless I have thought it well to print them again here, and this for two reasons: first, the reader may be glad to have the opportunity of making some acquaintance with Lydgate's source without being compelled to have recourse to my *Échecs Amoureux* or the 2nd volume of this present edition; and secondly, because my last collation of the Dresden MS. brought to light some inaccuracies in the earlier transcription which I am now able to avoid. A list of these errors with the proper corrections may also be found in *Englische Studien*, vol. xxviii, p. 310–312.[1]

1. Description of spring. *Échecs Amoureux*, p. 230 ff. *Reason and Sensuality*, l. 87 ff.

Estoye en assez grant delit Fol. 1a.	Quelle voit ainsy estele
Une matinee en mon lit	De tant de flourettes plaisans
Ou doulz printemps delicieux	Plus cler questelles Reluisans
Cest le temps sur tous gracieux	Les Arbres aussy (se) Reuerdissent
Qui toute plaisance appareille	Et font fueilles et se flourissent
Ou la nuit au Jour est pareille	Pour fruit porter en la saison
Cest la doulce saison nouuelle	Tel quil doiuent selon Raison
Ou toute riens se Renouuelle	Li fleuue aussy et les fontaines
Et Resioist aucunement	Se Renouuellent en leurs vaines
Si quil appert communement	Et commencent habondamment
Es herbes qui de la terre yssent	A croistre et courre Radement
Et qui croissent et se nourrissent	Et grant prouffit au monde font
Et font mainte fleur merueilleuse	La naige se degaste et font
Dont la terre est si orgueilleuse	Li airs sadoulcist et attempre
Et si se cointoye et se pare	Si quil ny a ne tart ne tempre
Quil samble quelle se compare	Ne trop chaleur ne trop froidure
Au ciel destre mieulx estellee Fol. 1b.	Pour le souleil qui par mesure
Pour ce quelle est enmantellee	Ses Rais a la terre presente
De son verd mantel pincele	Zephirus voulentiers lors vente

---

[1] The corrections of H. Spies in *Englische Studien*, vol. xxvii, p. 439 ff., are inaccurate.

Qui fait Resioir les flourettes
La rousee sur les herbettes
Y descend aussy voulentiers
Dont Il est souuent bien mestiers
Pour ce voit on rire les pres
Et tout Reuerdir loingz et pres
A brief parler toute semence
A esmouuoir lors se commence
Et veult de la terre yssir hors
Pour lumeur qui habonde lors
Et la chaleur amesuree
Dont la terre est moult honnouree
Ainsy se cointoye la terre
Et sesforce ou printemps de querre
Tous ses plus beaulx aornemens
Pour mieulx moustrer aux elemens
Et au ciel qui tournoye au tour
Sa grant beaulte et son atour
Comme fait la Josne puchelle
Qui pour sambler estre plus belle
Et plus gente et plus gracieuse
Le Jour quelle est nouuelle espeuse
Sappareille et Raisons le veult
Le plus noblement quelle peut
Aussy samble Il que faire vueille
La terre qui adont sorgueille
Pour la doulchour quelle est sentans
Au Renouuellement du temps
On voit aussy les oyselles
Plus mignos et plus genteles
Et demener plus grant Reuel
Pour la doulchour du temps nouuel
Qui mue leur condicion
En meilleur disposicion
Et pour ce meismez le samble
Se Raparient Il ensamble
Et font leur nidz moult soubtilment
Par naturel enseignement

Qui les fait ainsy maintenir
Pour leurs lignies soustenir
Briefment a parler qui vouldroit
Faire Induction Il verroit
Que toutes naturelles choses
Qui sont es elemens encloses
Se Resiouyssent lors et oeuurent
Pour quoyne sayquelles recoeuurent
Qui leur estoit tolu deuant
Par le froit temps dyuer greuant
Creature nays humaine
Plus Joyeusement sen demaine
Et en est asses plus Jolie
Et plus amoureuse et plus lye
Et plus Jouans et plus aperte
Cest chose certaine et experte
Ainsy dont comme Je vous comptoye
Ou point que Je dy lors estoye
Pensans ou doulz temps gracieux
Qui tant estoit delicieux
Et datempree qualite
Quil nest cuers a la verite
Qui Resioir ne sen deuist
Quelconques anuy quil euist
Si my delittoye trop fort
Et y prenoye grant confort
Non pas en dormant ne en songe
Mais tout en veillant sans menchonge
Riens ne meuist lors endormy
Car li oysellet entour my
Chantoient si Joliement
Et si tres efforciement
Que de dormir neuisse soing
Et en euisse grant besoing
Tant les ooye voulentiers
Finablement en dementiers
Que Jestoye sy ententis
Doir les oyselles gentis . . .

2. The enemies of Dame Nature. *Échecs Amoureux*, p. 9. Cp. *Reason and Sensuality*, l. 369 ff.

Car attropos le fil desront   Fol. 3 a.
Et desface les pourtraitures
Les ymaiges et les paintures
Malgre lachesis et cloto
Dont moult a grant Joye pluto
Et cerberus qui tout engoule

Quan quil happe a sa tripple goule
Riens ne len pouroit saouler
Ains vouldroit tres bien engouler
A vn cop par sa desmesure
Toute la cotte de nature.

3. The ways of Reason and Sensuality. *Échecs Amoureux*, p. 12. Cp. *Reason and Sensuality*, l. 647 ff.

LI vns commence en orient   Fol. 4a.
Et sen va deuers occident
Et sans riens quen ce se bestourne

En orient arrier Retourne
Qu Il prist son commencement
A lexemple du firmament

LI aul*trez* doccident se part
Et sen reua de lautre part
Vers orient la voye droite ₁᷒Fol. 4 b.
[1]Et de puis tant arriere esploitte
Quen occident tout droit Repaire

Par maniere a laultre contraire
Or enten oultre et tu orras
Comment congnoistre le porras
Et le quel tu deuras tenir.

4. Dame Nature charges the author to go the way. of Reason. *Échecs Amoureux*, p. 13 f. Cp. *Reason and Sensuality*, l. 817 ff.

[1]PRen dont le chemin de Raison
Et de vertu toute saison   [1] Fol. 5a.
Et fuy ce que Raison desprise
Loe de tout ton cuer et prise
Ton createur sur toute Rien
Aoure le et croy et crien
Et soit toudis deuant les yeulx
De ton cuer si ne pourras mieulx
Ayme dont dieu sur toutes choses
Et pour ce que mieulx te disposes
A sieuir de Raison la sente
Ayes tousdis lueil et lentente
Aux choses haultes et celestres

Et despis les chosez terrestres
Et la mondaine vanite
Ayme Justice ayme pite
Et fay a tous de prime face
Autel que tu veulx *com* te face
BJaulx se tu ne te veulz tordre
Ad ce te conuient Il amordre
Car cest li chemins que Je voye
Qui maine au ciel plus droite voye
Dont tu vins et aussy tu dois tendre
Se tu sces bien ta fin entendre
Quant a mes loys especiaulx
Soyez y Justes et loyaulx.

5. Lines referring to *The Romance of the Rose*. *Échecs Amoureux*, p. 38 f. Cp. *Reason and Sensuality*, l. 4811 ff.

[1]Et pour ce ont en mainte escr*i*pture
De ceste amoureuse closture [1] Fol. 18 b.
Parle maint amoureux soubtil
Et de cest deduisant courtil
Et mainte auenture Retraitte
Entre lesquelx le mieulx en traitte
Et le plus gracieusement
Chilz qui fist le commencement
Du Joly Rommant de la Rose
Ouquel il desclaire et expose
Comment Il songa vne nuit
Quil vint au vergier de deduit
Et comment a pou de priiere
Oyseuse qui en yert portiere
Le mist ou bel pourpris quarre
Par le petit guichet barre
Ou Il vit m*o*ult de grans merueillez
Et y ot de dures bateillez

Et m*o*ult de paine et de traueil
Pour le plaisant bouton v*er*meil
Quil desiroit tant a auoir
Quil nen preist nul aul*tre* auoir
Mais sur tous nottable oeure fist
Chilz qui cest bel Rommant parfist
Ou Il desclaire apprez com*m*ent
Chilz amoureux finablement
Cueilla le bouton gracieux
Qui tant estoit delicieux
Et lot a sa voulente plaine
Comment que ce fust a grant paine
Sicom chilz liurez le deuise
Qui tant est de soubtil deuise
Et tant est plain de gr*a*nt mistere
Quoncquez mais de ceste m*a*tere
Ne fu nulz pl*us* biaulx liurez fais
Ne plus complex ne plus parfais.

6. Power of Love. *Échecs Amoureux*, p. 246 ff. Cp. *Reason and Sensuality*, l. 5391 ff.

Vous deues sauoir dau*tre* part Fol. 20 b.
Que chilz g*en*tilz die*ux* q*u*i depart
Amours tout a sa voulente
Auoit en coste luj beaulte
Ceste luy tenoit compaignie
Qui m*o*ult estoit b*ie*n ensaignie
Car m*o*ult lui plaisoit sacointance
Amours le tint par sa main blance

Aueuc ces deux fu doulz Regars
Qui ne sambla pas estre gars
Mais sur tous frans et deboinaires
Chilz portoit les deux ars co*n*traires
Et lez sayettez ensement
Dont amours trait crueuseme*n*t
Toutez les fois quil luj est bel.

7. Description of the chessmen.　*Échecs Amoureux*, p. 46 ff.　Cp.
Reason and Sensuality, l. 6155 ff.

*Des eschecz que la damoiselle auqit de sa partie et premierement dez
paonnes et de sa fierge.*

SI paonnet or escoutes
Estoient fait cest verites
Desmeraudez voire si bellez
Si finez et de vretus tellez
Quexperience masseure
Quil nen puet nulle es*tre* en nature
Plus precieuse ne plus digne
Si quil mapparoit par mai*n*t signe
Sestoient tuit dune mesure
Sans diuersite de figure
Fors des enseignez dessus di*c*tez
Qui en leurs escus sont es*cr*iptez
Li premiers qui assis estoit
Deuers sa main destre portoit
Vn croissant de lune nouuelle
Pourtrait par maniere mo*u*lt belle
Le second dencoste celly
Auoit en son escu polly
Vne Rose aussy figuree
A merueillez bien mesuree
Li tiers selon ma Ramembra*n*ce

Auoit la fourme et la samblance
Dun aignel simple et deboinaire
Larcq du ciel dont Juno seult traire
Vy pourtrait en lescu du quart
LI quins paonnez dau*tre* part
Y ot pourtrait vn anelet
Trop faitich et trop gentelet
Vn serpe*n*t y ot li sisiesme
LI aul*tr*ez qui estoit septiesme
Vne panthiere y ot pourtraitte
Et li huitiesmez vne Aiglette
Ainsy comme Je vous ay Retrait
Furent si paonnet pourtrait
Sa fierge aussi gente et plaisant
Fu dun fin Rubis Reluisant
De si p[r]ecieux appareil
Concquez nulz ne vit le pareil
Ceste precieuse Royne
Portoit senseigne en la poittrine
Vne balance y ot fermee
Pour peser chosez ordonnee.

*Des aul*t*rez eschecz.*

SI doy cheualier ensement
Furent fourme trop gente*m*ent
Dune matere saphirine
SI orientelle et si fine
Com tenist a mon escient
Tous aultrez saphirs a noyent
Or est droiz que Je vous enseigne
De chascun deul*x* la propre e*n*seigne
La destre et vne vnicorne
Ceste beste porte vne corne
Emmy le fro*n*t moult perilleuse
Dont elle est trop plus orgueilleuse
LI senestre portoit lymaige
Dun lieure fuitiz et sauluaige
Figure trop bien et trop bel
SI Rocq estoient aussy tel
Que leur valeur toute aul*tre* passe
Chascuns fu fait dune topasse
Sus toutez precieuse et digne
Sauoit aussy chascuns son signe
LI destrez ot vn oysellet
Moult plaisant et mo*u*lt gentellet
Qui est la callandre appellez
Et li aul*tre*z de lautre lez
Portoit vne monstre de Mer

Que Joy seraine nom*m*er
Dune pierre de gra*n*t Renom
Qui selon les*cr*ipture a nom
Elietrope aussy fait furent
SI doy aulphin qui ta*n*t valure*n*t
Que*n* leur valeur not poi*n*t defin
Les enseignez que chil aulphin
Orent en leurs escus pourtraittez
Estoyent bellez et bi*en* faittez
Vn coulombel y ot li destrez
Et vn pellican li senestrez
Or vueil dire appres de son Roy
Qui Reffu de moult noble arroy
Dun dyamant estoit tailliez
Tel que tout fu esme*r*ueilliez
Ou si beaul*x* dyamans fu pris
De tel grandeur et de tel pris
Chilz Roys auoit aussy sans faille
Vn cheual de trop belle taille
Dune pierre moult Renom*m*ee
Qui estoit abeston nommee
Selon ce qui mestoit auis
Et auoit chilz Roys que deuis
La fourme dune tourterelle
Pourtraitte en son escu mo*u*lt belle.

*Des eschecz de lautre partie et premierement de ses paonnez
et de sa fierge :*

TElz eschecz et de tel deuise
Que chilz liurez chi *vous* deuise
Auoit la dame en sa bataille
Or est Il droiz apprez que Jaille
A ceulx dont Je deuoie traire
Si vous en vueil briefment Retraire
Et la fachon et la matiere
Qui Restoit de moult gra*nt* mistiere
Car tous dor fin estoie*nt* voir
Si deuez aueuc ce sauoir
Quil auoient aussy figurez
Appartenans a leurs naturez
Tout aussy que ly aultre auoient
Car de ceulx ne se differoient
Fors es materez et (es) formettez
Quilz orent aux escus pourtrettez
Mes paons premiers qui estoit
Vers ma main senestre portoit
La fourme dun secq arbre vvyt
Sans fueilles sans flours et sa*ns* fruit

LI secondz portoit vnez clez
LI aultrez qui estoit delez
Vn tigre portoit ensement
Fourme moult gracieusement
Li quars y auoit vn oysel
Qui chante doulcement et bel
Cestoit vne merle Jolye
Li quins en sa targe polye
Portoit la fourme dun luppart
Et li siesmez daultre part
Auoit aussy vn mireoir
Concaue moult bel a veoir
Vn cygne portoit li septismez
Et la chienette li huitismez
La fierge qui me fu baillie
Estoit figuree et taillie
Bel et bien Je le vous affiche
Et sauoit en guise daffiche
Ou pis vn pappeillon trop ·bel

Des eschiez.

MI cheualier estoient tel
Aussy quil affiert *par* Raison
LI senestrez en son blason
Portoit vn lyon tres bien fait
LI destrez y ot contrefait   Fol. 24 b.
Orpheus qui tient vne harpe
Et qui ce samble en Joue et harpe
My Rocq aussi daul*tre* part furent
De tel fachon com estre durent
Et seignie sicom drois Requiert
Lenseigne de mon Rocq destre yert
A vne coulombe samblable
Pour grant fais soustenir ayable
Lenseigne aussy de lautre Rocq
Fu de la figure dun cocq
De mes Aulphins dire apprez doy

Il est vray qui furent touz doy
De tel fourme quil doiuent estre
Chilz qui estoit au coste destre
Auoit aussy qun Ray de feu
Et chilz qui a senestre fu
Auoit lenseigne dune nef
Garnie de mas et de tref
Et de tout ce qua nef falloit
Mon Roy aussy qui *moult* valoit
Estoit briefment de tel arroy
Quil affiert en bataille a Roy
Sestoit sus vn cheual assis
Qui dor fin restoit tout massis
Et sauoit son escu pare
Dun paon trop b*ien* figure.

The manufacturer's authorised representative in the EU for product
safety is Oxford University Press España S.A. of El Parque Empresarial
San Fernando de Henares, Avenida de Castilla, 2 - 28830 Madrid
(www.oup.es/en or product.safety@oup.com). OUP España S.A. also acts
as importer into Spain of products made by the manufacturer.
Printed and bound by CPI Group (UK) Ltd, Croydon, CR0 4YY

05/05/2026

02102998-0005